Seltzertopia*

The *Extraordinary* Story of an Ordinary Drink

Barry Joseph

BEHRMAN HOUSE

www.behrmanhouse.com

I dedicate this book (in a paraphrase of
Walter Backerman, seltzer man extraordinaire)
to all who have played custodian for
the next generation.

Project manager/editor: Dena Neusner
Editor: Tova Ovits
Design: Anne Redmond
Copyright © 2018 by Barry Joseph
All rights reserved
Please see page 298 for permissions and photography credits.

Published by Behrman House, Inc.
Millburn, New Jersey 07041
www.behrmanhouse.com

ISBN 978-0-87441-975-7
Printed in the United States of America

Library of Congress Cataloging-in-Publication Data
Names: Joseph, Barry, author.
Title: Seltzertopia : the extraordinary story of an ordinary drink /
  by Barry Joseph.
Description: Millburn, N.J. : Behrman House, [2018] | Includes
  bibliographical references.
Identifiers: LCCN 2018005014 (print) | LCCN 2018015608 (ebook) |
  ISBN 9780874419757 (ebook) | ISBN 9780874419757
Subjects: LCSH: Seltzer Works (Pittsburgh, Pa.)—History. | Pittsburgh
  (Pa.)—History.
Classification: LCC HD9349.S634 (ebook) | LCC HD9349.S634 S355 2018 (print) |
  DDC 338.7/663620973—dc23
LC record available at https://lccn.loc.gov/2018005014

CONTENTS

WHY WRITE A BOOK ABOUT SELTZER?

In which begins a decade-long quest to uncover the history of seltzer water and learn how and why it became such a sparkling source of pleasure.

NEW YORK CITY

"Why does she want me to write a book on seltzer?" I wondered. We were having lunch on Madison Avenue, at the upscale restaurant she had chosen, and I was confused. (*Spoiler alert: I wrote it.*)

I ordered pasta; maybe it was fettuccine Alfredo (hard to say, it was over a decade ago). I tried to calm my rising panic. This seemed like the nuttiest idea in the world. Why a book on seltzer? And why me?

But first, who was she? And why did she care so much about seltzer?

When I first received her email, I had no idea who she was. It was January 6, 2005. There was no subject. All she really said was, "Please give me a call," and signed it Carolyn Starman Hessel. I

1

didn't know who Carolyn Starman Hessel was; the email said she worked at the Jewish Book Council, about which I knew even less.[1]

Still, I could imagine why she wanted to speak with me, if she was anything like the others. I'd been receiving emails all week from people sharing their memories of growing up with seltzer in their homes, recollections of climbing on the seltzer man's truck, or siblings spritzing each other when mom wasn't looking. The tales were nostalgic with a hint of urgency, shared as if racing an unspoken deadline. This was all in response to my article.

It was a product review, really—at least that's how I pitched it to the *Forward*. There was a new kitchen appliance for making seltzer from scratch that had just come to America from overseas. I knew little about seltzer at the time, but I thought it would be fun to get the appliance for free from the manufacturer if I could Google enough to write about it. In my byline I included my email address and invited readers to send me their own seltzer stories, opening up a floodgate of memories from around the country.

My piece was barely 650 words long. There just wasn't much to say. This was more than a decade ago, before I began to drink a few liters of seltzer a day, before I tended my collection of seltzer machines (one for work and one for home), before I accidentally became one of the world experts on seltzer. In fact, here's the article itself; after you read it, even if you knew nothing about the topic when you first picked up this book, you will now at least know as much as I did when I first sat down with Carolyn for lunch, the meal that would launch me on my quest to understand what I've come to term *Seltzertopia*.

MIXING UP THE SPRITZ

By Barry Joseph

December 31, 2004

Like Chinese food and pickles, seltzer—an effervescent spirit that has inspired dreams of cures for such diverse ailments as scurvy and indigestion—is often associated with Jews. An ad for an at-home seltzer maker touts its product as part of the history of Jewish ingenuity: "Matzo, circa 1440 B.C.—Chicken Soup, circa 1280 A.D.—Homemade Seltzer, 2004." Anecdotally, it is said that Jews came from Eastern Europe, the land of soda water, and brought this unique taste along with their baggage. But if this were true, why don't our non-Jewish countrymen hold this same association?

I turned from oral history to medical experts, seeking the advice of my doctor. "The Jewish people suffer from a thousand and one gastrointestinal problems," he said. "But once they could burp? Wow!" (Unfortunately, since my doctor is also my father, it was not clear whether he was referring to all Jews or just to me and to my family.)

A character in Ben Katchor's graphic novel, *The Jew of New York*, envisioned an endless supply of seltzer piped to homes from a carbonated Lake Erie. My seltzer dreams paled in comparison. All I wanted, in the privacy of my apartment, was to make my own seltzer.

An English chemist named Joseph Priestley created the first man-made glass of carbonated water. He had hoped to develop a means for slowing the decay of a rotting corpse. Priestley described his process with elaborate detail and hand-drawn diagrams in a 1772 paper to The Royal Society, titled "Impregnating Water with Fixed Air." My own home brewing, however, needed no such diagrams. Recently I made my own discovery: the Fountain Jet Home Soda Maker, self-described as the number-one "home carbonation system in the world."

Of course, in modern times, such efforts at home carbonation no longer are required. Centuries ago, I would have had to travel to Niederselters, Germany, wherefrom the word "seltzer" derives, to drink from their natural pools of carbonated water. But because of entrepreneur John Matthews, who left England in 1842 and turned New York City into the epicenter of the seltzer revolution, now I can travel downstairs to my corner grocer for a two-liter bottle. Convenient, yes, but who wants to lug a bottle home every week?

The Israeli-owned Soda-Club manufactures the Soda Maker in its Jerusalem plant. It is a surprisingly simple device. The night before our Hanukkah party, after hours frying latkes, my wife and I decided to try it out. We filled the specially designed one-liter bottle with Brita-filtered, previously chilled water. I pushed back a small black lever on the top of the fountain to tilt the nozzle at a convenient angle. I inserted the open bottle and twisted a few times until it was good and stuck. It was that quick. Everything was in place. To turn water into seltzer, all I had to do was push a button.

With each firm press, a burst of carbonation shot through the bottle from the carbon dioxide canister hidden in the back. One. Two. Three times. Then a fourth for good measure. With a sharp twist of the bottle it fell free from the nozzle, ready to be capped.

If this actually worked, if this machine could turn my Brooklyn tap water into seltzer, it would feel as miraculous as one night's worth of oil lasting for eight days. We poured our first glasses of homemade seltzer and raised them in a toast to Priestley, Matthews, and all who followed in their visionary footsteps. I tipped back the glass, partly expecting the dullness of flat water. Instead, delightful bubbles danced down my throat and I let out a delicate belch, exquisitely satisfied. I had in my hands the holy grail of soda water, something only dreamed of in the crazy works of Ben Katchor: a supply of seltzer as accessible and plentiful as all the water in the New York City reservoirs.

You might have noticed I was grasping at straws, interviewing my dad and quoting in desperation from a graphic novel to fill space. So, yeah, when Carolyn recommended I turn these 650 words into an entire book, I couldn't imagine what she had in mind.

But Carolyn, she knew. She came from seltzer. Her dad was in the seltzer business, her kitchen sink as a child rigged to run tap and carbonated water.

Carolyn also knew books. I would later learn that since 1994, when she joined the Jewish Book Council and became its executive director, she had become known for helping new authors find their audiences, which led some to call her the "Jewish Oprah." Over lunch she explained why she had asked me to lunch. "There are books on bread and salt," she told me. This was back in the day when microhistories were blowing up. "There should be a book on seltzer. And you can write it."

Me? Write a book? For fun, once a year, I might write an article on something that caught my fancy. But I had never before considered writing a book.

"I like your writing style," she told me. "It flows well."

Still, I had little relationship with seltzer. Unlike those emails from my readers, I had no exciting childhood memories of seltzer. As a child, seltzer was just "gross." No flavor, or too sour, I might have said. My family's kitchen table was an altar to bottles of Coca-Cola. If my family had a crest it would certainly have framed a plastic two-liter Coke bottle. They filled out our meals, one or two a night. Many a photo from family trips proudly show us after an exciting culinary adventure gathered around the empty remains of Coke bottles, the higher the number the greater our pride.

After college, however, to the dismay of my family, I left behind the cult of Coke. It was not that I had decided to live a healthier life, but I sensed there was something wrong about the constant caffeine running through my system. So, for a year or two I did without, and what I found I missed more often than anything else, especially at mealtime, was the fizz. Meals felt flat without it. Then I began to see seltzer in a new light. I drank a bottle, almost in desperation. It no longer felt gross but refreshing. The thing I had disliked as a child, its clear, sharp taste, was now its main appeal. I was far from a fan, but it became my drink of choice, motivating me to write an article so I could stop schlepping bottles home.

Still, to Carolyn, I pleaded seltzer ignorance. How could there be enough for a whole book? What was there actually to say?

She was unrelenting, insistent I would find the story of seltzer. I wanted to give her the benefit of the doubt while showing appreciation for her kind words, faith in my abilities, and the lovely lunch.

We agreed I'd think on it for a month then get back to her.

During those four weeks I didn't think so much as listen, quizzing everyone I knew on the topic: if you had to write about seltzer, I asked, what would you want to write about?

I was surprised at how quickly a pattern emerged among their answers. First, bemusement—"Seltzer? What's to say about seltzer?" Then, interest—"Actually, what about . . ." To be followed by near rapture—"Ooh, and what about . . . And don't forget . . . And wasn't there a scene in . . . And did I mention . . ." Before long it was evident I was onto something. What exactly, however, was far from clear.

I told Carolyn I thought she was right and embarked on a project that grew, over more than a decade, into *Seltzertopia*. At first

I decided to spend a year interviewing people wherever I went. I bought a tiny digital recorder that fit in my back pocket and struck up conversations with random people as I went about life in New York City, just to see what I could turn up, searching for patterns along the way. I spoke with cabbies and businessmen, waiters and policy makers. And I always asked the same four questions:

- What is your name?
- What do you do for a living?
- What comes to mind when you hear the phrase "seltzer water"?
- How would your life be different without seltzer?

This original research was supplemented by the few books I could find that mentioned the topic. It turned out there had never been a book on seltzer—children's books, sure, but nothing comprehensive that explained what seltzer is and why we drink it. I had little I could rely on to point my way beyond the informal experts hidden in plain sight. I needed to expand the effect created by my byline in the *Forward*, to become a beacon attracting the attention of seltzer fans around the world. I created a blog, a podcast, a Facebook account, and more. There was just a trickle at first, but that trickle turned into a stream. Over the years hundreds of people have contacted me, helping me piece together the geological, industrial, and cultural history of seltzer. More importantly, they helped me to understand what made each and every one of them so passionate about the subject: who, in a world of syrupy sodas, smoothies, and fruit juices, aspired always to keep it seltzer.

When I sat down for that lunch more than a decade ago, I could never have imagined it would ignite a passion within me to track down every seltzer lead I could find and shape them into the story you are now reading, the exciting and often unexpected tale of how we are approaching Seltzertopia.

What I would learn, as well, is that I was far from alone. Throughout history, and across America today, seltzer's charismatic carbonation has attracted people who have developed a loyalty and passion that often defies logic. How did seltzer come to lay claim to such a broad and diverse swath of human experience? What is it about this simplest of concoctions—$H_2O + CO_2$—that has allowed it to make a difference to so many people in such different ways? How does it manage to absorb and reflect the cultural desires of those drawn to its effervescent spirit?

So, join me in an adventure into the past, present, and future of seltzer.

In the first part, we will discover the untold story of seltzer's history and meet the men and women across America who have found themselves building a path to Seltzertopia. You'll learn where seltzer comes from, the science of seltzer, and more. And in the fascinating tales shared by those running century-old seltzer works or those collecting seltzer siphons, you might recognize a kindred soul who shares your fondness for the fizz. Or, instead, you might marvel from outside, looking in at people who have discovered seltzer passions that have overtaken their lives, forcing us to ask: why are people so passionate about something that seems so ordinary?

In the second part, we will explore why so many people care so much about seltzer (and if you don't, perhaps why you should). We'll uncover the different ways people have brought meaning to their fizzy friend, such as healthy living, the joy of soda fountains, slapstick humor, and ethnic identity. We'll explore local food connoisseurs, egg creams, European spas, and the Three Stooges.

In the third part, we will enter the effervescent age, when seltzer is freely available in plastic bottles, in corner stores, now in a wide range of flavors. We'll meet the first flavored-seltzer entrepreneurs and learn how they upended an industry, then explore seltzer's global appeal. Finally, we'll meet the new generation of seltzer professionals, opening seltzer works around the country and redesigning the profession as they guide us all toward a state of Seltzertopia.

Once upon a time, only the most elite had access to carbonated water, by going on holiday and traveling to distant health spas. It was this inequality of access that motivated the character of Francis Oriole in *The Jew of New York*, which I referenced in my original article. His seltzer-utopic dream of carbonating Lake Erie, as he declares it, is for seltzer to be "piped into every American home!" Oriole's dream was a populist fantasy, to provide the average person with the same rarefied benefits enjoyed by the most well-to-do.

Today, at the start of the twenty-first century, we are surprisingly close to Oriole's dream. Few might have access to a local seltzer works, but seltzer is available by the liter in supermarkets and single servings in corner delis. SodaStream's "home carbonating system" (described in my article above under its old name, Soda-Club) allows the average big-box shopper to manufacture seltzer on demand using nothing more than simple tap water.

It might not be from Lake Erie, but America is slowly turning its local water supply into seltzer, one faucet at a time. My aim in this book is to help us understand why.

I

THE NEW MO
SYPHON F
MANUFACTURE
BARNETT & P
ENGINEERS
LONDON ENGLAND

PITT
SEL
MA
CLUB

John Seekings at the Pittsburgh Seltzer Works

PART ONE

The World According to Seltzer

Learn the untold history of seltzer and about the people across America who have found themselves building a path to Seltzertopia. Discover where seltzer comes from, the science of seltzer, and how people can become so passionate about something so ordinary.

More specifically, meet John Seekings, a public relations executive in Pittsburgh, Pennsylvania, and join him on his unexpected journey into the modern world of old-fashioned seltzer bottling.

ODE TO SODA WATER

Delicious drink, albeit unsubstantial —
  Fraught with fruit syrup, or extraneous essence,
Mighty, monarchic in thy reign, though man shall
  Scoff at thy evanescent effervescence!

Concoction beautiful, inimitable!
  By every girl art thou assimilated
In quantities unparalleled, illimitable,
  While man's finances become abbreviated.

— anonymous, 1884, *National Bottlers' Gazette*

1

THE BIRTH OF A MODERN
SELTZER MAN

*In which John Seekings, a Pittsburgh-based public relations executive, learns
that a more-than-a-century-old seltzer works is up for sale.*

BOTTLES OF DEATH

John Seekings drove himself to the emergency room in Shadyside
and presented his self-bandaged hand wrapped in a bloodied rag.
"It's a pretty deep cut," he said, explaining that it was in that meaty
section right underneath his thumb.

The nurse was far from impressed. This was an emergency
room, after all. "How deep can it be?" she asked.

Then she removed the bandage and saw the blood. "Oh," she
said. "You're right."

She called over a young intern to take a look. He, too, was
surprised.

The head of the emergency room came over and looked at the
hand. He looked at John. Then he asked, "How did this happen?"

As the attending physician began to sew up his right hand, John answered with his left by drawing a picture of the seltzer siphon that had bought him his ticket to the hospital.

"Well," John then explained, "if you really want to know, I have this seltzer company. I was walking, and I wasn't paying attention, and I tripped." Unfortunately, his hands had not been empty: he had been holding a seventy-pound wooden crate containing ten siphons full of seltzer. When he tripped, the case fell.

When the case fell, the bottles spilled out.

And when they hit the cement floor of the factory, the thick glass bottles, all older than forty-year-old John, shattered. The bed of glass spreading out before him became the sharp cushion that broke his fall.

John's seltzer company was the Pittsburgh Seltzer Works, located in a modest warehouse in Pittsburgh, Pennsylvania. Certainly not a beautiful space, but there was beauty nonetheless in the 110-year-old carbonators, in the bottles that were everywhere, and in the wooden cases. The carbonators that made the fizz certainly caused no lack of difficulty—try finding a replacement part for a machine that hasn't been manufactured since the Great Depression—but what broke most often were the computer and credit-card machines, the only modern things in the space. Everything else predated World War II. John was still looking for one of those old cash registers with the handles on the side. Then the only modern technology would be his computer, for Facebook, which he logged onto as soon as he returned from the hospital with his twenty-eight stitches.

He had to—his customers were waiting.

Typing was difficult, what with being down to one good hand, but with text messages and voicemails collecting, he knew he couldn't put it off much longer. But John didn't know what to write. He had purchased the temporarily shuttered Pittsburgh

Seltzer Works eighteen months earlier, in September 2009. Back then he knew little about what he was doing. He was just a public relations executive, constrained in his suit and tie, who thought he had come across an interesting side investment. Now he looked like he belonged on the fishing show *Deadliest Catch*—dressed in sneakers and ripped jeans, with a baseball cap up top and his body wrapped and waterproofed from head to foot, soaking wet on the outside, with a smile from here to there. He now claimed membership among a handful of experts around the country with deep knowledge of an arcane art—bubbling water.

When John reopened the factory, former customers came out of the woodwork. It was as if a favorite television show had been cancelled then picked up by a different network, just years later with a different cast. "We have been waiting for our delivery for a couple of years now," wrote one customer on Facebook, mentioning she still had six siphons from the last order all ready to be exchanged. Customers learned to use the Facebook page to connect directly with John, letting him know when they were ready for another delivery, while others simply posted gushing testimonials. When clients of the Pittsburgh Seltzer Works became fans on Facebook, they declared their passion for seltzer, their commitment to take meaning from its iconically simple mix of water and carbon dioxide, time and time again.

At first it might seem odd to use twenty-first-century technology to promote a business that was at its peak before television was born, back when telephones were far from ubiquitous and traffic signals were a new idea. But John and his partner, Jim Rogal, both came from an advertising background. They enjoyed this direct and open communication channel with their customers. John loved to sit back and watch what people were saying, telling him when he was doing a good job or when they had a problem. It kept their relationships fluid.

Still, John needed to post time and again, especially when business was going to be delayed. In the past, John had posted just enough photos to give customers a feel for the Works: John standing in front of the carbonator, mugging for the camera, surrounded by thousands of bottles. Or a close-up of a customer visiting the Works, reading the children's book *The Seltzer Man* by Ken Rush. If people looked carefully at the photo, just over John's shoulder they could see the special shelf featuring siphons missing significant parts, the siphons he calls the "Bottles of Death."

The bottling machine that filled the siphons with carbonated water took six at a time. The thick glass bottles each weighed five pounds empty; they were designed to take the high pressure pushing out from the seltzer within. But sometimes the sturdy bottles were flawed and had a crack or other deformity. The pressure caused those bottles to explode. Even if it happened *inside* the machine, toward the back, glass shards flew. John had been hurt a few times and received stitches for those injuries as well.

"John proudly displayed the remains on a shelf behind his desk."

To mark each explosion, and to remind himself to be careful (and duck!), John proudly displayed the largest of the remains on a shelf behind his desk: the Bottles of Death. So no, this was not his first injury in the shop, or the first of the year. He had broken two fingers trying to fix one of the machines. Another time he had slipped on the wet floor and cracked his ribs landing on a case of siphons. But this new injury was going to leave the best scar for sure, a real war wound. All in all, John just considered it an occupational hazard, the price he paid to keep the seltzer running and, at times, possibly saving other people from a worse fate.

Take the previous year, when a man came in with a bottle purchased at a flea market, an old European model that took a small CO_2 cartridge. He asked John how he could use it to make seltzer. He wanted to get a large canister of CO_2 and regulate the pressure. "What you'll ultimately make is a bomb," John informed him, "and it may blow up and kill you." The bottle was beautiful and ornate. John recommended putting it up on display and, if he really wanted good seltzer, becoming a new customer. Instead of winding up in the hospital, he followed John's advice. Nothing could make John happier than his hard work keeping someone else both safe and seltzer satisfied.

So, sure, his hand hurt. But he was a committed seltzer man—committed to his customers—and what really mattered were those depending on him and the Works to keep their thirst quenched. John was not about to let any Bottles of Death keep the seltzer from flowing. When he and Jim first bought the Works, they could have turned around and made a quick profit on eBay selling off the machinery and all the bottles. It would have been easy. But it would have been dishonest. When they bought the Works, they promised to keep it going. This was a commitment to the clients. This was a commitment to the former owners—not just the last ones, but a chain that went back over a century. This was a commitment to their peers around the country, a handful of seltzer makers who fought the odds to maintain a practice that should have died out long ago. How could John turn away from that now, even for a short time? No, the seltzer must flow.

No clients on Facebook would learn of John's injury that day. All they would know is that bottles were being prepped for the next delivery. John, however, did not leave the computer right away. He still had one more task to complete. He entered his newest client into the customer list: the attending physician from the emergency room.

John looked at his stitches and thought, "We got a customer out of this, so it was a win-win at the end of the day."

SELTZER FOR SALE

Two years earlier, all Seekings had known about seltzer was from mass-produced bottles he brought home from the market and the antics of the Three Stooges he had enjoyed as a child. He had no idea that people had first discovered seltzer's promise of pleasure more than two centuries earlier, that pleasure coming to overshadow its original medicinal role. He knew nothing of Joseph Priestley, the radical minister who invented seltzer; or of John Matthews, the seltzer industrialist; or of William B. Keller, who more than anyone nursed the emerging bottling business in its infancy.

Born in 1969 to parents who flew—his mother as a flight attendant for the precursor to British Airways, his father as a former pilot in the British Royal Air Force—John Seekings was raised in Connecticut, had family all over Long Island, and was schooled in New York and New Jersey. One day in the late 1980s, his brother in Pittsburgh coaxed him to come for a visit; once he arrived, John never left, completing his education at the University of Pittsburgh. The city was less hectic than the tristate area. He liked the people. He had found a new home.

Before long John began working at the local PBS affiliate in advertising and public relations, supporting such shows as *Where in the World Is Carmen Sandiego?*, a joint coproduction with the Boston affiliate. And that was where he met Jim Rogal.

Also in advertising, Jim had been a journalist and had worked for Major League Baseball. In some ways, Jim became John's mentor, a generation older with his kids already out of the house. They decided to set up shop together. For tax purposes, they created their own separate businesses (John's was Caroline Communications and Jim's was Century Communications), serving different clients and doing different things in the area of communications, media relations, and public relations. But they shared the same office and worked together every day. They complemented each other perfectly. Jim was Jewish; John was Catholic. Jim was a native Pittsburgher, his family going back three generations; John was a transplant. Jim considered himself "technologically challenged," but John thrived on technology.

"Some work will come in through John's company," Jim explained, "and he and I work on it together." Other times it was the reverse, with Jim's company bringing in the business and retaining John. Occasionally opportunity arose for them to become business partners dabbling on side projects small enough to fit, as Jim said, in his "hip pocket."

In the spring of 2009, John kicked back at the end of a long day at his public relations company. As he took a few minutes to drink some seltzer and opened the day's paper, he had no idea his future was waiting inside. Right there, in the *Pittsburgh Post-Gazette*, he encountered the headline that would change his life: "Pittsburgh Seltzer Works Fizzes Away After 120 Years in Business."[2]

The article was off by just a few years. The seltzer factory was founded in 1898, part of the first generation of bottlers that had risen to meet the needs of America's newfound love for carbonated beverages.

The article featured a photo of Evan Hirsh and his business partner, Paul Supowitz, surrounded by blue, green, and clear siphons. Evan and Paul, along with their friend David Faigen, had bought the Works on a lark. But after a dozen years, the three men were now calling it quits, citing work responsibilities from their day jobs. That week's seltzer delivery would be their last, and the final from the Pittsburgh Seltzer Works, unless a new owner could be found.

"It's a funny business, where the profits are marginal," Evan said in the article. "But they exist." The article described how over time the friends increasingly pulled back more and more from the business. They even stopped returning calls from new customers. "They hope someone more ambitious, with more time," John read, "would approach it differently."

And their terms were rock-bottom: all they wanted for the bottles and machinery was the same thirty thousand dollars they had paid twelve years earlier. They seemed to feel almost guilty for stepping down from the business, as if they couldn't bear the weight of disappointment that might hang over the city.

"We would love to see someone take it over," Evan concluded.

As John Seekings read the article he wondered, "Could I be that person?" The idea was crazy—he already had his own business with Jim, had two small children at home, and knew nothing about the seltzer business—but the idea was something he just couldn't shake. So he called Jim to his desk.

"Hey, look at this," he said as he handed Jim the article. "Do you know any of them?" People from Pittsburgh like to say it's a big small town. Everyone knew everyone, especially in the East End, where they both lived. It turned out Jim knew the previous owner from the 1980s, Sam Edelmann, from when they both worked at WQED, the public television station. Meanwhile, John lived two blocks from Evan and coached his son on lacrosse. Jim was especially interested when John explained the financial angle. "They are selling it relatively inexpensively," John said. "Why don't you look into it?"

"Well," Jim cautiously told John, "let's go through the motions."

The next day John called Evan to learn the terms of sale. They were unusual, to say the least. The friends had already made it clear in the article that they were looking not for a profit but for a commitment, to preserve the Works and its local nature. They had come up with a plan: host an event, invite all interested buyers to attend, and give them a tour. While the visitors were evaluating the Works, the prospective buyers would be evaluated as well. At the end, they would see who was left standing.

When John hung up the phone, he didn't know exactly what might happen on the tour, but he knew one thing: he had to come prepared. He could easily imagine the expertise of his competition: soda manufacturers, seltzer bottlers from other regions, and who knew who else. And at that point he couldn't tell a can of soda from a carbonator.

But how much could there be to know about seltzer anyway? Some bottles listed carbonated water, just water (H_2O) injected with carbon dioxide (CO_2), as the only ingredient.

So what accounted for its crisp, refreshing taste? The bubbles, perhaps, dancing across the tongue?

Think again.

THE SCIENCE OF SELTZER

In 2009, a research paper published in the journal *Science* forever changed our understanding of seltzer's sharp bite and silenced, once and for all, the seltzer haters who insisted it tastes no different than water.[3]

"When you drink a carbonated drink you really think you are detecting the bubbles bursting on your tongue," reported Nicholas J. P. Ryba, one of the coauthors of the paper and a National Institutes of Health researcher focused on how people perceive taste.[4] But he and the other scientists on the paper were curious. Was perception reality? They had heard of a research study in which participants drank carbonated beverages in high-pressure chambers set up so no bubbles could form. Did it taste flat? No. In fact, the subjects reported tasting the fizz! They wanted to understand why and thought Ryba's ongoing study of mammalian taste might provide an answer.

To test the hypothesis that the zest of carbonation came through taste, not touch, Ryba worked with mice that had been bred to lack specific taste receptor cells (bitter, sweet, sour, salty, or umami) on their taste buds. The mice who could taste everything but sweet flavors, for example, all responded to carbon dioxide. In other words, "sweetless mice" might enjoy a cold glass of seltzer (if they could be convinced to ignore the fizz and drink it). And this was true for all the mice, save one batch: the mice missing their sour receptors. "Sourless mice," so to speak, were the only mice not to respond. For these unfortunate mice, all seltzer would seem flat.

(Let us please take a moment of silence to thank the sourless mice for their noble sacrifice.)

So it turns out that seltzer's carbonation is experienced through sour taste receptors. But seltzer doesn't taste sour. Here's what's so amazing: by the time the taste is experienced, at a chemical level it's actually no longer seltzer. The secret is something that comes between the seltzer and the taste bud, an enzyme in mouths called carbonic anhydrase 4. This enzyme, which lives right next to the taste buds, greets the newly-released CO_2 by transforming it into bicarbonate; this process leaves behind a free-floating acidic proton that triggers the sour taste bud receptor, giving the sensation of "feeling" (instead of tasting) zesty carbonation. That acidic proton is the car key turning on the taste of the seltzer.

In fact, Earl Carstens, a researcher at the University of California, Davis, reported that without the carbonic anhydrase 4 enzyme, anything carbonated tastes flat. A high-altitude-sickness medication, for example, which temporarily suppresses this enzyme, is known to cause great disappointment to mountain climbers who open a bottle of champagne or a can of soda at the end of their climb only to find that it tastes "like dishwater."

So seltzer's sharp kiss, it turns out, is more than just physical. Those little bubbles, playfully jumping out of your seltzer glass to tickle your nose, are not what provides the delightful feeling of effervescence as you drink. That sparkle, that crisp edge that rejuvenates the soul, comes not from the bursting of bubbles but, instead, through a rather fortuitous reaction to the bubbles by a well-placed enzyme with a certain attraction for seltzer.

THE OPEN HOUSE

For John Seekings it was game time. What little he had learned or thought he knew about seltzer would have to suffice. As he arrived for the first time at the Pittsburgh Seltzer Works to satisfy his curiosity, the open house was about to begin.

John parked close to its entrance at 221 East Ninth Avenue in the town of Homestead, right outside Pittsburgh's city line. Homestead was famous for having been one of the largest steel-making centers in the world back when it had played a key role preparing America for World War II. Mere blocks from the Works, the neighborhood once hosted one of the most important labor strikes of the nineteenth century.

While his seltzer knowledge had been enhanced through some targeted Google research, when John approached the front door he still had little idea what to expect.

Twelve years earlier, when Evan, Dave, and Paul had bought the Pittsburgh Seltzer Works, their first task had been to find it a new home. They carved out a niche in their twenty-four-thousand-square-foot futon warehouse, previously a Buick dealership, and set up the bottling equipment in a cold corner of the concrete basement. The rest of the floor was filled with storage for the futon store and, where some room remained, Evan's 1972 Cutlass convertible.

As John approached the bottling line, the tables topped with siphons and crates upon crates of stacked bottles, he saw he was far from alone in his interest. His call was one of over one hundred received by the Pittsburgh Seltzer Works in the days following the article, far more than the three owners had ever anticipated.

John stood among a few dozen men and women who had responded to the challenge, some there on their own, others with a friend or colleague. Some were looking for a side project, a way to supplement their income. Some were out of work, with little to lose. Some just saw a seltzer company for sale and thought it was interesting. One came brandishing a business plan. Another's family had been in soda for many years. But most, like John, knew little about the business of seltzer and had a lot to learn. If John wanted the business, and he was still far from certain he did, he had his work cut out for him.

In many ways, it was like the Roald Dahl classic *Charlie and the Chocolate Factory*, in which the eccentric Willy Wonka leads a group of children on a tour to determine who would take over his business. Only this time the visitors were not children, there would be no chocolate, and the only Oompa-Loompas in their way were the guidelines laid down constraining the pool of potential buyers. There would be no regular sales pitch, as seltzer bottling in the twenty-first century was no regular business.

Evan and his friends began the presentation by explaining how they ran the company. They bottled once a week and delivered twice a month. They quickly clarified that they had intentionally slowed down the business, so their efforts were far from meeting the existing demand; the future of the Works should not be determined based on their current sales.

To demonstrate, they pulled out their prop: a store-bought bottle of seltzer. They had paid $2.00. Their seltzer siphons, in contrast, sold for $1.50. Clearly there was room for a price increase. Yet if anyone fantasized about getting rich on seltzer, they had better look elsewhere to find their fortune. At best, the Works could be a good sideline business, not a sole-income provider. Nor was a seltzer business something to be done alone. All three owners were required to pull it off. What with the pickups and drop-offs, the cleaning and filling, the paperwork and community outreach, running a seltzer plant took time, care, and a lot of physical labor.

Tremendous effort. Little profit. If it was not yet clear to the others, it became increasingly so to John: for these three friends, running the Works was less a business venture than a labor of love. The more he listened, the more he understood what had moved them.

Evan lifted a wooden crate. Packed with six full siphons, the crate weighed forty pounds or so, he explained. He and his partners bottled roughly thirty cases at a time, several times a week.[5] From among a collection of glass bottles colored blue, green, and clear, he lifted one up. "The whole story of seltzer is linked to these bottles," he said, quoting his predecessor Sam Edelmann. The three thousand or so bottles owned by the business were some of their prime assets. Filtered water could always be found. Customers could always be reached. But the siphons were irreplaceable. Most dated from World War II or before and had been in use for decades. Older customers might very well have encountered the same siphon as a youth, if not from the Works than at a cafe, bar, or ice-cream counter.

Siphons are the crux of a seltzer delivery business, whether delivered to a home or local bar. They are the only containers strong enough to withstand the high pressures that distinguish its content from that offered by store-bought plastic seltzer bottles. More pressure means greater carbonation, smaller bubbles, and more fizz.[6]

Siphons also carry their own pedigrees. The siphons at the Works were marked with the names of cities and towns from around the region: New Castle, Verona, New Kensington, McKees Rocks, and Warren. Others were from further afield: Brooklyn and Long Island, Michigan and Wisconsin.[7] Some had unique marks, such as a balloon, to identify the plant from which they had originated.

With each marked location, John fell deeper for the history they carried. As Evan spoke, John found his mind wandering, speculating on historical reconstructions suggested by the bottles. "Maybe Andrew Carnegie, the American industrialist who founded Pittsburgh's Carnegie Steel Company, sat down with this bottle," he thought, "right here, in town, meeting with his business collaborator, Henry Clay Frick. And this one, from the Camden Club in New York: who drank cocktails mixed with its seltzer, and where is their family today?" The speculative possibilities were endless.

The more John understood, the more he fell in love, including with the machines.

At almost a hundred years old, the collection of assorted pipes, containers, and contraptions was showing its age. Amazingly, this jalopy of a factory was healthy enough to produce seltzer and fill those siphons, one of only a handful of seltzer works active across the country. To the newcomer, the mechanisms were undecipherable. But to the initiated, the machines used for each of the four phases of converting water to seltzer were clear: the triple filters, the chiller, the carbonator, and the filler. Having explained the nature of the business, Evan now revealed to John and his competitors the magic trick that turned plain water into sparkling seltzer.

First, municipal water, no different from tap water, traveled through pipes to undergo a triple filtration process. Sand filters removed particles. Charcoal, like that found in a standard home water filter, removed unwanted odors and tastes. Finally, a paper polisher removed any remaining particles. At the end of this first stage the filtered water was purer than some bought in stores.

Second, the water poured into a ninety-gallon chiller. Good seltzer depended upon cold water. Here the water sat, pushing past cold plates

The carbonator

that lowered its temperature to approximately forty-three degrees. At the end of the second stage the water was both chilled and filtered.

Third, a loud pump in the carbonator sucked in water from the chiller. At the same time, pressurized liquid CO_2 was pulled into the carbonator, turning into gas upon release. A paddle beat the two together, as if mixing a cake, transforming them at a molecular level from two to one, from H_2O and CO_2 to H_2CO_3, otherwise known as carbonic acid. Carbonic acid formed best in the cold, thus the need for the chiller, and it only maintained its bonds under pressure. At the end of the third stage the water was now pressurized, chilled, and 100 percent seltzer.

Finally, the filler. The filler machine took an empty siphon and returned it after a few seconds with pressurized, chilled seltzer water. For that to happen, the human bottler had to place one bottle at a time upside down on a circular belt in the machine, which turned like a revolving door. Placing the bottle required smooth, fast action. The person feeding the bottles was at risk of breaking his arm—or worse, if his hand got caught on the splash guard. As the bottle moved into the filler's dark chamber, outside of view, the machine pressed the siphon head's trigger to open the spout as the filler's valves opened. The pressure from within the carbonator shot the seltzer into the bottle spout, sending it through the glass straw down the center until the bottle was full. As the filler completed its revolution, the seltzer's journey ended when the human bottler removed the siphon from the machine and, with a flip, placed it back in its wooden case on the conveyor belt.

John was handed a glass of seltzer to taste, real seltzer, not the low-pressure variety he had enjoyed all his life. It came as a revelation, as if the low-pressure variety had stolen the name, because the siphoned seltzer tasted that much better.

But as complicated as the process may have seemed, at its core it was all rather simple: mix cold water and carbon dioxide. All else was extra. Without that process, there would be no seltzer works, nothing mass produced or distributed, no source for seltzer lovers to find their refreshment. And this process, upon which the entire works relied, was invented in 1776 by the most unlikely of people, a radical priest-turned-scientist in Birmingham, England, named Joseph Priestley.

THE INVENTION OF SELTZER

John Seekings had turned up the name of Joseph Priestley time and again during his research before the tour of the Works, one Google search after another. The minister and self-taught scientist was still renowned as the eighteenth-century Brit who discovered oxygen and brought the then-radical religious practice of Unitarianism to America. But among Priestley's vast scientific, religious, and political achievements, one reigned supreme, at least for soda aficionados: Joseph Priestley invented seltzer. Yet, in Steven Johnson's recent Priestley biography, *The Invention of Air*, the event barely rates two pages. Within the history of seltzer, however, it was paramount, the oft-recounted origin story without which modern seltzer could not exist.

To be more precise, Priestley invented a way to manufacture carbonated water, to put fizz where none had gone before. What would soon become a common practice was, at the time, revolutionary, like stealing fire from the gods. Priestley had enabled humans to produce what for millions of years had been beyond our grasp. Once people had the power to re-create what was found in nature—carbonated water mixed with a variety of minerals—it was only a matter of time until science discovered how to adjust that water to meet the shifting streams of popular taste, how to domesticate it by removing harsher elements and turn it from a source of medicine to a delightful drink. Priestley is credited with beginning it all.

Priestley was born on March 13, 1733, in Fieldhead, England, a small, rural town six miles southwest of Leeds. His aunt encouraged him to enter the ministry due to his love of books and brilliance evidenced at a young age. While he spent his twenties preaching to small congregations of religious nonconformists, his future income lay in his writings, such as "The Rudiments of English Grammar." These writings would move him into teaching and—due to an unlikely confluence of three things: his speech impediment, Benjamin Franklin, and a brewery—put him, soon after, on the path toward experimentation that would change the world.

Many factors influenced Priestley's early career path as a minister. His unorthodox religious views (he believed Christianity's Holy Trinity was two too many) and the politics of the time (he supported both the American and French Revolutions) held clear importance. One personal trait, however, rivaled those in significance: his stammer. Despite being proficient in six foreign languages, he stammered from an early age, which made the public speaking required of a minister or teacher somewhat of a challenge. Over time, as writing became an effective vehicle for him to communicate his ideas, he spent less time administering to parishioners and school children, and more time experimenting in his laboratory and writing up his results.

Portrait of Joseph Priestley by Rembrandt Peale, circa 1801

Priestley's scientific interests were in a field then called "natural philosophy." He saved his meager salary and purchased the three essentials for a "modern" scientific lab: a well-calibrated scale, an air pump, and what was known as an "electricity machine"[8] (an electromechanical generator that produces static electricity). During Priestley's childhood, a brilliant American discovered a series of fundamental facts about electricity that excited amateur scientists like Priestley and still hold true today. That man was Benjamin Franklin.

When Priestley began dabbling in science, Franklin was living in London, having been sent by the Pennsylvania Assembly as a colonial agent in the years leading up to the American Revolution. Active within the scientific community of London, including the Royal Society, Franklin often met with a group of freethinkers he termed "The Club of Honest Whigs." If one wished to connect with this slice of London society, or just meet Franklin, there was no better entry point than at the London Coffee House in the shadow of St. Paul's Cathedral, where they would often debate late into the night.

Priestley met with Franklin and his Honest Whigs, convincing them to share their research in a popular book he would write. In 1767 Priestley published *The History and Present State of Electricity, With Original Experiments* to critical acclaim. It had its desired effect on both scientists and the public, viewed as the definitive source on the subject for almost one hundred years.

The scientists offered Priestley advice that would prove instrumental to the development of seltzer. Don't just write about our research, they encouraged. Conduct and write about your own. To quote Johnson: "Priestley had arrived in London as a dabbler. . . . By the time he left, he was a scientist."

First, Priestley's stammer drew him to writing. Next, Franklin led him to seek research opportunities. Now, a brewery near his new house in Leeds would soon provide a subject for Priestley to explore, and doing so would change the course of history.

Priestley moved with his wife and child to Leeds, England, when he became minister of the Mill-Hill Chapel. Waiting for their official residence to be readied, they bided their time in a house on Meadow Lane, adjacent to Jakes and Nell, a public brewery.[9] Priestley's limited responsibilities to the congregation left him ample time to experiment and follow his scientific whims, and he was fascinated by the brewery.

Budding scientists like Priestley were interested in a hot topic identified only twelve years earlier: "fixed air" or "mephitic air," today known simply as carbon dioxide. Visiting the brewery, Priestley learned that as beer brewed, carbon dioxide collected above the cauldron. His creative mind went to work, turning the brewery into a laboratory and testing whatever notion came to mind as he played with the "fixed air." As Johnson describes it, "Priestley discovered that pouring plain water back and forth between two cups while holding it over the vats suffused it with the fixed air after a short amount of time, adding an agreeable fizz that was reminiscent of certain rare mineral waters."

Priestley took great pleasure in his discovery, later calling it his "happiest,"[10] but, never a businessman, saw in it little immediate scientific or practical value. He may never have fully appreciated that it transformed the rare into the common, upending the economics dictating who could access seltzer and where. With no drive to publish his findings, for years his technique remained the providence of the Honest Whigs and other members of the Royal Society. The world had no idea that humanity had just gained the power of fizz.

All that changed at a dinner party in 1772, during a conversation with the Duke of Northumberland about sea scurvy, which plagued the Royal Navy.[11] The British might rule the waves, but they were no match for scurvy. Its cause was unknown at the time. The simple solution, eating fruits full of vitamin C, eluded the duke. But Priestley had an idea. Within the week, Priestley found himself before John Montagu, Fourth Earl of Sandwich, the Lord Commissioner of the Admiralty, describing his plan. A few months later everything was in place. In June, when the *Resolution* and the *Adventure* set sail, led by the famous explorer Captain Cook, they were armed with the latest British weapon against scurvy: seltzer machines administered by the ships' doctors.

Excited by interest from outside his scientific milieu, Priestley was inspired to finally publish his findings, offering them to the world: *Impregnating Water with Fixed Air; In order to communicate to it the peculiar Spirit and Virtues of Pyrmont Water, and other Mineral Waters of a similar Nature.* The short pamphlet described in detail, supported by diagrams, the technique he had refined for infusing ordinary water with the "peculiar spirit and virtue" heretofore available only within waters bubbling up from the ground. It opens with a dedication: "To The Right Honourable John Earl of Sandwich," thanking him for his support of the recent "trial of . . . medicated water" for the Royal Navy. And should the Admiralty desire to furnish additional ships, Priestley explained, and to make the process more generally known, he was now writing up "easy directions for making it."

Priestley's logic was understandable. Mineral water healed people who were sick. Mineral water contained "fixed air." Such air, impregnated in water and drunk upon a ship at sea, must surely offer some positive effect to those afflicted, or so he thought. As Priestley would later write elsewhere, "There can be no doubt that water thus impregnated with fixed air must have all the medicinal virtues of genuine Pyrmont or Seltzer water."[12]

Priestley, of course, was wrong. While seltzer might taste exceedingly pleasant, it cannot prevent scurvy without a vitamin C–filled slice of lemon. Because seltzer water had always been associated with medicinal properties, the potential for controlling those powers inspired the invention of artificial seltzer. Efforts like these to harness seltzer as a medicine continued to drive its popular consumption, so Priestley's key contribution should not be seen as just a failed medical experiment. What changed the world was not why he did it, but how, and that he chose to share what he learned.

His process, it turns out, was remarkably simple. As he would later write in his autobiography:

> The readiest way of impregnating water . . . is to take two vessels and to keep pouring the water from one into the other . . . held as near the yeast as possible. . . . In this manner, I have sometimes, in the space of two or three minutes, made a glass of exceedingly pleasant sparkling water, which could hardly be distinguished from very good . . . Seltzer water.[13]

Priestley was a minister and scientist. He would have been appalled by the suggestion to protect his innovations with anything like a patent and use them for his own advantage. Instead, he informed anyone with interest and ingenuity how they could manufacture their own seltzer. "If this discovery (though it doth not deserve that name)," Priestley wrote in his pamphlet, "be of any use to my countrymen, and to mankind at large, I shall have my reward."[14] As a result, the process he detailed was soon put into service by those who could apply it for commercial use and spread the practice far and wide.

One of the first who capitalized on Priestley's discovery was a German-born Swiss jeweler named Jacob Schweppe. By 1783 he had perfected the craft of mass-producing seltzer. In 1790 he was ready to go public with his innovations. He formed a partnership with his previous competitors and brought to market the first artificially produced commercial mineral water. Their success with

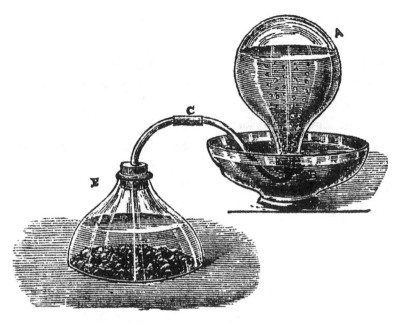

Dr. Priestley's apparatus for aerating water

exports to Britain, however, led Schweppe to leave the partnership, move to England, and sell the same product under a new business name: Schweppes. Within a few decades Schweppes was the official "Supplier of Soda Water and Mineral Waters" to the king and queen. Today, under the ownership of the Dr Pepper Snapple Group, it remains one of the top producers of seltzer.

Since Jacob Schweppe, hundreds if not thousands of seltzer manufacturers have come and gone. John Seekings, as he stood in the Pittsburgh Seltzer Works, could begin to appreciate that and something more. While far from the first or the largest, Pittsburgh Seltzer Works had something over most others: against incredible odds, it had survived.

Still, John had to wonder: "But for how much longer?"

As he concluded his first visit to the Pittsburgh Seltzer Works and climbed into his car, John felt not bewildered exactly, but perhaps enamored. There was just so much more here than he realized—the outdated machinery, the beautiful bottles, the rich history—and he could feel it getting under his skin. Purchasing the plant would be no standard side investment, he now knew, no weekend hobby.

If he wanted to pursue and develop the passion he felt emerging, it was time for some due diligence. It was time to get inside the Works' books and get a better understanding of the seltzer-bottling industry. And that, John knew, is where his partner Jim would come in.

2

THE ELYSIAN FIELDS OF BOTTLERS LITERATURE

In which John Seekings and his partner, Jim Rogal,
perform due diligence on the Pittsburgh Seltzer Works, learning the
history of seltzer as an industry and the role it played in the temperance
battles that came to a head during Prohibition.

"NO BOTTLES, NO BUSINESS"

The more John spoke with the three partners, the more interested he became in buying the Works. Jim was not surprised that John had called the owners the very night of the tour to say they were interested. John's enthusiasm could provide energy for the project, but it could also be a danger. Now was the time to let the levelheaded numbers guy do his work. Although John's enthusiasm was infectious, Jim was intrigued but cautious. His primary interest was financial.

"So?" John asked. He sat at his desk across from Jim's in the office they shared, one half technically Caroline Communications and the other half Century Communications.

"So," Jim replied. A few days earlier, John had filled him in on the Pittsburgh Seltzer Works tour and given Jim their books to work the numbers. John had told Jim about the wonders of the carbonator, the beauty of the siphons, the depth of a history you could hold in your hands. Jim saw the seed of John's interest beginning to germinate not just into a new joint business venture but into something else.

Jim was surprised that the owners were willing to sell the Works at such a reasonable rate. John explained their point of view to Jim. The three friends sold seltzer as a labor of love and were understandably wary of someone who would buy the Works and bury it on the same day. "You look at all these beautiful bottles—someone could just purchase the assets and just sell them." In the world of eBay, anyone could make their money back, and possibly a profit, simply by selling off the siphons. Quick turnaround for quick money. "But I told them that we will keep this going. We have a background in advertising. We have roots in the East End of Pittsburgh where the company is based, and we will take it to the next level."

Jim considered. "Do you think we can deliver on that promise?"

John looked to Jim like it was still his turn to share his thoughts. "You tell me. If it works, we make money. If it fails, we sell it off and get it all back. Right?"

"Let's see the books."

John had returned with the books, Jim had reviewed them, and now John was prepared to hear the story they told.

"First of all, we aren't talking about buying General Motors here," Jim began, his desk covered with the Works' customer lists and inventory. "It's pretty simple. We know what the numbers look like, in terms of money in, money out." He moved the papers around as he spoke, as if conjuring the Works itself. "The inventory is also clear, all the bottles and equipment. And the customer list."

"Is that it?" John asked.

"That's all you need. The bottles, the equipment, and the customer list. It's not complicated." John's initial instinct had been correct, and Jim told him so. "It would be hard to get hurt from a business perspective," he agreed. "If we went completely bust on the business, the value of the inventory was enough, if it ever came to that, to offset the cost. If we did nothing but sell off all the bottles we'd at least break even." It was starting to seem like such a small risk, and so simple.

"So?" John asked once again.

"So, I think from an investment perspective it'd be hard to get hurt, and if we're able to make it go, just a little bit, it'd be profitable for us—"

"Okay," John interrupted with excitement, "then—"

"But wait," Jim said. "But from a business perspective, that doesn't mean it makes a whole lot of sense. You know, this is hard work. The margins are very small." They would have to sell a lot of seltzer to make any significant profit. And the current owners were far from reaching those numbers.

"Can it get bigger?" John wanted to know, referring not to the margins but the business. "Can you see that? Because I think I can. I think we can do it, reach more customers, maybe increase prices."

"John," Jim said to his partner, to his friend. "We've done other ventures before. But this one is different. What do you know about seltzer? What do you know about running a seltzer factory? Talk to people—"

"I've talked to people," John said, and he had.

"Yes," Jim replied, "locally. Just customers. We need to learn about the industry, about the work it will take. Do that, and let's talk more, okay?"

John thought a moment. "Okay. That sounds good. Real good." He helped Jim reorganize the papers to return to the Works. "Anything in particular you're curious to know?"

"Yes," Jim replied, "but I think you've already figured this one out. We can't grow without new customers, and we can't support new customers if we can't give them siphons. But no one makes siphons anymore, right? And growth aside, without a way to renew our inventory, our reach will grow smaller with every broken bottle."

Jim was right: John had already figured this out and was concerned. Very concerned. "No matter how good a job we do," he agreed, "without new bottles, we're going to hit a wall at some point. Some bottles are going to get cracked, or broken, or lost." And the bottles were only one part of the siphon. There's the metallic siphon head on top, the glass straw inside, and who knew what else?

John picked up the papers from the desk. He turned to his partner. "If we can't find siphons, we can't buy the business."

HISTORY WRITTEN ON BOTTLES

By all accounts, the modern seltzer siphon originated in mid-nineteenth-century Paris, tragically promoted by the arrival of the deadly Asiatic cholera.

The carnivalesque Mi-Carême, a French festival that dates from the Middle Ages and is held in the middle of Lent, was scheduled for celebration on March 29, 1832. Mocking fear of the pandemic, which was spreading around the world, guests at balls across the city wore off-color, misshapen caricature masks, drank all sorts of cold drinks, and danced the cancan. Later that evening, however, the laughter died as many at the balls were struck by leg chills. The removal of their masks revealed violet-blue faces, the mark of their imminent demise. They were carried by the wagonload to Hôtel-Dieu, the main hospital. Before the month was out, Asiatic cholera would claim more than thirteen thousand victims.

In 1832, Parisians' annual consumption of carbonated or mineralized water was around half a million bottles. Five years later,

Antoine Perpigna patented the first seltzer siphon, known as the "Vase Syphoide," essentially a modern siphon, its head fitted with a valve that was closed by a spring. On the introduction of the siphon, and the recommendation supporting "carbonic acid" for preserving health from the "Academy of Medicine" and the "Hygienic Committee," sales of carbonated water increased tenfold, from five hundred thousand to five million in a short time. The use of siphons for dispensing seltzer spread throughout Europe, and for many years, the French dominated their production.

"Siphon heads were made by melting pure tin in a crucible and pouring it into molds."

The United States, however, was not seduced by the siphon's allure for at least another half century. Carbonated mineral water finally struck the public's fancy by the end of the nineteenth century. By then bottle production had shifted east, from France to Bohemia, today a region of the Czech Republic, where it would remain until the decline of the industry. The Bohemian bottles, exported to the United States, were fitted with American siphon heads, filled by American workers, and washed in American machines, encouraging a whole new industry largely centered in and around New York, at such companies as the Alfred Schneier Company, the Starman Siphon Company, the Majestic Siphon Company, and Consolidated Siphon Supply. Siphon heads were made by melting pure tin in a crucible and pouring it into molds. Each siphon head required six molds—shell, spindle, collar, valve, handle, and cap.

For many years, the siphon bottle flourished in high-priced, fashionable restaurants and resorts, as well as in Jewish households on the Lower East Side (more on that later). But after 1939, the industry experienced a precipitous decline. From that point on, no new patents were filed. Progress ended and the industry crumbled. No new bottles from Bohemia, especially not during World War II. No new heads made in America. Eventually, even the molds would disappear.

At some point, the last Bohemian bottle was formed and shipped. From then on, the only source to replace a cracked bottle was from the existing pool. Each broken bottle removed one from circulation.

John knew that he needed to get his hand on thousands of siphons so someone could continue that history, keep making seltzer accessible, and extend the stories its siphons could tell.

THE ACCIDENTAL COLLECTOR

Could one source of siphons be antique dealers? People collected all sorts of things. Was there a collectors' market for these fascinating pieces of history, with dealers who could provide the quantity of bottles required for John and Jim to feel confident about purchasing the Pittsburgh Seltzer Works?

As it turned out, the seltzer-bottle market rarely fluctuated, nor did it attract the same level of fervor as stamps, coins, or marbles. "Seltzer bottles are a funny collectible," antiques reseller Richie Strell explained. "There's never been a lot of interest in collecting them." People collect soda. They collect colored glass. They collect things with advertising. Seltzer bottles have all that. They came in different shapes and colors. "They should be the most collectible thing in the world," Richie marveled. Perhaps so. And yet there has never been a book about them or a price guide. "I've probably only met twenty collectors in my life." But there is a market: hundreds of thousands, in fact, of "people out there who want one, just one—for the bar or their kitchen. They don't even much care what it looks like. They just want one." Richie took some credit for making seltzer bottles more collectible. "I push seltzer on people. I present it at shows. It's a little more collectible now thanks to me." Thanks to him—and an increase in nostalgia. "As people get more nostalgic for the old days, when things were simpler," Richie said, "seltzer collecting is starting to weave its way back into the tapestry of our lives."

Richie Strell accidentally started collecting siphons in the 1980s. His passion, however, came late in life. Yes, he had a photo of himself with his brother, waiting on a wintry street for the seltzer delivery man. But when his family moved from Brooklyn to Long Island the deliveries stopped, and aside from after-school egg creams, seltzer was just not a part of his life.

Richie's brother, Alan, waiting for the seltzer man, Brooklyn, 1947

Richie's father once ran the Roxy Gift and Card shop, close to Radio City Music Hall. Decades after the shop closed, Richie began to take the nostalgic relics stored in his family's Valley Stream basement to the Baldwin Antique Flea Market, held on Thursdays on Long Island. He was hooked on antiques after discovering he had a knack for selling old postcards for fifteen dollars. He soon launched Richie's Red Barn antique shop behind the flea market property. And one day, in marched New York City seltzer man Walter Backerman with his wife, Zila, hunting for old seltzer siphons. A seed was planted.

Walter invited Richie to his house on the edge of New York City, taking him down into his basement, which was filled floor to ceiling with gorgeous seltzer siphons. Richie came to realize siphons were collectible on so many fronts—color, glass, bottles, advertising, decoration, function, and humor. "Between Walter's focused zaniness and the look of his basement," Richie recalled, "my mind got hooked on seltzer."

One day in the late 1980s, Richie was in New York City and wandered into an auction. "And the man was auctioning off this multi-panel, fluted, green seltzer bottle," he recalled. Fancy ones. When the auctioneer got to twenty dollars, Richie raised his hand and won the bottle. Then he found out the lot was not for one siphon, as he had presumed, but sixty. "So now I suddenly owe the guy sixty times twenty," Richie recalled with a laugh. Not twenty dollars but twelve-hundred dollars. But it worked out. They sold well.

He climbed out of that financial hole and, once out, jumped back in, time and again, buying and reselling old seltzer siphons, developing an appreciation then a taste for the rarest, and building his own collection. "I like different, unique, and fabulous shapes and the most unique colors." Other collectors preferred labels like Coca-Cola, but not Richie. For him, it was all about shape and color. Lined up side by side on his windowsills, they looked like brightly colored candy sticks at a soda shop. A light blue bottle, labeled a Marquis but called a "Mae West," had a full and rounded top that tapered to a conical shape at the bottom. A peach-colored one from France sported a red, white, and blue glass tube that siphoned the seltzer up and out and gave seltzer bottles the name "siphon." Like a barber's pole, the bottle's vertical ridging spiraled up and around the outside, bending light into interesting patterns. A French green glass siphon composed of uranium framed the dark cobalt blue straw within; black light made it glow. A squat bottle was called a "send-up" because it was used by hotel room services. Richie's absolute favorite might have been a pink bottle with a footed bottom, from Geneva. With concentric circles going around the entire bottle, it has a pink straw inside.

Richie featured his favorite 120 bottles on his eBay "About Me" page, not for sale but to share his pride and joys. "I do enjoy looking at my collection of unusual ones as they reflect the colors

"Walter's basement was filled floor to ceiling with gorgeous seltzer siphons."

of the sun," it read. "From pink and cobalt to Vaseline glass, from miniature to extra-large, they sit recessed in my windowsills." The number stayed constant, but occasionally he needed to sell the least favorite of his favorites. When times were really tight, he sold off the top, his favorites, replacing them when his finances improved. The bottles lined his windows like a fiscal health meter. "That's kinda how I know if I'm doing okay," he explained. "Look, the bottles are still on the window," he told himself now and again. "I haven't gotten desperate enough to sell them yet. Okay. I'm okay."

Richie's bottles

One night in 2005, Richie Strell just couldn't let himself go to bed. He wouldn't let himself, not if he wanted to prevent someone else from buying the seltzer siphons he was tracking on eBay. He sat at home in San Diego, staring at the eBay auction on his computer screen, undecided. A good night's sleep would certainly help, but there was no guarantee the "Buy It Now" deal would still be available when he awoke. Unlike in typical eBay auctions, the first person who agreed to the asking price would become the instant winner, claiming each and every one of the fifteen to eighteen thousand bottles. It was so tempting and, at only fifteen hundred dollars, a steal to boot.

When Richie had logged on earlier in the evening, he had not planned on encountering such a treasure trove. He had just wanted to update his "About Me" page. An eBay "power seller" since 1998, he knew that on eBay your appearance, and your reputation, was everything. With over twenty-five hundred positive comments to his credit, he understood that on eBay you sold more than just the Maxfield Parrish collectibles, vintage magazines, surfing memorabilia, and seltzer siphons that made up your successful antiques business. On eBay, you sold yourself.

It was clear to anybody viewing his page that Richie was both a bit silly and quite infatuated with seltzer siphons. His eBay storefront was more like an online siphon museum, exhibiting seltzer siphons reflected in popular culture. Clarabell the Clown. The Three Stooges. He found examples of siphons in use from all over: with leprechauns, on the cover of *Mad* magazine, in a photo from *National Geographic*, and more.

Richie did the math as he stared at his computer screen. Fifteen hundred dollars was not significantly more than his first accidental auction win. Only this time, what a bounty! Rather than sixty bottles, the haul was closer to sixteen thousand. This was unheard of. A Los Angeles–based seltzer man had aged out of the business, and his entire collection was up for sale. And the price was fantastic—about eight cents per bottle. At that price, even if many were worthless and missing their heads, he would still do fine. It lowered the risk. And there was always risk involved in a collection this large. Where did they come from? The dealer said they were being stored in Los Angeles in a twenty-by-thirty-foot area. But what condition were they in? And how many "fancies," as Richie would say, might it contain?

It was late at night. There was little more he could learn before the morning. He thought, "Should I do this?" Then he clicked the "Buy It Now" button. The bottles were his.

The next morning, over breakfast with his wife, he casually mentioned his latest eBay acquisition. Securing new siphons happened all the time. It was business as usual. "How many?" she inquired. "Oh, about eighteen thousand," he responded, "but probably closer to fifteen thousand." She practically fell out of her chair. "She thinks I'm crazy," Richie later related, "and she's always right."

Richie continues in his professional pursuit of siphons. "Watch my auctions," his eBay page exhorts, "as I continue to liquidate the last great treasure trove of seltzer bottles on the West Coast." His unabated excitement would be contagious. "Discovered and uncovered for your collecting pleasure will be many scarce ACL [Applied Color Label], acid etched, and embossed seltzer bottles from the West Coast and the Midwest and the East Coast. Watch for an occasional Coca-Cola and a Hawaii or a Nevada beauty as I am still looking through the bottles and discovering new treasures every week." His windowsill favorites, for now, are all in order, magnificent in their assortment of shapes and colors, reflecting the brilliant sun across his room through a rainbow of colors. One can imagine Richie looking out his window as he concluded his eBay page with this final summation: "Here I am bewildered by the enormity of it all!"

"BY OUR WORKS YE SHALL JUDGE US"

John Seekings continued learning about the seltzer industry as he searched for a siphon source to make a go of the Pittsburgh Seltzer Works. Even a collector like Richie Strell, rich in bottles, would be of little help. Richie might have bought each bottle for pennies, but put back up, individually, on eBay, he could ask anything from twenty dollars to over one hundred. "We can't spend those kind of dollars, not one bottle at a time," John reported to Jim. And they should be as lucky as Richie was, to stumble across a seltzer man liquidating his entire collection.

As he searched for a solution, John's research gradually revealed a fascinating and quirky history as the seltzer industry moved from England and France to plant roots in emerging urban centers like New York City, led by entrepreneurs like John Matthews.

John Matthews emigrated from England to New York City in 1832, opening a shop at 55 Gold Street, a few blocks south of where the Brooklyn Bridge would later rise. He produced and sold his own seltzer, as had others whom he had left behind in Europe, but this is not what earned him his place in history. When Matthews passed away four decades later, in 1870, he was known as the "soda fountain king" for the fountains he designed and sold—grand marble monuments dominating countertops in pharmacies around the country, helping to popularize drugstores as the new social centers. Matthews similarly was called "the father of American soda water"[15] and "the Neptune of the trade."[16] Matthews's two sons took over the business, one focusing on the technical side, the other on the business side. Within a short time, the company employed more than three hundred people and had sold more than twenty thousand fountains. Along with manufacturing fountains, the factory was engaged in thirty-seven other related trades.

Matthews's final resting place in Brooklyn's Green-Wood Cemetery, which he had co-designed and his company helped build, cost a hefty thirty-thousand dollars and won the award for "mortuary monument of the year." A thirty-six-foot Gothic granite canopy and spire rose above a marble sculpture of Matthews in a state of repose. The monument, carved with gargoyles as well as likenesses of Matthews's relatives, scenes from nature, and milestones from his life, resembled the type of Victorian soda fountains manufactured in the very factory that produced it.[17]

By the time of his death, Matthews's company had provided the infrastructure for a new industry on the cusp of reshaping the future of popular consumption. But someone was needed to provide a rallying cry to unify Matthews's ragtag collection of customers into a coherent economic force.[18] Someone had to organize

the bubbling seltzer industry the same way that Joseph Priestley had compiled the electric scientific research of Ben Franklin and his friends: through publishing. That someone was William B. Keller, a journeyman printer who had traveled Pennsylvania, Ohio, New Jersey, and New York in the years after the Civil War.

William B. Keller

Keller could not have picked a better time to launch his publishing venture. New proprietary brands were being introduced, those still enjoyed today (Coca-Cola, Pepsi, and Dr. Pepper) and those long since forgotten (Kola Phosphate, Red Banana, and Filipin Fizz). Direct home delivery was expanding. Developments such as these would forever change the industry. A wide range of social, economic, political, and technological changes were being introduced, changes whose disruptions would be addressed in Keller's new publication, including the meaning of seltzer.

In the eighteenth and nineteenth centuries, seltzer was all about health. In the twentieth century, seltzer was about the promise of pleasure. This transition was both documented and actively promoted by Keller. Many of his printing customers were beverage bottlers and suppliers whose work he would observe, filling many hours of late-night conversation. Keller was excited by this new industry just gaining a hold. He felt he understood the needs of bottlers and others in the business and, using his handbills expertise, produced a new form of publication: a trade journal.

Trade journals combined personal and professional journalism, providing Keller an opportunity to inform and organize the industry while boldly addressing issues of concern to them all. When Keller launched the *Bottlers' Gazette*, beer was the main product of most bottling plants, with seltzer just a sideline. Saloons were the principal customers of bottlers, accounting for 70 percent of bottle sales.

The first issue of the *Bottlers' Gazette*, in March 1882, opened in what would soon become classic Keller style: boosterism and bravado mixed with matters more mundane. "The bottlers of this country deserve a journal, a practical journal, and that is just what we propose," his first editorial began, practical enough. Then slowly his language began to take flight. "With our experience to guide us," he continued, "we start anew into the elysian fields of bottlers literature," referencing the ancient Greek idea of the afterworld, "and we shall ever aim to keep abreast of the time." He concluded with a boisterous adieu: "Give us a hearty welcome, brother bottlers, and . . . by our works ye shall judge us."[19]

The first issues addressed a broad range of concerns: the need for cleaner bottling plants, the elimination of price cutting, advice on the care and feeding of horses ("Never allow anyone to tease or tickle your horse," "Never beat the horse when in the stable"),[20] and tips on wagon repair. Two issues, however, were of primary concern to Keller—bottle thievery ("the monstrous evil which every year saps the life from this otherwise prosperous trade")[21] and the need to organize the industry—and both came together in the same year, with Keller as the glue, through the creation of the United States Bottlers' Protective Association.

Bottle thievery was wreaking havoc on the intended life cycle of soda bottles, with no solution in sight. Bottles were filled, distributed, emptied by the customer, returned, cleaned, and refilled on average five or six times per bottle. This cycle was crucial to the bottlers, for whom the costs of bottles shipped from Europe were substantial and the savings from recycling bottles critical to their profits. However, there was one simple, intractable problem: there was no motivation for customers to return the bottles. They were bulky, sometimes dirty, and returning them accrued no material benefit to the customer in exchange for his or her efforts. It was a precarious setup, with the smooth functioning of the entire industry built atop hopes for its customers' voluntary efforts. At the same time, there was great incentive for bottlers to, essentially, steal the discarded bottles of their rivals, remove any sign of their previous owner, and then reuse them or even sell the stolen bottles at a discount to bottlers in other locations. In fact, there were unscrupulous bottle dealers who even bought empty bottles from stores and saloons and then turned around and sold them back to the bottlers who had originally produced them.

"The trade is very much annoyed with the junk dealer who buys stolen bottles," read one letter in the *Gazette*, written on behalf of a local Bottlers' Association. "They wish to know when their funerals will take place, as they wish to inscribe on their tombs the following:

Here reposes the soul of a heartless bottle adventurer.
May he remain 3,000 feet below hell, in company with
his customers."[22]

As Keller launched the *Gazette*, he advocated for and then became secretary of the newly founded United States Bottlers' Protective Association, the first attempt to organize the few hundred members of the trade. The diverse group—brewers, soda and seltzer bottlers, cider and vinegar processors, wineries, and an assortment of tonic and elixir promoters—immediately picked up thievery as its signature cause. Despite their differences, they all had one thing in common: as one hand was selling a bottle, the other was itching to snatch it back. The issue would continue to plague bottlers for decades, until bottle deposit laws were enacted in the 1930s. For the first time, customers had a financial incentive to return the bottles. Reclaiming a few pennies fixed, at last, the broken life cycle of the bottle.

The *Gazette* tried to maintain a congenial relationship with bottlers, as if Keller himself were dropping by for a chat. The trade journal included silly jokes, stories, and rhymes—all bottle related, of course, such as the following ditty:

> I would not marry a farmer,
> who works in the dirt
> but I'll marry the young Soda Bottler
> who makes the soda squirt.[23]

But Keller wasn't there just to cater to bottlers' needs. He wanted to whip them into shape. Price-cutting competitions plagued the industry from time to time. In a March 1899 editorial he concluded: "Don't rob your business. Say, rather, to yourself, 'I must make a living profit.' And stick to it!" He was as much friendly neighbor as irascible uncle to his readers. Using the royal "we," he asserted in an editorial entitled "The Relations of a Newspaper to Its Subscribers" that "so long as we handle the quill for *The Gazette* we shall do it to please our own sweet will, in the interests of honesty, justice, and equity."

Keller knew what was in their best interest and didn't hesitate to use the full force of his publication and powers of persuasion to fight for it. The lead editorial in October 1883, entitled "The Use of Mineral Waters," excoriated bottlers who chose to take the winter season off, when bottling and distributing sodas was impractical due to their thin glass bottles, rather than adding mineral waters in thicker-glassed siphons to their offerings, since the heavy siphons and popular demand now made it a year-round product. "Don't wait until next spring," he exhorted. "Go at it now. . . . Make up your mind to make some money this winter, instead of sitting about the stove, swapping 'yarns,' and otherwise fooling away your time and money." If they were already bottlers, the next step was simple: a siphon filler and about a hundred bottles would make a good start. The siphon head has been brought to such perfection, he asserted, and the siphon glass so superior, that there are practically no costs for upkeep. "If you don't know how to go about it," he addressed those interested but hesitant, "write to us, and we will put you on the right track, and help you all we can."

Keller, however, went far beyond mere words. He incentivized bold action as well, through "fast bottling contests," or, as Keller liked to call them, "tests of speed at the bottling bench." Each year, Keller would announce the rules for the latest "friendly rivalry for superiority" and challenge bottlers around the country to step up. During a designated week, they would claim a bottle category, such as seltzer siphons, and, before official witnesses and their community, see how many they could fill in an hour. Notarized results would be tallied and winners announced in the next edition. His stated goal was to "encourage and suitably reward the skill of the operator, make a record of the feat, and . . . demonstrate the capacity and capability of different machinery, appliances, etc." Like today's contests, in which private companies compete to develop a desired innovation (like offering private space travel or improving Netflix's algorithm), Keller used competitions to boost industrial progress by providing "these knights of the syrup gauge and treadle a chance to prove their mettle." For example, the siphon champion of 1885, John H. Friedler of Rochester, New York, filled almost four dozen twenty-six-ounce bottles in one hour, a far cry from the measly eighteen filled by the third-place finisher. "In regards to siphons, I do claim to be the boss," said Friedler upon his win. "I will challenge any man in the country."[24]

The *Gazette*'s clientele grew to almost three thousand subscribers in the first two years, and Keller never failed to let them know his appreciation. "A publication without a regular clientele of paid subscribers and readers," Keller wrote in an early editorial, "is like a waif on the street, a homeless, wandering, aimless, useless nondescript, fit only for one thing—the ash barrel." More importantly, he wanted bottlers to think of the *Gazette* as their office away from home. He offered the *Gazette*'s conveniently located downtown Manhattan address at 114 Nassau Street as a place travelling bottlers could hold meetings, forward their mail, or simply work at a desk. "We shall be pleased to attend to any business matters," Keller invited, "which may be entrusted to our charge—WITHOUT COST." Keller was eager to please, and please he did. Before long, bottler associations around the country were voting to give the *Gazette* their official support and endorse it as their official organ.

The *Gazette*, true to Keller's intentions, strove to take stands on matters of concern to bottlers. Keller wrote in the magazine's fourteenth-anniversary issue that the *Gazette* "stands for something. It stands for right, honesty, courage, bravery, brains, and pluck." More than that, it knew who its enemies were. "It hates cowardice," Keller continued. "It despises the namby-pamby, opinionless, wishy-washy, colorless nobody who is afraid to say his soul is his own or take any decided stand without consulting the powers that be." With language such as this, Keller made bottling sound less like a business and more like a moral crusade.

Keller and the bottlers took a stand on subjecting imported seltzer to tariffs. They argued that once pulled from the ground, Britain's Apollinaris brand water was enhanced with new minerals and carbonation. Yet in the halls of Congress the debate centered on two questions: was seltzer a necessary medicine (and therefore not subject to a tariff) or a luxurious beverage (and thus worthy of a tax)? Although bottlers fought for recognition of seltzer as a beverage, a source of pleasure, it could not shake its medicinal roots. Congress decided Apollinaris would continue to enter the United States duty-free, and all artificial mineral water was added to that coveted list as well. There was a silver lining for bottlers, however: While mineral water could now be imported tax free, the bottles could not. A new tariff was placed on all imported bottles containing liquid for consumption. It was an unexpected victory that Keller would savor for some time.

Something as mundane as tariff legislation grew to have profound implications for American bottlers. The carbonated beverage business was witnessing the emergence of a new era, Keller would proclaim, one in which theirs was now a chief industry symbolizing the country's new "age of invention and progress."

New drinking customs were developing, he would write in 1883, and this "greatly enhanced consumption has in turn reacted upon the mineral water manufacturer, which has been, and, in fact still is, undergoing something very like a revolution." Keller then detailed the industrial changes sweeping the country. "The old rough and ready methods of production have been to a great extent discarded, scientific accuracy in the factory has taken the place of rule of thumb, chemical knowledge and skill have been brought to bear, and ingenious machinery nicely adapted to the special requirements of the trade has been freely introduced and generally adopted."

The *Gazette* focused as well on the social impact of these changes. "Three or four or five years ago," a bartender reported in 1885, "a man looked more or less ashamed of himself when he ordered ginger ale, lemon soda, or seltzer. Nowadays, however, everything is changed. . . . There was a time when a saloon keeper looked upon a bottler and his goods as barely to be tolerated, but that is all changed now. Their beverages are the taste of the day." Keller was both documenting and accelerating that change with every means at his disposal.

Ultimately it wasn't the esoteric vagaries of tariff policies that shaped the meaning of seltzer at the end of the nineteenth century, as informative as those battles were. Rather, these public engagements simply prepared Keller and the industry for a bigger battle, one that would do considerably more to shape the meaning of seltzer while shaking society to its very core. Seltzer would no longer be just a pawn in battles between waters foreign and domestic, natural and artificial, but align itself with other beverages against a greater foe in one of the grand struggles of the age: the drive for Prohibition.

TEMPERANCE DRINKS

Nowadays, seltzer and alcohol are the best of friends. Along with club soda, tonic water, and ginger ale, seltzer is one of the four standard mixers that no self-respecting bar or restaurant could be without. But one hundred years ago, they were not just at odds. They were at war.

When Keller founded the *Gazette*, bottlers and brewers may have found common cause in their fight against bottle piracy, but year after year, as Keller walked a fine line between the two, the center could not hold. Originally, the masthead proudly displayed a wide range of beverages side by side—a champagne bottle, a seltzer siphon, and bottles of other alcohol—but that portrait of peaceful economic camaraderie was revealed by history to be no more than an illusion framed by Keller's attempts to unite the industry.

Carbonated beverages came of age at the dawn of modern medicine, when science took precedence over charismatic hucksters with sharp sales pitches. At the same time, society began to shift away from the workforce's centuries-old consumption of brain-dampening alcohol, such as beer, and looked instead for beverages that could sharpen minds for mental stimulation—first tea, and now, in Keller's era, alcohol-free drinks increasingly being termed "temperance drinks."

Keller, of course, tried to blow against the historical winds pushing the two apart. In February 1883, he penned an editorial noting that in recent years "the drinking customs of the people have been sensibly modified by . . . the wholesome and refreshing beverages known as temperance drinks." Sure, seltzer and other carbonated drinks could be "pleasant and wholesome drinks for foes to alcohol," yet they also "lend admirably with almost any stimulant." For example, "Hock [German white wine] and Seltzer has the recommendation of Lord Byron." Seltzer could be something for everyone, Keller seemed to suggest—both an alternative to alcohol and a great way to improve it. He concluded the piece with the same argument: they "promote the cause of temperance" on one hand, "while to those who can use without abusing, they form a pleasant and wholesome adjunct to almost any alcoholic drink."[25] The palpable anxiety underlying his calm demeanor pleaded: we're all friends here, right?

When the Prohibition began in the 1840s as a religious movement, the focus was on personal abstinence. But toward the end of the century, the movement broadened its focus from liquor to all related behaviors and establishments. Alcoholism, once primarily

VOLUME XIV.—(Fourteenth Year.)   NEW YORK, MARCH 5, 1895.   NUMBER 157.

"The masthead proudly displayed a wide range of beverages."

viewed as a personal failing, was suddenly seen as a social problem. For the brewing industry, the pressure was on.

Founded in 1874, the Women's Christian Temperance Union (WCTU) was one of the most successful Prohibition players. Its members successfully advocated for bringing anti-alcohol lessons into every state's education system. In 1881, two years before Keller launched the *Gazette*, the WCTU had 22,800 members. By the turn of the century, membership soared to over 154,000 and more than doubled over the next two decades to 344,000.[26]

Despite Keller's efforts to unify both wet and dry industries, the terms of debate were shifting around him. Before long the temperance movement called for full prohibition of alcohol via a constitutional amendment. Keller was challenged to frame seltzer and other beverages as temperance drinks without appearing to take a side. His solution? Support temperance while attacking the movement—support the principle but not the practice. More specifically, and audaciously, he painted members of the Prohibition movement as a bunch of extremists, while claiming bottlers as the only real force for moderation.

This adroit spin underlay his 1884 column "Carbonades and Temperance." Seltzer and other carbonated drinks, he argued, "are strictly temperance beverages and merit the support of all who wish to inculcate temperance principles." Yet the "remarkable eccentrics" leading the temperance movement are "incapable apparently of reasoning outside of a very narrow groove." To Keller, these "so-called reformers" were no less extreme than "vegetarians, the anti-vaccinationists, the free-traders, [and] the anti-tobaccoites."

Keller's efforts to co-opt the movement while delegitimizing its leaders was stretched to the extreme with claims that none have done more for the cause of temperance, including the temperance movement, than the bottling industry. "The temperance man may have done much good by his eloquent harangues in declaiming against strong drink," he offered, "but the mineral water maker has been quietly manufacturing, supplying, and pushing by every means in his power, the harmless and refreshing substitute." While Prohibitionists spend their time making pretty speeches, Keller concluded, the bottlers are the men of action, delivering temperance drinks to saloons each and every day.

As much as he tried, Keller found it impossible to keep walking the fence between the two forces. He had to pick a side. In October 1891, Keller announced that from then on the *Gazette* would dedicate itself exclusively to carbonated beverages and mineral waters, divorcing itself from wine, beer, cider, and vinegar.

The tensions that emerged between the "wet" and the "dry," the alcohol and the temperance drinks, would occasionally boil over, no doubt to Keller's consternation. In November 1908, he reported that in San Francisco it was as if "a bombshell had been dropped in the camp of the local soda water manufacturers." A newspaper advertisement published by Weiland's Beer, under the headline "Beer and Soft Drinks," decried carbonated beverages, claiming all of their "sparkle and life" derived from a pollution of marble dust and sulfuric acid. Beer, meanwhile, was the healthier alternative, derived from "the pure brew of hops."

This tale, in Keller's eyes at least, had a happy ending. The local Soda Water Manufacturers' Association immediately arranged a delegation to confront the brewer, Mr. Alton, who fell all over himself apologizing. He explained that his advertising company was wholly to blame and offered to do anything the association asked. "What I want is boosters, not knockers," he reportedly said. "Nobody is hurt more than I am by my own ad."

For the next four days, all newspapers in San Francisco ran a laudatory ad about both soft drinks and beer, proudly declaring their common cause in its title: "Beer and Soft Drinks—Both Are Temperance Drinks." Yes, both. If seltzer can define itself as a temperance drink in opposition to alcohol, why can't beer do the same, united with other temperance drinks in opposition to the harder alcohols? Or so the argument went.

This public lovefest, however, cut against the grain. Just a few months later, a full-page ad ran in the February 7, 1909, *Chicago Tribune*, asserting that beer was a temperance drink, while throwing all other alcoholic beverages under the bus. Entitled "the world's favorite beverage," it stated, in part, "Soft drinks sold at the soda fountain and other so-called 'temperance bars,' when not a combination of bad water and decayed fruit juices, frequently contain such deadly drugs as cocaine or caffeine." Beer, however, "contains so small a percentage of alcohol as to render it absolutely harmless when taken in moderation." Furthermore, "beer does not create an appetite for whisky or other strong liquors but acts as a tonic." In other words, beer was not a "gateway drug" to harder alcohol but acted in some mysterious, unexplained way as a deterrent and thus a force for temperance. It seemed that everyone was out for himself, frantic to prove that his was the best, and perhaps only, temperance drink.

Of course, Keller would hear none of it. He always sought unity, but he wasn't an ideologue. When attacked, he didn't pull punches. In the March 5 issue, he took it on in the lead editorial, entitled "Brewers to Blame: A Scandalous, Unwarranted, and Uncalled for Attack on Soda Water." Keller called the ad "one of the meanest, lowest, and most contemptible pieces of literature ever issued for public consumption." The Chicago Brewers "ought to be radically ashamed of such a miserable piece of work."

Keller clearly connected the dots for his readers: this was not an isolated incident, as "the brewers' journals . . . with an unctuous disregard for the truth . . . never fail to speak ill of soda water." But the brewers were not alone. By now separate trade journals had emerged for beer, whiskey, and wine, and when not sniping at one another, they, "with one accord and acclaim, never miss an opportunity to publish the meanest trash and falsest lies about soda water."

> The poor soda water bottler is clubbed, lampooned, traduced, spat upon, and otherwise ridiculed—all for the purpose of selling a few more intoxicating drinks. The public is wise, however, and it prefers soda water, thank you. And the legislature cannot legislate it out of existence, either. Another thank you.

Keller wanted to be clear that lies and other malicious attacks would not be tolerated. "IT IS TIME TO CALL A HALT," his all-cap sentence cried out. "THE BOTTLING TRADE DEMANDS IT."

> Call off your dogs of war, Mr. Brewer; for just as sure as fate, if you and your ilk do not desist and abstain, hereafter, from slandering and libeling soda water, it will as surely lead to a trade war such as never before existed.

Ten years later, nearly to the day, the Eighteenth Amendment to the US Constitution was ratified, taking effect the following year. It declared illegal the manufacture, sale, and transportation of alcohol.

Saloons were replaced by speakeasies. Within just a few years, New York City alone harbored tens of thousands of them.[27] And before long, Prohibition became unpopular and was repealed by the Twenty-First Amendment. But Keller never saw its repeal. On March 8, 1929, a *New York Times* headline reported: "Founder and Editor of the *National Bottlers' Gazette* Dies Suddenly." At seventy-seven years of age, Keller passed away at his Park Avenue home. The obituary in the *Times* called him a "pioneer in the field."

Today, Prohibition is marked as a historical blunder that temporarily sent alcohol underground while giving rise to a problem that plagues us still: organized crime. Harder to recall, however, is the uniqueness of Keller's desire for a unity between bottlers and brewers, for his *National Bottlers' Gazette* to be able to speak to them all as one, in part, because few today have ever experienced the two in conflict. Seltzer is still used as a "temperance drink," an acceptable alternative to a glass of beer, yet it is just as popular when mixed with alcohol.

After Keller's death, generations of family members remained involved with the *Gazette*. By 1975, when its name changed to *Beverage World*, it had reintegrated beer, wine, and other alcoholic beverages into its pages. Nearly a century after its birth, Keller's vision for an industry united under one periodical finally became reality.

Now John Seekings had to decide whether to make their reality his as well.

3

SELTZER WORKS

In which John Seekings speaks with seltzer works owners
around the country to learn what it takes to run a contemporary seltzer
business with nineteenth-century technology.

THE PITTSBURGH SELTZER WORKS

"How do I run a twenty-first-century business with nineteenth-century technology? How can a door-to-door business model, in decline for decades, be revived in the age of digital downloads and Amazon warehouses? And how can I build a consumer base for home delivered siphons when most people already fill their seltzer fix at a corner deli or supermarket—pitting a labor-intensive product against the efficacies and supply chains of big soda companies mass producing plastic-bottled seltzer?" These are just some of the big questions that John Seekings needed to answer in order to decide whether it would make sense to purchase the seltzer plant . . . or if it would just make him crazy. His next step was coming to understand the history of the Pittsburgh Seltzer Works and the industry it had outlasted.

In the decades before the Civil War, according to the US Census, there were no more than a few dozen nonalcoholic bottling plants, with small windows and dark basements lit by gaslight. Bottling was a summer business because the thinner glass bottles would freeze in the winter cold during delivery. Plants locked their doors after Labor Day until the warm, spring sun returned.

But by the end of the Civil War there were nearly four hundred bottlers operating with a wide array of newly invented machinery under more modern conditions. In 1889, the number had risen to fourteen hundred, and ten years later, when the Pittsburgh Seltzer Works filled its first siphon, the number had doubled to twenty-eight hundred bottling plants producing one billion bottles of soda and seltzer a year.[28]

The growth of bottling plants reached its peak in 1929, at just over eight thousand; during the Great Depression, many bottlers closed or were gobbled up in consolidation drives. While the number of bottlers would continually shrink over the rest of the century, the number of bottles sold would climb and climb.

However, what people drank changed dramatically during World War II. While the rest of the country recovered from the Great Depression, seltzer bottlers would not. As sodas like Coca-Cola became more available through supermarkets and represented the ultimate symbol of assimilation and acceptance, seltzer bottlers began to lose customers, close their doors, and lose access to new equipment and bottles. The rise of mass-produced beverages, not just of sugary soda but eventually seltzer as well, made the local, tiny seltzer works less viable with each passing year. If seltzer works wanted to stay in business, they had little choice but to scale back and just make do.

Pittsburgh Seltzer Works was not immune to these changes. In the 1930s, Jimmy Rosen and Molly Rosenberg, a brother and sister team, took ownership of the Works. The siblings added soda to their business, delivering bottles first to homes, then cases to pizza and sandwich shops, until, one day, the tail wagged the dog. By the 1970s, they spent no more than a morning a week maintaining their seltzer route; they focused their time instead on the new core of their business as reflected in their new name: Pop Beverage, *pop* being the regional word for syrupy soda.

Back in the '50s, before the business had shifted, one of Jimmy and Molly's customers was a little different from the others. The Edelmanns were a Jewish family transplanted from Long Island; their son, Sam, had arrived in Pittsburgh at age six with no love for the fizz-filled siphons that filled his family's fridge. But the boy grew. In the late 1970s he got engaged to his college sweetheart, a local girl named Marion. His parents passed. His tastes changed, and Sam found he enjoyed seltzer. When he saw the "Pop Beverage" truck drive past, his childhood came back to him—the father he missed, the home deliveries of seltzer, the neighborhood in which he grew up—and he pursued it, not just the truck but the entire business.

Sam introduced himself to the seltzer works siblings, who were well into their seventies at this time (with their helper a young sixty or so). It was 1980, and, although proud of their business after half a century, they were sort of disillusioned. Sam explained that he was self-employed and interested in seltzer.

How far could the siblings trust Sam? Anyone could buy a business and sell off the assets. So they agreed to let Sam volunteer part-time, helping out, learning the seltzer business along the way, like an old-fashioned, no-salary apprenticeship. For the next year, as his interest bubbled into a passion, Sam worked one day per week for Pop Beverage, supporting himself with his freelance counseling and expert-witness work. The siblings taught him how to work the route, how to bottle the seltzer, and how to fix a busted siphon. Sam saw that their seltzer route was a pale shadow of its former glory; they delivered no more than one or two dozen cases a week. This wasn't good business, but still the siblings hung on, with Sam at their side.

After a year, it was time for a change. As Sam and Marion made wedding plans, they also discussed seltzer. Sam's intention was not to ask permission from his fiancée to go into seltzer full-time. He wanted something more, for both of them. Instead, he invited Marion to be his partner, in both marriage and business. Marion was working as an assistant manager in a clothing store. She was the one with business experience. And she loved the idea. It sounded exciting and creative, edgy and a bit romantic. They could make new something old, reviving a flagging enterprise. They could travel the country, visiting bottlers in New York, California, and Connecticut, as they learned from the masters.

Sam spoke with Jimmy and Molly, who, after all this time, still resisted the lure of retirement. "I can't do this anymore for free," he told them. "Sell me the damn business."

And they did.

With that, in 1981, Pop Beverage and its soda business was discontinued while Pittsburgh Seltzer Works, helmed by a pair of newlyweds with a dream, was reborn.

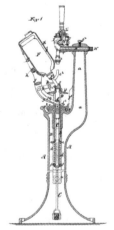

Diagram of a manual, single-bottle siphon filler

For thirty thousand dollars they acquired six thousand seltzer bottles, the machinery, and the franchise. Sam and Marion ran it together. Marion handled most of the bottle repair and loaded the trucks. Sam delivered the seltzer. And together they filled the siphons, first on the ancient, manual, single-bottle machine that came with the business and then on a glorious upgrade, an automatic hand-bottling machine from 1905 that could manage six bottles at a time. They fell into a smooth routine. Marion would hand Sam an empty bottle, which he would insert into the machine. Inside the machine, the waiting siphon was filled with seltzer. Marion would remove the freshly filled bottle, test the pressure with a quick spritz, then hand Sam the next empty bottle.

The business grew to one hundred customers a week, but never too big. It was always a part-time affair. Pittsburgh was a small city, after all. The city paper ran a piece on their unlikely story, and before long, the national press, including the *Wall Street Journal,* picked up on it. Sam and Marion's customer base rose to four hundred families a week. They brought in help to deliver the siphons. And over the next sixteen years Sam and Marion made a good run of it.

But by the time Sam turned fifty, it had switched from a passion to a business. And while his body aged, the workload never let up. "It was difficult," he said in an interview, "and it's a lot easier to sit in a courtroom and give opinions," referring to his former occupation. Marion, too, felt it was time. "I'm pretty strong and I did my share of lifting," she said. "I was actually glad I didn't get hurt," Sam also reflected. "We just reached an age where it was time to stop. It's a young man's game, I guess." They were ready to see the Pittsburgh Seltzer Works go to the next person.

Three people, it would turn out, Jewish friends who had grown up together in Pittsburgh: David Faigen, Evan Hirsh, and Paul Supowitz. Learning that the Pittsburgh Seltzer Works was for sale, Evan decided to check it out. When he visited the plant for the first time, Sam expected him to act like the others who had expressed interest in buying the Works, asking about cash flow and the books. Instead, Evan headed straight to the machinery, totally intrigued. Before long he was thoroughly in love with the old, simple equipment used to make something so classic and pure. "It's nuts and bolts," Evan would later say. "Cams and levers." That is when Sam knew he had found the new owners.

Some guys go away on hunting trips. Others hole up playing video games for hours on end. But on weekends, David, Evan, and Paul, at thirty-four years of age, could now bond through something no one else could touch—seltzer bottling. They started in 1997 with two hundred customers, restricting their activities to the weekend, managing all pickups and drop-offs on Saturday. Each found an area to focus on. Paul got into the siphon bottles, Evan became the mechanic, and David worked with him on the bottling. All three took their turns cleaning. But over time their clients dropped to only 120, due more to neglect than any measurable lack of demand. By then, all three friends were in their forties, married, and with kids. Dave and Evan had both developed back problems. Life required them elsewhere. Their hobby, their bonding activity, had become a burden.

Still, the friends felt the very same way about the Pittsburgh Seltzer Works as they had when they first bought it from Sam. "The company has been in Pittsburgh forever," they had said at the time. "It's someone's responsibility to keep it going." They weren't about to sell it for parts and let one of America's last remaining seltzer works go out of business. They held conversations with potential buyers, but nothing panned out. Something dramatic was necessary to get someone to bite the bullet and buy the Works. So they wrote a letter to all of their customers saying that, yes, they were shutting down the Works, but they hoped it would be temporary until someone else could take it over. As luck would have it, one of their clients worked for the *Post-Gazette*, which took up their plight, publishing a piece about the Works and their struggle to find an appropriate caretaker.

This *Post-Gazette* article is the one John Seekings had read, which brought him to the open house and led him to consider writing himself in as the star of the next chapter in the century-plus history of the Pittsburgh Seltzer Works. To inform his decision Seekings needed to find others like him, contemporaries who had already decided to run their own seltzer works, to hear their stories and decide if he should proceed.

It was not long before he had identified the two most prominent seltzer works still active, each dominating its coast: Gomberg Seltzer Works in Brooklyn, New York, and the Seltzer Sisters, servicing the San Francisco Bay Area of California. If the owners of these companies could not answer his questions, if they could not help him decide whether to claim some of the landlocked middle ground between the two, then no one could. It was time to make some calls.

THE SELTZER DOCTOR IS IN

John began by calling the Gomberg Seltzer Works and speaking with one of its proprietors, Kenny Gomberg. Kenny was not averse to taking calls from strangers. He enjoyed talking about seltzer and his family history. In 1953, four years before he was born, his father and grandfather launched Gomberg Seltzer Works, the family business that still operates in the industrial heart of Canarsie, at 855 East Ninety-Second Street, on the corner of Avenue D and East Ninety-Second Street in Brooklyn. Back then it was one of dozens of local seltzer works, with its own cadre of a few dozen seltzer delivery men. These men owned their own bottles and managed their own customer lists, relying on Gomberg to care for their empty siphons and refill them for the next delivery. Gomberg, in turn, relied on the seltzer men to stay in business and buy its seltzer water. It was a marriage of convenience—the seltzer men could not run their own machines, and Gomberg Seltzer Works preferred not to make deliveries. And like many such marriages, they tolerated one another the best they could, at times experiencing something akin to respect.

For more than a dozen years before John Seekings called, Gomberg had been the sole surviving seltzer works in New York

Kenny Gomberg bottling seltzer siphons

City, providing seltzer for fewer than half a dozen seltzer men. Kenny bristled with discomfort at the notion that this somehow made him special. "It's just a job," he insisted to John. "I come to work every day. I do what I have to do." Kenny spoke with a relaxed confidence and a tone as crisp as his product, his Brooklyn accent only coming through on words like *seltza*. Kenny found it, as he put it, "interesting" how taken people were by the nostalgia and the romance of the bottles and, just, everything. It is a part of their history, and they need someone with whom they can relive it. "Sometimes I feel like a therapist listening to their stories," Kenny said, with a hint of pride, about strangers who just called out of the blue. "They just like to call and tell me about what they remember. They're not calling because they want seltzer. They just want to talk to someone." A smile in his voice can be heard when he announces with a hint of pride, "The therapist is in."

Kenny Gomberg grew up in a household always stocked with ice-cold, well-pressured seltzer. In his teens he began working after school at the family business, but he had no plans to take over. However, armed with his new college degree, he found himself there, and there he remained (and remains to this day). His grandfather and father passed on, as had his aunt, who kept the books. Her position was soon filled, however, by his new brother-in-law, Irv Resnick, with whom he has continued to run the business since 1979. The business, however, might be hardly recognizable to Kenny's grandfather.

As an accommodation to the seltzer delivery men, the Works began to offer them both beer and soda. It was just an extra. Something on the side. Sometime in the 1970s, as seltzer declined and beer and soda rose in popularity, they switched places. Seltzer water, specifically siphons, became the extra. Gomberg Seltzer Works remained, but growing around it in a cavernous space large enough to dwarf its predecessor was a beer and soda distributor.

Gomberg Seltzer Works was, of course, not the only company to experience this shift. By the 1990s there was barely a handful of seltzer plants left. By the turn of the twenty-first century, only one remained in New York: Gomberg Seltzer Works. If you were a seltzer man, lucky or crazy enough to still be servicing customers, it didn't matter how many bottles you owned, how strong your truck, or how important your clients. If you didn't fill at Gomberg, you were out of business.

Even today, watching a siphon pass through Gomberg is exciting, a demonstration in how to repurpose the past in service to the future. When visitors pass the residential houses to enter the industrial neighborhood surrounding the Works, the first thing they notice is its long, tall, red-bricked outer wall speckled with black bricks. The windows are closed and barred. One section is marked with graffiti. Its only identifying feature is an aging white sign with faded black letters—"Gomberg Seltzer Works"—dated by the old-fashioned phone number underneath, "NI9.9883." There is little to suggest the wonders within.

Gomberg Seltzer Works

A metal door opens onto an alcove offering the seltzer men a special vise for fixing siphon heads and a wrench on a chain for opening or tightening the heads. To the right, the space opens up and out into the warehouse, its gray cinder-block walls bare save for a handful of cigarette ads. An old-fashioned analog clock hangs down from the high ceiling, its black hands ticking down time.

Along the street-side wall rises what can only be described as a seltzer-scape: seltzer bottles piled as if mimicking the city they serve, hundreds upon hundreds of bottles collected in old wooden delivery crates, some stacked as high as four stories, sixteen boxes deep and five boxes wide. The peaks of these miniature skyscrapers shine silver, the color of the traditional metallic siphon head, but a profusion of the new Argentinian plastic colors dot the scene in blue, green, yellow, and red, aligning or contrasting with the clear, blue, or green glass beneath. Each neighborhood in this seltzer-scape has a name sketched on a tall strip of cardboard. Mike. Or Tom. Or Eli. Or any of a half dozen or so seltzer delivery men for whom Gomberg ensures the safety of their bottle collection. These are the bottles waiting to get filled or delivered.

Across from the siphons are two bottling machines, one functioning as the backup filler should the other one break. Before them stands the manual conveyor belt, on which empty siphons are lined up and from which they will be removed on the other side of the bottling machine when they are filled. On a yellow metal sign attached to the top of the vintage bottler, like a caption at a museum exhibit, red letters spell out the imported machine's pedigree.

On the side, a silver-boxed on/off switch hangs in close reach. The slots in the machine for each fully assembled empty seltzer bottle hang at a diagonal. Each siphon is secured in a cradle, like a babe in arms, during its brief, circular travel inside the machine. The machine presses the trigger handle to open the siphon spout as it rotates into the machine, and a slight hydraulic hiss is heard as seltzer spritzes through the open spout into the glass straw and fills the bottle. Behind the bottling line stand the three water filters, the chiller, the carbonator, and all the water lines connecting them.

"Along the wall rises what can only be described as a seltzer-scape."

Kenny warned of the inherent danger in handling any pressurized vessel. "Use common sense," he told John. "Handle the bottles with care. Don't drop them. Don't bang them together. The bottles are under pressure. If they break they will explode. Glass will fly."

This was all of interest to John Seekings. It helped to fill in the gaps. But he had yet to hear the advice he was looking for. Then Kenny began to get into the finances.

"We're manufacturing a product and we are selling it," Kenny said. That was the long and short of it. What they charged covered expenses, but at the end of the day, there was not a lot of money in making seltzer. "It's essentially a volume business. If we were selling more volume we'd be doing better." Seltzer is just water and CO_2, so the profit could not be in the pricing. "We're not losing money," he said, "but we're not going to get rich making seltzer, not with the volume we're doing now."

Would Kenny go into the business now, knowing what he knows? "This is something we are doing because it is here," Kenny explained. "The machinery is here, and it's working. And as long as it continues to work and everything continues to run, we will be here." But this line of work was not something he would expect anyone to begin now.

Unfortunately, Kenny couldn't recommend a source for seltzer siphons, but he promised to let John know if one turned up.

Kenny had been generous with his time. And brutally frank. John hadn't found a source of siphons to expand the Pittsburgh Seltzer Works. But he had heard something else, perhaps something more important, that spoke to the feelings that had been growing inside him since that first day at the Pittsburgh Seltzer Works. John listened to Kenny's nostalgia-laden tales of seltzer calls from customers and sensed his pride in receiving them, and suddenly John experienced a hint of envy and a growing excitement that one day he might be taking such calls.

So, it was a discouraging conversation for his short-term objectives, but it provided long-term motivation and additional incentive to seek those siphons. It was time to call the Seltzer Sisters in California to see if they could help.

THE BENZINI BAPTISM

John was not the first to call Kathryn Renz, the head of the Seltzer Sisters, for help. (There is no sister, actually, just Kathryn.) Years earlier, after one such call, she found herself marveling at a circus scene before her, and the surprising path, spritzed with seltzer, that had led her there.

Before her stood the charismatic ringmaster. The circus performers gathered around him, hanging on his every word. He spoke to them about tradition, about how they are a family. Part showman, part mock minister, the ringmaster asked them to close their eyes to give thanks. "It is because of his discovery," he continued, as one man, Jacob, was pushed forward, "that we have the greatest star attraction in the Benzini Brothers' history!" Cheers and applause filled the circus tent. "And so, to officially welcome him into our family, we open our eyes," and as they did, the ringmaster took something silently into his hands and continued, "and we give him the traditional Benzini Brothers' baptism!"

With that he tilted back the seltzer siphon hidden in his hands and sprayed Jacob full in the face. The surrounding circle of clowns unleashed a torrent of seltzer, too, their separate streams coming together into a brilliant seltzer star with Jacob at the center. Everyone cheered; the women lined up to plant kisses on his dripping, beaming face, and others added cream pies to the celebratory mess.

The baptism lasted as long as the siphons sprayed and ended with a film director crying, "Cut!" The cameras stopped rolling, and the actors prepared for another take on the historical romance *Water for Elephants*.

The crew swarmed around the film's lead actress, Reese Witherspoon, to touch up her makeup, while the protagonist, played by Robert Pattinson, needed to be cleansed of pie and seltzer. The circus performers got back into position.

The clowns easily reset for the next take, as did the actor Christoph Waltz, who played the ringmaster. But what about their seltzer? Once sprayed, there's no putting that beverage back in its bottle. Those siphons were spent. And in the middle of the desert there's no place to find a seltzer plant outside of a mirage.

So the prop master needed siphons, scores of siphons, and not just any siphons: they had to be identical, even though they were produced before anyone on the set was even born, or at least look identical to an audience in a darkened theater. Ah, the magic of Hollywood. And the magic of the Seltzer Sisters.

"So, what they needed was a hundred matching bottles," Kathryn Renz recalled, a few years later. "I told them, 'When you find them, call me.'" Still, in the end, she came through for the production. "What we did was we pored through all these bottles and we found fifty matching that we knew we had, and then we found ten of a specific kind, enough to fill their order." She and a driver took them down to the set where the two were warmly welcomed. They were invited to stay and watch for the day.

"Each clown had to do each scene," Kathryn explained. "He had to do ten takes and have the same bottle in his hands every time." She marveled at the attention to detail, detail that required her seltzer siphons. "If you want authenticity in what you're doing, that's what people do." When the film was released on DVD, she finally saw it. "There they were, spraying seltzer bottles in the movie. And I'm, like, cracking up."

Kenny Gomberg and Kathryn Renz were opposites in so many ways. Kenny was the East Coast to Kathryn's West Coast. Kenny was embedded within a complex seltzer economy, composed of at least a half-dozen delivery men, while Kathryn controlled every step on her supply chain, delivering what she produced. Kenny entered the business right out of college, extending the family ownership to a third generation, while Kathryn, after twenty-eight years in sales at 3M's fiber optics division, knew nothing about the professional seltzer world until she bought the flagging company a few years before John Seekings contacted her.

Yet, with all that, Kathryn and Kenny were similar in the only way that mattered to John Seekings: They both made seltzer. And, like Kenny, Kathryn was just a phone call away.

Kathryn's voice was reminiscent of actress Julie Kavner's: warm and confident, with character (Julie Kavner voices Marge on *The Simpsons* and, back in the day, played Brenda Morgenstern on the 1970s sitcom *Rhoda*.)

As soon as they began talking, Kathryn could tell she liked John. John was fully engaged in the conversation but in his arms, he had explained, lay his son being rocked to sleep. "What a heck of a nice guy," she thought. And, in any case, she always felt proud of someone attempting to start up a new seltzer works, partially because it was good press for her and her handful of peers around the country. She decided to tell him all.

Growing up on the South Shore of Long Island with a Brooklyn grandmother, Kathryn was no stranger to seltzer. The soda shops. The candy stores. The luncheonettes. But those disappeared when she moved out west, so she was delighted to meet and bond with Susan, another transplant from her hometown. They were friends for years before Kathryn learned something about her new acquaintance that would forever change her life.

Susan's sister ran a seltzer delivery business. She had made a pretty good run of it since the mid-1980s, but then her husband took over. He ran the Seltzer Sisters into the ground. At the same time, Kathryn had recently been laid off from 3M. The seltzer company had been closed a few months before Susan recognized a possible confluence between her sister and her friend: maybe Kathryn could take over the business and restart the stream of seltzer. "You don't know what you want to do," Susan told her unemployed friend after introducing her to the idea, "so you should buy the Seltzer Sisters."

What a radical idea, Kathryn thought. She was ready for something different, but was this *too* different? On the one hand, Kathryn felt overwhelmed by the idea of owning the one-hundred-year-old machinery. What am I going to do if anything breaks? she wondered. I don't know how to fix anything. She knew nothing about how these machines worked, or if she could learn, and was concerned that she might be overwhelmed. John could sympathize.

On the other hand, a seltzer works brought her back to her roots, as both an entrepreneur and a New Yorker. "I have always had to run someone else's P&L [profit and loss statement]. In my own business unit with 3M, we always had to know where we were saleswise, profitwise, you know?" Kathryn had always done it for others. Maybe it was time for her to do it for herself.

At the same time, she missed New York. She wasn't always happy in California. "Buying the Seltzer Sisters was a perfect way to blend my childhood back in with my current life."

So, after a few months, she just did it. She bought Seltzer Sisters. "Eventually I just thought I could make a go of it. I don't know why. I don't really know."

And what she didn't know she learned, fast, or found someone who already did. Machine repair shops. Carbonators. And in October 2003, the Seltzer Sisters reopened. Reinvented.

"So, when I bought the business we were heavily dependent on the home-customer base," she explained, "and within a year we changed that and started selling more to restaurants." And in restaurants she found her niche: the high-end cocktail market. "San Francisco has an incredible cocktail business." Home delivery spread through word of mouth, as one friend introduced it to another. It was fairly organic but small-scale and unpredictable. Bar delivery, on the other hand, spread through bartenders. When bartenders leave, they go somewhere else and start a new business. "But the place he leaves doesn't drop you, and the place he goes to picks you up. So, you're not losing clients that way; you're just picking up more bars." And these are big bars. "We have bars that use thirty cases a week."

Kathryn took the Seltzer Sisters from total dependence on home delivery to a much broader-based restaurant delivery service. "The restaurants, shall we say, are what pays the bills." The first year in business she took in between sixty and seventy thousand dollars. Almost ten years later, she was running closer to half a million dollars. "We're going to add our fourth truck, and hopefully it all goes well." When she first bought the works she had a vision for growing the business, but never this big. "Now I can easily see it almost tripling, if I do it right," said Kathryn.

John told Kathryn about his life as well as his plans for growing the business, about doing it all on the side while he ran his marketing firm. Kathryn was far from convinced that would work. She had once had similar thoughts. "I was looking for something that was not going to intrude in my life," she confessed, "where I was like a corporate person getting sixty hours a week." There is no way, she told him, that he was going to keep his day job. "You just don't walk in here and set up routes," she warned. "You need someone on the phones, you need trucks, you need scheduling."

"We'll see," John replied. "Let's just do this and see how it goes."

John's son was asleep. Before he ended the call he raised his biggest concern, the key challenge preventing him from moving this deal forward: "Do you have bottles to sell?"

Proud that he wouldn't let the Pittsburgh Seltzer Works close, Kathryn decided to anoint John into the small community of seltzer producers with her own version of the Benzini Baptism.

"Yeah, I have a hundred here," she said. "But I know someone up in Rhode Island sitting on all of their assets." David Meisel had bottles, she told him. Thousands of bottles. Enough to expand an ambitious seltzer works.

John reached out with a short but direct email. "My name is John Seeking," he wrote Meisel. "I live in Pittsburgh. We are purchasing a company. Katherine said you may have some assets. What's the story?" Within ten minutes, Meisel responded. It turned out he had bought a seltzer company but developed other business entities over time, quietly letting the seltzer part go out of business. He had a strong customer base but just did not have the time to dedicate to it. He mothballed everything. All the Stella Brothers Seltzer machinery and bottles had been put into storage and were available for purchase.

Finally John had found a source for siphon replacements. If he and Jim purchased the Works, they would have the means to expand.

THE SIGNING

With fall just around the corner, temperatures had been fairly mild. August had ended in the low seventies with clear skies. Wednesday, September 2, 2009, was little different, with a high of seventy-five. A perfect day for John Seekings and Jim Rogal to become the new owners of the Pittsburgh Seltzer Works.

With Jim's blessing, John had met in July with the three owners of the Pittsburgh Seltzer Works and had offered to buy the plant on their terms: the same thirty-thousand-dollar price they had originally spent. The price included the client list, the machinery, the bottles, the company name, and six months' free rent until they found their own space.

The three friends were still quite impressed with John after the summer. They had spoken with other interested parties but none like him. John seemed to have the wherewithal to run the Works. And as important as anything else, John was someone with whom they felt comfortable. Like Jim, they, too, could feel John's excitement.

"He was enthralled from the beginning," owner Paul Supowitz had noted after one of their early meetings. "You could tell his mind was just racing with the possibilities, thinking about all he could do with it," Paul observed to his partners, who were not necessarily looking for the best businessman to take over the business; they were looking for the most passionate person to carry on the tradition. Over the course of the summer, John had become that man, perhaps to no one's surprise more than his own. John's energy

was exactly what they wanted—and what the Pittsburgh Seltzer Works needed.

Jim had liked what he had heard of John's summertime research with Kenny and Kathryn. John's enthusiasm continued pulling him in, as it had ever since this project first began. And the financials were as strong as ever.

"So," John asked, "what do you think?"

"What I think is," Jim replied, "if you're still interested after all this time and all you have learned, I encourage you to go for it."

John was grinning, but repeated back, "'You?'"

"Us. Yes," Jim replied. "This is going to be a fun little enterprise we can run out of our hip pocket and give us a little extra kick in our lives. But let's be clear about one thing: you will be doing all of the heavy lifting, and I mean that figuratively and literally."

As they had discussed earlier, Jim would play the CEO to John's COO. And as chief operating officer, John would be running the day-to-day business concerns, taking on the lion's share of the work. He would be lifting the heavy bottles filled with seltzer. Jim would be lifting paper.

This was just fine with John, and he reiterated his commitment to their role sharing. John was confident he could figure out how to manage the machines, bottles, and deliveries, but he needed his partner to coordinate the financing and help oversee the strategy, contributing now and then to key management decisions. And now, John most needed Jim's help arranging the purchase of the Works.

Within weeks, and after a few exchanges, the papers were signed on September 2. The torch was passed. John and Jim now owned a seltzer works.

On that day, Paul, the now former owner of the Pittsburgh Seltzer Works, reiterated his first impression upon meeting John Seekings: "I hope his actions match his enthusiasm."

Jim could not help but turn to John and ask, "What now?"

4

BECOMING A SELTZER MAN

In which John Seekings is mentored by two generations of
Pittsburgh Seltzer Works owners as they usher him into the esoteric practices
of seltzer production, siphon bottling, and seltzer delivery.

MAN VERSUS MACHINE

After preparing for months, by October 2009 John was ready. Or maybe not. In any case, he was about to find out: the bottling machine was running, and it was not going to stop. There was no one there but him to feed it. He had been taught to recognize if it was moving too fast or too slow. He needed to get as many bottles through as quickly as he could. There was no doubt about it: seltzer would flow.

Had he not invested so much effort learning the ins and outs from the previous owners, it all would have seemed so alien. And intimidating. John and his partner Jim were preparing to use all the vintage equipment inherited with the Pittsburgh Seltzer Works: four chillers that cooled the water to a perfect thirty-seven degrees, a carbonator that transformed H_2O and CO_2 into seltzer, and a six-headed bottler that filled the siphons.

When all the machines were on, it was loud. And dangerous. Water came out of everything: really, really cold water. The siphons were bulky and heavy, and the bottling machine did not care if a finger got stuck in one bottle as it sucked the next one inside.

Perhaps that's part of what gave John such a thrill: because everything was done by hand, he was responsible for it all. There was no sterile, automated, computerized system monitoring each step. Everything came down to him. A real old-fashioned man-versus-machine story.

There had been a huge amount to learn. How do you set the siphon heads? How do you get the temperature just right? How do you balance the temperature and the CO_2 levels? In the midst of the noise, the water, the bottler's unforgiving rotation, John kept an eye on the carbonator and ensured the machinery was working in general. And when it was, when everything was flowing smoothly, it all really came down to one job: feeding the machine. As the insatiable bottler screamed its constant requests for more siphons, all John would need to do was manage that line.

He could never have learned all this on his own. There are no manuals, no "Seltzer How-To" section at the bookstore. The knowledge required to maintain and run those machines resided in the minds of a select few individuals, three of whom had just sold him his company: Evan, Paul, and Dave.

Like an apprenticeship in days of old, John at first spent his time sitting and watching the masters at work. Sam Edelmann, the previous owner, even came to the Works and showed John how to operate a single-head machine, used for manually filling one seltzer bottle at a time, to demonstrate how it should sound and how the machinery would react. Next, John became the person handing over the bottles, and then the one removing the filled siphons, finally reaching the point of getting out in front of the machines. He was learning how to ask the right questions: How does the carbonator work? Where does the pressure come in? How do I regulate that pressure? He was driven in part by the knowledge that he was learning the almost lost art of handmade seltzer production. John's teachers were similarly driven by their shared incentive to pass on their collective knowledge: they wanted the Works to continue, and for that, John was their last, best hope.

One of the first lessons was designed to teach John how to take the machines apart and rebuild them from scratch. It was also designed to divest the previous owners of the remaining vestiges of the Pittsburgh Seltzer Works, as it was time to move. The Works had found a new home.

John's plans to expand required a larger facility than the space shared with the futon company. He also needed a location that would be convenient for customers wishing to drop by for a pickup or just to chat, close enough to John's home for him to come in late at night, and safe enough for him to bring his kids. John's business partner, Jim, offered advice on selecting a new location. After one and a half months of looking, finding the right size location was taking longer than John or Jim expected (rather surprising, since Pittsburgh is a manufacturing town). The Works, however, had more modest needs than most factories, and the search was becoming a challenge. And then a fortuitous drive turned their bad luck into good.

As John and a real estate friend were heading from one point to another, checking out possible spaces, they passed a nondescript warehouse sporting a "Space Available" sign. John would not have given it a second thought had his knowledgeable friend not commented, "You know, there's an artesian well in that building." An artesian well occurs when the groundwater, under pressure, is naturally pushed to the surface when tapped with a pipe. The word "artesian" derives from the former province of Artois in France, where many such wells were drilled by twelfth-century monks.[29] Yet here was a well right in the middle of Pittsburgh, in the middle of a warehouse.

"Really?" John said. He couldn't believe it. He needed a warehouse to produce seltzer, and here was one practically built for the purpose. It seemed like fate. "You're kidding, no?"

"No," his friend replied, and so they called the owner, who was quite amenable to the transaction. A little research on the building revealed that in the 1970s it had been home to a different seltzer company. The company was no more, but its bottles were actually still in use by the Pittsburgh Seltzer Works. Many of the water lines and filtration systems were still in place. After a wall was moved while refitting the space, John found the artesian well. If the room was quiet, he could even hear the sound of trickling water trying to get in.

Jim had full faith in his partner rebuilding the seltzer lines. John and Jim used to joke that if Jim went near the machine it would break—and sometimes it wasn't a joke. Jim liked to describe himself as "mechanically challenged," as someone who couldn't change the oil in his car. John not only was willing but enthusiastic; his energy and knack for figuring things out sometimes made Jim envious.

To learn everything he needed to know, John put that energy into overdrive. With customers waiting for the business to reopen, his partner waiting for the money to come in, and a landlord waiting for the rent to be paid, John's training was forced up a notch of intensity.

After the new place was secured, in the crisp chill of late October, Paul, Dave, and Evan helped John take the machines apart, load them in a truck, and reassemble them at the new address. Transporting big pieces of equipment and pallets of stacked bottles was a lot of work. Once complete, however, John took over his own training. He had already been reading up on the chemistry of CO_2. If the carbonator broke down, he would be able to diagnose the problem. He was ready to be his own Jedi Master. John could call the previous owners for help, when needed, but his training continued "on the job" as it were, waiting for a gear to break or a belt to fall out of alignment and then figuring out how to get the machines back up to speed.

Before the bottles went into the machine for the first time, there was work to do: John had to make sure each was strong enough to handle the pressure and that its head functioned properly. He had learned how to manage the heads and make sure the bottles were sterilized. He used the special wooden wrench to remove the head that contained all the magic—the collars, the trigger, the spring, the washer. Sans head, the siphon was little more than a beautifully shaped bottle. After removing the head, John washed all the parts with soap and hot water, inside and out, then scrubbed with a wire brush until they shone. Then John placed a flat, white washer atop the neck of the bottle, creating a half-inch cushion between the glass below and the hard metallic head. John inserted the glass tube that the seltzer would move through; its upper end was covered in metal and splayed out like a flower to rest on the white washer. With the washer at the top of the neck, the two parts of the collar snapped across the bottom to form a groove. The head was then screwed back into place along the groove of the collar, buffered by the washer. The head held the glass straw in place and contained the spring that activated the trigger. That special wrench finished the job and tightened everything in place. John had learned to make sure the siphon-head triggers opened properly to release the seltzer but held in the carbonation when closed.

John hauled the first crate of ten empty siphons to the start of the line, placing them side by side in preparation. Once aligned, he stood before the bottler and began the process: lift a bottle from the wooden case on the conveyor belt, invert it, insert the siphon into the bottlers' next revolving grip, then release it in time to reach for the next bottle. Repeat until the machine is full. Out of sight, deep inside the machine, John could hear the seltzer streaming from the carbonator into each siphon. It was working. He was making seltzer. But not just any seltzer—really cold, sharp seltzer. After all his training, he could hear that the carbonator sounded just right. When the first bottle emerged, having completed its revolution through the machine, his suspicion was confirmed by the frost that appeared on the outside. This was a handmade, labor-intensive process, and he wanted each bottle to be the best it could be.

Once the bottles were filled John completed the process by working in reverse order: he removed the filled siphon before it revolved back into the bottler and placed it on the belt on the other side of the machine, until all of the empty bottles previously lined up on his right transformed into a line of filled siphons in the wooden case on his left.

Once all of the crate's siphons had passed through the machine, John had to confirm their internal pressure by sharply tapping on the bottles. When properly carbonated, one sharp tap produced a sound like a pop. John watched small bubbles rise and smiled with the satisfaction of having produced a perfect bottle. Then and only then would he know the bottler had done its job and the siphon was sound. But if the pressure wasn't right, if there was no pop, if all he saw was a kind of weak fizz, something was wrong. It might be a sign of a small leak in the siphon head. Or perhaps the one-hundred-year-old bottling machine was in a bad mood. In any case, if John couldn't hear that satisfying pop, the siphon would not be allowed to pass. The bottle would be emptied and passed back through the bottler.

If not confident, John was at least competent. And now that he had completed the purchase of bottles from David Meisel, the

Pittsburgh Seltzer Works would continue, even if some bottles needed to be put out of commission.

The Seltzer Sisters' information about the Meisel's siphon collection had helped both John and Jim feel confident moving forward with the purchase of the Pittsburgh Seltzer Works. After they bought the Works they proceeded with the siphon negotiations. Buying the bottles and their mothballed equipment gave them their next task: transporting thirty-five hundred seltzer siphons and the enormous machines all the way from Rhode Island to Pittsburgh.

John and Jim hired five people to load the bottles and equipment into a fifty-foot box truck, a tractor trailer, and a flatbed truck and drive it from Rhode Island to Pittsburgh. Unloading at the new location must have looked to passersby like a scene from a comedy. A local college student drove a forklift as the guy from the box truck, which was filled with seltzer bottles from front to back, tried to figure out how to fit all of them into their new Pittsburgh home. The siphons were everywhere, just everywhere, like a flock of penguins.

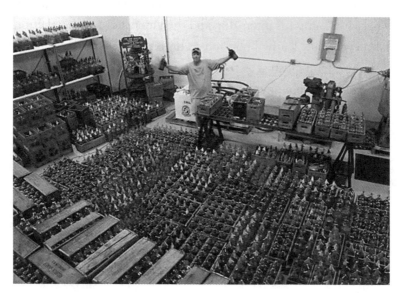

"The siphons were everywhere, just everywhere, like a flock of penguins."

A photo from that day ended up on the Pittsburgh Seltzer Works' Facebook page. Clad in tan shorts and a gray shirt, John stood small in the back of the room brandishing a bottle in each of his outstretched hands; hundreds of siphons, perhaps thousands, closed in around him like zombies on the attack, peppered with red, green, and blue from the Argentinian plastic bottle heads in the collection.

The purchase doubled their inventory of siphons and, more importantly, the Works' output capacity. The Works was now positioned to grow bigger than anyone in recent memory had allowed it to become.

But once John was on his own, his mentors all back in their own lives, of course things started to break down. "It's like when you buy a used car," John said. "It works great on the test drive, but the minute you leave the dealership that's when all the funky noises start happening." He could have called for help, but he needed to learn to do it on his own. If one of the metal heads no longer fit on a bottle, he had to get it back on. If the bottler was broken, he had to get out his tools and figure out how to get it working again. That's how, after his internship and then months of trial and error, John eventually learned how to run his own seltzer works.

Once John finished testing the bottles, he collected his first ten perfect seltzer siphons and lifted their heavy, thick Czechoslovakian glass into the awaiting crate. They looked beautiful. "Why did people stop doing this?" he wondered. Then he remembered. It's dangerous. It's dirty. It's heavy.

And he wouldn't change it for the world.

Over the next few months, John worked the line and developed his skills. Each night John powered down the machines, sending them to their own quiet slumber. And in the silent warehouse, when he turned off the lights, he could hear the whisper of water underneath the Works, bursting to escape, drop by drop.

More difficult to discern were the winds of the approaching storm.

THE BLIZZARD OF 2010

Winter was just under way when John announced they would be ready to reopen the Pittsburgh Seltzer Works at the beginning of February.

"We said we'd be in business in a few months," John explained, and people waited. They waited as the bottling system was rebuilt. They waited as the siphons were prepared. As a delivery truck was purchased, requirements by the Department of Health were met, and the Facebook page launched. Articles were written announcing the Works and its plans to reopen. And still they waited. At last, John was ready. "We say we're gonna begin delivery again. Everyone signs up. We're all set to go. We say, 'Here comes your seltzer.'" And so it did, for a few days. "Then the storm of storms hits Pittsburgh."

The snow might have been fun initially, but then the first foot of snowfall toppled power lines and trees. As accumulation approached a second foot, public transportation was halted, roadways and businesses were closed, and the city declared a disaster emergency. This was just the first day of the blizzard, in a city accustomed to no more than a foot of snow all year. Before long almost two feet more would arrive, along with 470 members of the National Guard equipped with 117 Humvees, 6 ambulances, and 2 tactical vehicles. While 150,000 homes were without power, the governor told everyone in town to stay off the road, warning, "You will risk your life and, potentially, the lives of others"[30] if they did not.

When his cell phone started ringing, John knew something had changed. As John described it to me, "Everyone's on the TV saying, 'Don't go anywhere.' The supermarkets are closed. The city is paralyzed for literally two weeks." And yet the calls kept coming, all asking a version of the same question: "Are we still going to get our seltzer?"

John was dumbstruck. "These people don't have power. They don't have cable. And what's primarily on their minds is if we can get there to get them their seltzer."

It was then that John of the Pittsburgh Seltzer Works knew he had done more than just buy a bottling plant. "It's not just a drink," he realized. "It's a lifestyle," one loved more deeply by his clients than he had ever realized and which had now, at long last, infected him as well. He was not about to let the Great Blizzard of 2010 disrupt the relationship between seltzer connoisseurs and his bottles. Undaunted by the challenge before him, he recommitted himself to defending this sacred bond, now placed in his trust, forged long before he was born.

This was John's first month bottling seltzer, ever. All he knew about filling siphons he had labored to learn in the past few months. He knew even less about seltzer delivery, having made his first deliveries only the week before. He had so much still to learn.

But he knew without a doubt, as his phone kept ringing that wintry mess of a day, that he had over three hundred siphons to bottle and deliver. He was not about to let anything—not the National Guard or nature—get in his way. He had made a commitment. "Pittsburgh is a big small town, and everybody does know everybody." He wanted to conduct himself honorably and do it well, so he said he'd deliver.

"Whether we had to walk it there or drive it," he said, "we got them their seltzer."

It was one thing to learn how to run the factory. But delivering seltzer, driving it to the customers in person, building relationships every stop along the way, was a new world.

John's inauguration as a seltzer man had been a baptism by snow. "And," he explained, "it has been non-stop ever since."

When John officially reopened the Works, his city crushed by snow and buttressed by the National Guard, he became more than just a seltzer manufacturer. Delivering seltzer was a profession with its own rich and varied traditions and history.

Eli Miller and Walter Backerman were two exemplars of that trade. When John was just getting started, these two men delivered seltzer in New York. As different from one another as night from day, Eli and Walter were each willing to share "a day in the life" of a seltzer man as they filled their bottles at Gomberg, in Brooklyn, and delivered their siphons.

"BRING ME YOUR EMPTIES"

Most who meet him would be inclined to agree: Eli Miller was a myth-making machine. He greeted one client, "Hi, Sweetheart. How ya doing?" His crisp Brooklyn accent, each word highly articulated, made him sound as if he were performing on a radio show. After fifty years of delivering seltzer door-to-door in New York City, Eli had earned the right to tell it like he saw it. In August 2010, at the age of seventy-seven, with two heart stents, he was one of perhaps a dozen active seltzer men (and a few women) in the country. Most likely he was the oldest.

Eli was still regularly delivering seventy pounds of siphon-filled wooden cases to over 150 clients across Brooklyn and occasionally Manhattan. At the first delivery for a new client, a young mother in a fashionable sundress and white wedge heels raved, "I've been wanting it for a long, long time. I felt very lucky when I first saw you carrying seltzer into our apartment building. I stopped you and said, 'I would love for you to deliver seltzer to my house.' I love seltzer." Eli corrected her as he maneuvered his hand truck. "I'm the product. It's not the seltzer," he joked. "It's all about Eli." It was her first day, but she quickly learned the routine. "It's all about Eli," she repeated, "sorry." But then she said in all sincerity, "You're renowned in Brooklyn. When we met, I felt like an angel came."

Eli's stories about his life as a seltzer man often presented an industry approaching its end. They addressed the work of bottlers who carbonated the water, the desires of housewives and other clients that caused it to flow, and the backbreaking labor of delivery

Eli's siphons

men like himself, all connected through an invisible network that flowed through the city. With his stories, Eli claimed a space in the collective consciousness for a dying profession. When he quipped, "I'm an anachronism, what can I tell ya?" he was almost pleading, "Remember us, for soon we'll be gone."

His client Ken Rush immortalized Eli in a children's book, *The Seltzer Man.* Rush painted this beautiful children's book in the 1990s, imagining his daughters spending Eli's last day of work driving around with him, visiting clients and Brooklyn landmarks along the way. By the end of the tale, the girls had inspired Eli to stay in the business, for at least one more week. "This is my five minutes of fame right here, my seventy-seven years in a children's book. This painting here," the lanky, 6'2" Eli pointed out to anyone who would look, "you see me in the clouds, my hat, my nose." The cloud was shaped like Eli's head as his old truck flew through the sky, spilling seltzer siphons behind like a vapor trail. "Fifty years after I'm dead kids are gonna be reading about Eli the Seltzer Man."

Eli filled his bottles before the start of his route at Gomberg Seltzer Works, in Canarsie, Brooklyn. Gomberg had been one of many plants in the city that filled siphons for hundreds of seltzer men. Now they were the only game in town and supported around six. "And I don't see no new guys coming into the business," Eli shared with concern.

Eli went into the seltzer business in 1960, when he was twenty-seven years old. "I was a dividend clerk on Wall Street, making maybe $125 a week," the equivalent of around $1,000 today. One day, Eli visited his uncle's collision shop in Canarsie, across from a soda and beer distributor. Watching the delivery men come and go, he wondered what it would be like to have a business of his own. With his cousin egging him on, Eli crossed the street and spoke with the proprietors. His uncle vouched for him so he could get himself a van, a liquor license, and his first forty cases of beer. When he returned the next day, having sold the entire load on credit in the poverty-stricken Brooklyn neighborhood of Bedford-Stuyvesant, the distributor erupted. "Are you crazy?" Reflecting common prejudices of the time, he continued, "You gave forty cases to black people without getting a nickel?!!" Eli's face

"His client Ken Rush immortalized Eli in a children's book."

always shone when he shared his response. "I said, 'These people are like any other people. The reason I went to Bed-Stuy is because nobody goes there.'" Nobody meaning white delivery men. "They're afraid. I wasn't afraid. And I believed these people were going to pay me back." When he returned to Bed-Stuy a week later for the empties, everyone paid him, justifying Eli's belief in them. Within two years, he had switched from soda and beer to seltzer.

On Eli's head a black baseball cap announced in white print, "ELI THE SELTZER MAN," with his phone number and a sketch of a siphon. Walking billboards, seltzer men didn't need to advertise. Eli kept folded notes for the day's deliveries in the breast pocket of his gray-and-white-plaid camp shirt, unbuttoned almost halfway down; he wore comfortable brown shoes and blue pleated slacks with a belt to match.

In his gray 1989 Crown Victoria station wagon, Eli reviewed the stops planned for the day scratched on a sheet of paper with his left hand, due to the shaking in his right. He read the names of each family, of a pastry shop in Park Slope, of Mr. Holbrooke. "Now, Holbrooke—great family. Great patriots," he mused. "David has been with me a long time. I watched his children grow up, and of course he has a famous father. America's diplomat, the greatest one: Richard Holbrooke, a special envoy to Pakistan and Afghanistan." Eli often spoke of his customers like this, with pride, like they were family.

Before hitting the road, Eli swapped his bottles, replacing the cases of "empties" reclaimed from his clients the previous day with freshly filled siphons prepared before he arrived. Laboriously, but with great care, he removed one case at a time, piling them on a pallet to be taken in by the Gomberg bottler, Kevin Gilliam, who returned with a second pallet weighted with filled siphons ready to load into Eli's car. Eli hunched over, lifted each case, and placed it just so in the back of his station wagon. He treated the siphons with care. These were his, carefully collected and maintained over time, purchased from retiring seltzer men and entrusted to customers who could only hope to live as long as these bottles had been in service.

Eli's car was packed, not just with siphons but with news clippings, tools of the trade, and assorted ephemera. His odometer read 230,000 miles, counting not just the car's mileage but Eli's own across the borough. He had been driving the streets of Brooklyn professionally for over fifty years. Leaving Gomberg, his car weighted down with filled siphons, Eli wound through Crown Heights, passing the black-hatted Lubavitch Hasidic Jews and a favorite kosher bagel store, then turned left at Eastern Parkway, past the fountain of jumping water outside the Brooklyn Museum of Art, past the entrance to the Brooklyn Botanic Garden, then a hard right at the main branch of the Brooklyn Public Library, just before Grand Army Plaza.

Kevin preparing another batch of siphons

After a failed delivery attempt in Prospect Heights—most of his stops were in the afternoon, when people got home from work—he skirted around the traffic circle north of the Grand Army Plaza, then drove into the heart of Park Slope, chasing yellow lights and running a few reds every few blocks before unloading two cases for Sweet Melissa Patisserie, a fancy shop on Seventh Avenue.

Eli entered Sweet Melissa like he owned the place, walking right to a shelf where he dropped off their first case. Glasses tinkled as patrons sipped coffees and ate sweet pastries. "You have any more empties?" he asked a waitress. While someone went to check the refrigerator for more empties, Eli said, "Be right back," but not without a passing aside to Michele, the smiling lady behind the cash register: "CNN is doing a story about me."

Eli brought seltzer for their creamery, what others call an ice cream counter, where Sweet Melissa also served cherry-lime rickeys and egg creams. "We need the egg creams," Michele insisted. "It's a Brooklyn drink." Without siphoned seltzer, "we'd cry," she said with a laugh, as another waitress added, "I don't know if Sweet Melissa would be what it is without seltzer, right? I mean, right? Obviously."

Eli's visit was shaped by the well-rehearsed choreography of lugging twenty siphons in, then lugging out an equal number, initiating the fresh collection of empties in the back of his car. But it was also a publicity appearance: Having finished the seltzer transfer, he returned with his picture book, chatting up the staff in the creamery. "Watch, watch, watch," he said, holding it open. "This is me delivering seltzer." They ate it up. "Wow!" said Denise, her black knit cap failing to restrain her shoulder-length curls. "Look at you! Wow!" Eli told her how to buy the book on something called "eBay Amazon," then headed back to Michele to settle their bill.

Next, Eli drove through Gowanus to the southern end of Carroll Gardens, heading right up Clinton Street into brownstone

"Eli hunched over, lifted each case, and placed it just so in the back of his station wagon."

country, where old ways hang on. One case full of seltzer bottles can easily fetch a few hundred dollars on the collector's market, yet Eli stepped into the open foyer of a brownstone and without hesitation dropped off a fresh case, retrieved his empties, and picked up the check left under the mat, completing yet another transaction that went back who knew how many years, reifying a trust between customer and salesman, and between the two and their community, that is striking in its presumed normalcy.

The parking spot was across the street, in front of a funeral home that Eli didn't avoid, even though his father had died delivering seltzer. Previously a contractor, his father had spent his retirement helping his son on the job. He just felt more comfortable working, even though Eli didn't want him to. During one delivery Eli found his dad collapsed in the hall, already dead. Eli's attempt to revive him didn't help. Underneath the nostalgia for seltzer and the past it represented were men like this, who risked suffering the explosions of thick-glassed siphons, slipping under weighted loads in rain and snow, and literally working themselves to death. "It's not an easy way to make a living, but we're mavericks," he once explained. "We desire independence." And after some reflection added, "My dad died on a route, and the same thing will happen to me."

Jessica, the new customer in the fashionable sundress, waited inside an apartment building in Brooklyn Heights on a cul-de-sac overlooking the Brooklyn-Queens Expressway, the East River, and the Statue of Liberty. Eli argued with the doorman, who refused to let him enter with his handcart. Ten minutes later, Eli stomped back out. No dice. If Eli wanted to use his handcart, he couldn't use the front entrance. So Eli loaded his cart from the back of the station wagon and headed to the easterly service entrance, where there were stairs, all the while calling the doorman names he couldn't repeat on broadcast television.

The doorman placed a ramp on the stairs so Eli could lug his load into the building's basement. Jessica met Eli there and took him to her modern split-level apartment. Her first lesson in seltzer delivery began in the service elevator on the way up. A relationship with a seltzer delivery man is not a legal contract. It's an under-standing. "If you can't finish a bottle a week," he informed Jessica, "I can't use you as a customer." She nodded. "So, you've got to finish a case in two months." She nodded again, saying, "I can do that."

And without even a handshake, it was done. As Eli completed the drop-off, Jessica beamed. "I just got my first seltzer delivery!"

Eli then headed toward one of his oldest customers, the one to whom he was delivering seltzer the day Jessica first saw him. There was one problem: it was on the other side of the building, which meant exiting the eastern side and returning through the west. But the western entrance offered no ramp, just an imposing staircase for Eli and his handcart. At this point, Eli was far more than out of breath and beyond frustrated. "Look at this," he said to no one in particular, surveying the impossible challenge before him, then making a decision. He packed the handcart back into his car and, grabbing a heavy seltzer case, stormed into the main entrance, blew past the doorman, and into the elevator. Fine, he wouldn't touch their precious floor with his hand truck. But nothing was going to stop his delivery.

"The rewards in this business are my customers," Eli often said, referring to relationships that went back thirty, even forty, years. "We grew old together." At the next apartment a lady of Eli's generation, in thick glasses and a Bohemian printed tank top, opened the door. Here stood the archetypal seltzer-delivery customer.

"Mickey!" Eli greeted her with great enthusiasm. Mickey had been receiving seltzer deliveries for thirty years, having learned of his services from a neighbor who had since moved away. Mickey had a place in Eli's heart: She used to wait on her infirm husband twenty-four hours a day. Eli met him when he could walk and watched him move into a wheelchair and then into a bed. He asked Mickey about her husband, who had since moved into a nursing home, and about her two girls, both grown and moved out. "They were gorgeous kids," he said. "Gorgeous."

Mickey reminisced about how excited her husband had been when he had first learned of Eli. "He was like, 'Seltzer!' He grew up with it," before she admitted, "but we like you more than the seltzer." When she says *seltzer* it comes across more like *sell-za*, like in the famous Seinfeld "seltzer/salsa" routine. She told friends, "Eli has stents in his heart. I hate seeing him delivering seltzer, but it's all he wants to do, says he'll die doing it."

By 2010, Eli's business depended on word of mouth. If an old customer stopped buying seltzer and no one replaced him or her, he or she became the end of a long line of customers. One day, this could be how Eli and those like him arrived at the sunset of their profession, accepting the loss of their last customer. But with the delivery to the mother downstairs, hope was rekindled: a first delivery to a new customer. Mickey was no longer the last link on this particular chain of Eli's customers. This line had a future.

"You're really something, right?" Mickey announced. "You're an authentic New Yorker, and there's not many left like you." She suggested he be featured as the New Yorker of the Week, the feel-good piece that runs on the local twenty-four-hour news channel.

"Mickey had been receiving seltzer deliveries from Eli for thirty years."

"CNN," he said, as if correcting her. "CNN is going to do a piece about me. They are going to come around and interview you. You'll be famous."

"Yeah, sure," she replied dismissively, as if the paparazzi hounded her every day. "But I don't want a picture."

"You don't want a picture with me?" he asked, feigning shock. He sidled up next to her, as if the TV crew had just arrived.

"With you, I'll take a picture," she conceded with a laugh.

"My sweetheart," he said.

Eli picked up the case of empties. "Okay, Mickey," he declared, signaling it was time to move on. "Stay well, dear," he added, "and thank you for your time."

"CNN should make you a celebrity," she called as the elevator opened. "You deserve it!"

A few blocks north on Hicks Street was the magnificent brownstone of the Holbrookes. David Holbrooke, a tall man with a friendly face, opened the door and ushered Eli into the open kitchen. Eli narrated as if he were accompanied by that crew from CNN he kept talking about. "Okay," he proclaimed, while David Holbrooke, a filmmaker who runs film festivals, listened attentively as he enjoyed the show. "A great, great American. A great patriot. And a great diplomat. And I am so appreciative for having the Holbrooke family for customers. I love your dad."

David affirmed, deadpan, "You're a big fan of my dad."

"He's the greatest," Eli continued, quoting Holbrooke on Pakistan before adding his own in-depth analysis. "When I see him on TV, he says, 'Pakistan isn't the problem. Pakistan is the solution!' This guy should run for president."

David asked Eli to remind him how long they had been receiving seltzer. "Since the kids were babies," Eli replied. Around ten years. When asked about the dying art of seltzer delivery and how younger clients like himself represent a possible future, David replied, "Look, the real question is: How much longer can *he* do this? And I just don't know. That's the hard part about this." But for the time being, David and his family were experiencing the joys of seltzer—and Eli. "The kids are all growing up with it. They'll always remember these bottles and these boxes, and certainly remember Eli, who is unforgettable."

David settled his bill with Eli, who was still talking about David's dad. "Let me tell you, you know the strain this man has, as a special envoy, traveling? He's trying to bring peace and accommodation to these people, to understand their point of view and make the world a better place. This man is all about peace, and understanding, and caring for each other. He's just a wonderful human being." Eli obviously so admired a man whose labor came from traveling, from connecting with people to better their lives, someone whose very presence modeled a desired way of life.

"I appreciate it," David replied, walking Eli to the door. "As always, great to see you."

"I love this man," Eli announced. "Love his kids, his wife. Gorgeous daughters. Lovely wife. Nice family."

Before closing the door, David told Eli, "We're lucky to have you in our life."

In a little more than two hours, Eli had covered so much ground. In that short time, this seventy-seven-year-old had lifted so much weight, touched so many people, and spun so many stories. And he was far from through for the day: Eli still had five more deliveries.

Back at his car, Eli chatted up a passerby. "Come here," Eli told her, holding out his book. "I gotta show you something." She looked on while Eli turned the pages. "Wait'll you see me in the clouds. Look. Look in the clouds."

Eventually, Eli climbed into his car, prepared for at least two more hours on the road, with sixty siphons to deliver and empties to collect. He drove around the corner, toward the sun, hours to go before it set.

THE SELTZER-MAN PHILOSOPHER

The stories of seltzer men like Eli, with miles behind them, and those like John Seeking, with miles ahead, wove everyone together into a sprawling seltzer narrative. Walter the seltzer man, however, was a far cry from Eli's nostalgic, Frank Capraesque version of the profession. Walter was more unvarnished and unrelenting. Aside from the constant profanity and the lack of a filter, Walter Backerman was like a character escaped from a Quentin Tarantino film: brutally honest, full of chutzpah, with the charismatic power to spin dramatic stories packed with unexpected life lessons.

For seven hours a day, Walter took calls from customers and worked his seltzer delivery route, delivering seltzer around northern Manhattan, the lower part of the Bronx, and his home in Queens. Like an experienced taxi driver, Walter displayed a mastery of New York roads: hustling but never rushing and quick to point out the idiocy of other drivers.

To an eavesdropper, most phone calls sounded like this: "Hi. It's Walter the seltzer man. How are you doing today?" Pause. "I'm good. How are you doing for seltzer?" Pause. "All right. I'll see you in a few minutes." Pause. "Okay. Thanks. Bye." Or, if it was one of his children calling, "What? Anything important? Anything? What? Let me pull over. I'm driving. There is a cop over there. Talk fast. Later. Why? I don't know. I got a full route. I don't know when I'm getting home. You need something? I'll stop at the house. Let me do the route. I'll speak to you later."

Walter had just turned sixty and barely showed his age, his black moustache peppered only in the right light. "I could never stop delivering seltzer," Walter would say, despite forty years on the route, "even if I won the mega lottery." His work outfit was functional, not fancy: a dark blue sweatshirt covered a friendly light blue polo shirt above blue jeans and sneakers. He accessorized with a Craftsman Tools baseball cap and a phone clipped to his hip.

Walter's favorite bottles, on display in his living room

Like Eli, Walter was a consummate self-promoter, speaking to his listener and speaking for the ages. His stories were rarely linear; when he spoke, he started in one place and then meandered somewhere unexpected, through a complex syntax that built a whole greater than the sum of its parts.

Speaking to a passenger riding shotgun one day (a certain author researching a possible book on seltzer water), Walter recounted the ups and downs over the past century of the area they were passing through, 111th Street and Broadway, and then Harlem further north. "Manhattan is a whole mixed bag of population. The areas are changing." He added, "I go to parts of Brooklyn that twenty years ago I wouldn't have went through unless I had my guns on.

"I used to run around with two guns back in the days," he explained to his guest, "because New York was crazy. One time in the Bronx I see, out of the corner of my eye, I see some guy who wasn't kosher. He's wearing an army jacket, the kind a street thug would use to bury his gun." Because Walter was delivering seltzer, he carried cash payments and therefore had a target on his back. "I looked to him like, you know, a pretty woman to a guy that has been in jail for ten years." But Walter was on to him. Positioning himself at the back of his van, Walter pulled the end of the door in and looked as if he were preparing for his delivery. Out of the corner of his eye Walter saw the guy approach, hand in jacket. Swinging the van door wide, knocking both man and gun to the ground, Walter picked up the gun and stood over the man's head, saying, "You move, I'll blow your blocking head off, and I'm not playing." But Walter still had a route to finish. "Get the hell out of here," he told the thug and didn't surrender the gun at the local police station until his last siphon was delivered.

Back then, experiences like that made Walter feel helpless. But more recently, New York City was different. Now he walked in the street counting money. "I used to look like I was ready to kill someone if they looked the wrong way at me, and obviously I know what to do," Walter told his ride-along. But like Eli's customers, "I have people now leave the bottles out for me. They leave cash sticking out of the case and no one ever touches it." This made him proud to be a New Yorker. And what made him even happier: "I am one of the aspects of New York, one of the quirky aspects of New York, that still makes our city special."

Walter was a third-generation seltzer man. His grandfather, Jake, started his route in 1919 with a horse-drawn wagon. It was hard work, but a seltzer man could always depend on his horse. "If a customer quit, you were in trouble because the horse would stop anyway." Two years before starting his own route, Jake had survived the battles of World War I and gotten married. Now he needed work to support his new family. He partnered with a cousin who was a seltzer man delivering to the walk-ups on the Lower East Side. Walter would think about Jake when he carried siphons up and down stairs, figuring that's why his grandfather hated the business; the cousin had made Jake take the top floors while the he delivered to the easier lower stories. "My grandfather didn't like it, I'll tell you that," Walter told his passenger. "He didn't like it at all. He needed a way to make money. And seltzer was a way to make money." Back then, these were people who could have done so much more—"elevated" themselves, Walter would say—if they only had had the opportunity. "But it is what it is."

Walter's father, Al, became a seltzer man as well. In 1952, the year Walter was born, a case of ten bottles cost $17.50, equivalent to around $200 today. "But business was thriving then," Walter said, "with literally thousands of seltzer men and millions of seltzer trucks all over the city. Two or three seltzer trucks used to deliver to one block at the same time."

To get away from the competition, Al canvassed new buildings in Yonkers, north of the city. Sometimes, Al's wife Reba would join him, just to make sure she could see him, as his hours were so long. "My father would ring doorbells while my mother pushed me in a baby carriage." Walter liked to brag that, as a result, he made his first deliveries at six months of age.

Back then, according to Walter, doors were left unlocked and wide open, with people sitting out on porches in beach chairs. When they heard the doorbell or saw Al approaching, their interest would be piqued. Self-advertising was a seltzer man's tool of the trade even back then. He would say, "Look, I'm Al. I have a seltzer route, and I'm looking to build my route up." Virtually everyone back then bought from a seltzer man.

Al had never planned to follow in the seltzer path of his father. During World War II he was stationed on Staten Island, where he met Reba at a USO dance. One night Al won three hundred dollars in a crap game, a windfall. He called Reba up and said, "I'll never have this kind of money anytime soon. Let's get married." So they did, and by the time World War II ended Al had two kids and a wife to support. He came home to Manhattan as a returning warrior, expecting the streets to be paved with gold. "But the streets were paved with disappointment," Walter said, his dad lost among the wave of returning soldiers looking for work. Luckily, Al's father Jake knew of a seltzer route for sale in the Bronx and lent his son twelve thousand dollars to purchase it. That was a lot of money at the time, but routes then were lucrative. Walter figured when he was born his father was making anywhere from three hundred to four hundred dollars a week, "which was more than the doctors, probably more than president of the United States."

Buying a route meant buying specific bottles and specific customers. Walter still had his father's paperwork listing the bottles and to whom they belonged, and the deed to the business. To keep everything legit, there was the Good Health Seltzer Association, essentially a union for seltzer men. When someone bought out a retiring seltzer man, the new owner could keep the old seltzer man's name on the bottles. But by the regulations of the Good Health Seltzer Association, he had to acid sketch on the reverse side *his* name and logo and the year. The siphon manufacturers inscribed the seltzer man's name on the bottle, and when they made brand-new, chrome-plated tops, they inscribed his name there as well. The union representatives from the Good Health Seltzer Association checked the

The paper collar worn around a siphon's neck to show it was a union bottle. The Hebrew *seltzer shel Pesach* means "seltzer for Passover."

siphons, traveling from seltzer works to seltzer works, return-ing stolen siphons to their rightful owners for a ten-cent fee. Eventually the business waned, the seltzer association faded away, and seltzer men had to fend for themselves.

Walter once pulled into Gomberg Seltzer Works in Brooklyn to pick up his newly filled bottles, and there was a box of his finest siphons walking out on "Danny's" shoulder. "Danny, tell me some-thing," Walter had said, walking right up to him. "Why do you got my bottles on your shoulder?"

Danny looked at the bottles and put them down. "Oh, you're right," he said. "These are your bottles. I'm sorry."

Walter wasn't buying the apology. "Danny, are you really sorry?"

"Yeah, I am really sorry," Danny replied. "I'm sorry that if you had come in another five minutes, I would have had it on my truck."

And Walter's amused response, years later? Respect. "At least he was honest about it. The guy was a thief, caught him dead to rights, and he gave me back the bottles and was honest about it. You understand me? Could you get mad at someone like that? You have to hug them, right or wrong. That was a true seltzer man."

Seltzer men were once so important, everyone wanted to advertise on the side of their trucks. Fox's U-Bet, for example, the famous syrup company, would even paint the seltzer trucks every couple of years as long as they could put "Syrup by Fox's U-Bet" on the side. Walter's father Al drove a bright cherry-red truck, an International Harvester Loadstar. On the bottom were bays that could hold seventy-two cases of seltzer. A few years ago, Walter got himself a new van and decorated it with wonderful seltzer images and photographs, advertising not syrup this time but himself.

On the one hand, Walter hoped to follow in the steps of his late father and live up to the seltzer man Al was. On the other hand, Walter was haunted by the sense that his father wanted to do so much more with his life, so much more than delivering a cold beverage afforded him. On his father's dying day, Walter told him, "You know, Big Al, you lived a wonderful life because people remember you." Whenever film and television shoots hired Walter to supply seltzer siphons, he always sent "Al Backerman" bottles. "As long as I see my father's bottles up there, I think 'He is remembered.'" He didn't love the route, but at least he is remembered for his contribution. And for Walter, every day meant living the answer to the question: "What are you doing to make people know that you are a seltzer man?"

"Each bottle is a tombstone to a seltzer man," Walter once elaborated. "It is their way of being recognized even though they are gone. I'm just the custodian for the next generation, ya follow me? You don't own the bottle." Walter felt burdened at times by the weight of all the late people who had owned the bottles and his own place in their lineage, not just of his father and grandfather, but of all the men of their generations who had once worked their routes with these same siphons that now filled the back of his own truck.

Walter's gift of gab came from his father, and Al got it from who knows where—certainly not from Jake. "He never said a word," Walter remembered. Every Sunday Jake would read the *New York Times* from cover to cover, and he might talk about politics if

you brought it up. But not seltzer. He never wanted to talk about the route. Walter's last conversation with Jake, before he passed, was when he was ninety-five years old. They had just finished the Passover seder on Rochambeau Avenue in the Norwood section of the Bronx. As they were saying their goodbyes, Walter took his shot, aided by four glasses of Manischewitz wine, and said, "You know, Jake, I'm just curious. What was it like being the seltzer man back in the days of the horse and wagon?"

"It's a hard way to make a living," his grandfather replied, adding nothing more than, "I wish you would do something else." There was no nostalgia. No great sense of connection. Not something he felt as a passion. Seltzer was just a way for Jake to make money and, once, a way to help his son do the same.

But Walter felt a kinship with the past that made him feel happy and whole. "When I am walking out with a beautiful case of clean bottles, empty or full, I take pride in it."

Walter liked to say he lived by the Golden Rule. For example, once Al had traveled to the Bronx to find no one home and no empties waiting for him outside. Rather than apologize, the client called to curse at Al and insist that he return with filled bottles, threatening to throw the empties away if Al didn't come back right away. When Walter heard he flipped out, grabbed a wooden case, and drove up to her house. Instead of giving her filled siphons, Walter began to take back the empties that she'd threatened to toss. "You DON'T threaten to throw our property out! Give them back to me. You're done. Go find someone else," he had demanded.

"That's how mad I was," he concluded. "I'll take my bottles out and have three people waiting for that delivery tomorrow. Period. You understand me? If you ain't looking out for me, I'm not looking out for you. That's the reality of it. My father had a saying in Yiddish, 'One hand washes the other.' You look out for me, I look out for you. I hate when I look out for people and they try to screw me, 'cause I'm like a gangster: you screw with me, I'm gonna remember that; but you treat me good, I can't do enough for you. That's the way it's supposed to be."

Back in the day, Walter would befriend drug dealers in areas notorious for gang violence because they'd give him a good tip and watch his back. "Man, you're lucky we like you," they'd tell him. "You're the type of honky we love to stick up." Some days were fifteen hours of torture, everyone eyeing him wherever he went, deciding if and when to rob him of his cash.

One time Walter was sitting on top of his dad's truck, mixing soda. His dad, below, called up in a voice that was cracking. Walter looked down and saw his father's face turning colors. He was with two guys, one short and one tall, and they were riffling through his pockets.

Walter saw their gun as he jumped off the truck and they ran away. He took off after them, chasing them into a building. Things went south from there. The altercation ended with Walter sucking on the barrel of a gun. "And then he squeezed the trigger. Either it jammed or it wasn't loaded, but my head, I felt it like . . . exploding." That was when his customers in law enforcement helped Walter get a gun permit.

It's always good to have people in your corner, was Walter's conclusion. "That's the lesson to be learned here. Give 'em candy. Give 'em soda. It's always better than getting a gun behind your ear."

None of the danger lessened Walter's love of the job. "Seltzer is a wonderful old thing," he often explained, "and I actually enjoy bringing these bottles to people's homes."

Walter took pride, even if his father didn't. "Big Al, I think you're getting your strength back," he had told his dad on that last day in the hospital. "I think you're going to make it out of here. I miss you on the route."

Retired for two decades, Al would have none of it. "I have nightmares about the route," he confessed to his son. "People need me to bring them seltzer. I wish I could rest."

Walter didn't know how to respond. He looked out the hospital window and remembered all the times he had argued with his father. He thought about all the things that were out there in the fresh air, and the times that were good and the times that were bad, and he realized his dad would never be in that world again. Afterward, every time it seemed like life threw an obstacle in his way, Walter would "think about that window and I am glad I have a chance to have better days."

Walter's attitude toward his seltzer route was diametrically opposed to his father's and grandfather's. "I can't begin to tell you all the remarkable, wonderful experiences I've had that I would never, ever begun to experience doing anything else." Of course, it got tough: he was sometimes exhausted, or the snow was piling up. He could be running on three or four hours of sleep. People might piss him off. "On the other hand, in the scheme of things, you never really remember all that stuff," he would muse. "Usually you dwell on the things that are interesting, and I'm actually blessed. It's a powerful feeling to take something so ordinary like a bottle and make it your introduction to a world of people that would never have crossed your path before."

Walter first grew interested in seltzer siphons when he was about ten years old. It was a hot summer day in the Bronx, he recalled, and he was helping his father load the truck of a fellow driver, one of the last old-timers left, someone like Eli. Then the bottle came out. It was tall with green emerald-colored glass, ten-sided. Walter picked it up to admire. Condensation was forming on the outside of the cold bottle, and he held it up to spin it in the light of the sun, mesmerized, hypnotized. "It looked beautiful to me." He asked the aging seltzer man if he was up for a trade. "I'll give you a bottle for that one." The seltzer man agreed, asking for nothing more than "a bottle that works" in exchange. "And that was like the first bottle that I ever put aside that I collected."

Walter's budding interest couldn't have happened at a better time. In the early 1970s, most seltzer men were leaving the industry, finding no one interested in buying them out. So more often than not they unloaded their bottles into the trash. As a teenager, "I found it to be disgusting, revolting to me, that they were taking these beautiful art forms and chucking them into the garbage." Walter could not buy their businesses, but he could cobble together the change to buy the siphons, selling the metal tops for scrap at thirty cents apiece and keeping the beautiful bottles underneath.

Walter marveled at how reporters followed seltzer men around. "We are anachronistic, even when I was a kid in the '70s. The business shouldn't really exist now, of course: we are a mirage. We're absolutely absurd. Yet I'm on six different TV shows in five years. I don't know movie stars who get like that." He suspected the seltzer men appealed to viewers because the men were nothing more or less than hard-working people trying to support themselves and their families, trying to make life a little more pleasant for people in general. It was a simple, pleasant story. "These are

not multi-billionaires controlling money, manipulating people like Bernie Madoff, trying to screw people." Seltzer men just worked hard and wanted a little recognition. "Nothing wrong with honest hard labor, you know, in a world filled with chicanery."

Walter developed a talent for getting media coverage. But his first time on TV was in the background for a WNBC News piece about his dad. After spending twenty-five minutes on Nixon's impeachment, the anchor, Pia Lindström, came on with a piece about Al Backerman, the seltzer man, concluding with a focus on Walter. "Young Mr. Backerman," she said, referring to Walter, "is about to graduate from college and will be starting law school in the fall. And it is a shame that there are too many lawyers out there and too few good seltzer men." Looking back, Walter found the statement prophetic. "Every time I think about the route and the course of my life and how it turned, I think about what she said. Nothing was ever more profound and truer."

Within months of his graduation, Walter's dad almost died after collapsing with emphysema. "It was then that I put my plans to attend law school on hold for six months to help my father recover. Six months became six years became forty . . ."

Walter's phone rang and he talked to the doorman of the synagogue that was next on his delivery route. "How are you doing? Do you think it is good for me to sneak into that place or is it in shutdown?" Pause. "I'm on the upper part of Riverdale. I can get to you about ten or fifteen minutes." Pause. "Thanks. Bye." When the doorman helped, the delivery was always easier. As Walter approached the synagogue, he shared a joke with his passenger. "People ask me, 'Are you religious?' I say, 'I go to shul all the time. Every couple weeks to this one, to that one . . .' Delivering. That's my degree of devotion. Nice Jewish boy."

Walter was on a roll. "Fifty years ago, when I was a kid with my father, the seltzer man was dull, ordinary, mediocre, commonplace, nothing. When I was a kid, I saw my father coming home dirty, and my friends' parents had suits on, and, you know, the last thing in the world I thought I would ever do was become a seltzer man.

"Life turns, you know, and then you look back on your life, and in retrospect, you know, what did you become? Sure, you could have become a lawyer, but if you choose to be a seltzer man, be the best seltzer man you can be. You know what, people will come to look at you, admire you, and appreciate you. Instead of making it mediocre and dull, you make it exciting. You breathe life into it, instead of letting it get dusty.

"I go to shul all the time . . ."

"The route is . . . the route is the route. That's why I like seltzer. You know why? Doesn't change. You know what I'm saying? Doesn't change."

Nearly seven hours later, Walter would drive across the bridge from the Bronx toward his home in Queens, streaming past the panoramic skyline of Manhattan to the west, leaving the day's route behind. "I think seltzer, aside from being a drink, is part of, like, an art form. You know, in the changing world that we live in, in a world of disposability, in a world where values are erratic, where the vague areas of society are so precarious that people can't even get a true perspective on life, in a world like that, sometimes you need something that gives you permanence. I mean, there is something reassuring about consistency. Ya follow me?

"And for some people the fact that the seltzer man comes, you know, every week or two weeks, and brings something to their door, it's a wonderful feeling. Even on the route, it's a small-town atmosphere on wheels. In a world where you're being run around, rammed around like a number, it's good every now and then to know you are a person, and that somebody cares about you, and knows about you, knows about your life."

Like Eli, Walter connected with his customers. "When I walk into the homes of people, I form an intimate relationship with them. And for some people, it's multi-generational—they know my kids, I know their parents—and that's a wonderful feeling of, you know, like being a part of a broader community. And that community extends from borough to borough, wherever I travel, and I perpetuate that in the face of, you know, defying odds."

Even in New York City, where people live in an apartment for six months before moving on, Walter had found longtime clients. "I mean that's the sad commentary, they're gone. But the thing that makes it good are the people that are tried-and-true, year after year they still buy it, you are going to the same door. It can be ten years from now, you bat your eyes, it's twenty years from now, you know you're walking to the same door, to the same person, and nothing changes except the world around you. Your relationship remains the same, the bottles remain the same, and to have

something constant in a world of instability is the quintessential earmark of seltzer and seltzer men.

"Who am I? I am Walter Backerman, seltzer man, son of Al, grandson of Jake. I am a custodian of siphons. The route? It's an accumulation. The route is the route. It is what it is, and that's the truth.

"Ya follow me?" Walter asked as he turned into his driveway. "And that's it."

SELTZER AND COOKIES

Eli called it a family. Walter called it a community. Whatever it's called, seltzer men formed this web of human relationships and nurtured them over the years, one person to another, one seltzer delivery at a time.

When John Seekings went out into that Pittsburgh snowstorm and completed his first seltzer route, he was starting to weave his own web within the city, marking his transition from seltzer works owner to seltzer man. It had been a trial by fire (cold fire, as it were) but John loved every minute of his delivery days.

"There's not many things you can do now where you're out and about meeting people," John said, "and they'll come out and introduce you to their family. You start hugging people. You have no idea who they are, but you hug them regardless and give them their seltzer."

Sometimes he surprised a customer with a free case. "Here, this case is one from me," he would say, passing it over. "Thank you for your business. Enjoy the seltzer." People were so appreciative; almost no one connected this way in other day-to-day businesses. "It's such a simple thing but it makes their day every time. And that's a great feeling. It really is." All that care flows back as well. "There isn't one Friday or Monday," John says, referring to his delivery days, "that comes or goes that someone doesn't leave cookies. So, I'm well fed as I'm delivering."

John's partner Jim might have liked to share some of the cookies now and again, but he never regretted ceding this heavy lifting to his partner. "Look, I am not going to be out delivering seltzer at four in the morning," he had told John, who understood. "I'd be in the hospital." Jim knew John went into the business with Norman Rockwell dreams of taking his kids out delivering seltzer on a Sunday morning, not the reality of early on a Friday with two feet of snow on the ground, trying to get a piece of junk truck around the hills of the East End.

In the beginning, it was just John out there, without any hired help. "And he got it pretty much all delivered," Jim said, "and kept our customers happy."

And then the snow melted and it was time to build the business.

Walter Backerman's favorite siphons, on display in his home

PART TWO

Give Me Seltzer
(and the People Who Crave It)

During the blizzard of 2010,
John saw for the first time how much seltzer
meant to his customers. And they were far from
alone. From generation to generation, we fill seltzer
with meaning. Discover how that meaning can
change over time and place and how it is most
often associated with one of four categories:
health, refreshment, identity, and comedy.
Make a visit, not too far into the past, to
a time when seltzer found itself pitted in
a battle against another popular
drink: Coca-Cola.

SELTZER

River run through
with sky—what are you
if not a leaping up
of joy from stillness?
Enter Seltzertopia, land
of the purest ambrosia.
The sea becomes laden with bubbles,
little needlepoint pricks
as they pop. Perhaps lime,
perhaps blackberry, perhaps
soda-stream easy on your own counter—
but beyond it all, is the call
of the river dreaming up clouds.

—GennaRose Nethercott, 2017
(*www.gennarosenethercott.com*)

5

HOW SELTZER GOT HEALTHY

*In which we embark on a scientific, historic, and cultural
exploration of water, spa culture, the local food movement, and the fight
against Big Soda and learn that the most common reason people
drink seltzer is because of its health benefits.*

THE SELTZER WARS:
CAGE BATTLES, PART 1

Imagine arriving in South Africa at the international airport outside Johannesburg, the continent's busiest. As travelers walked
from their gate to the luggage carousel they passed by the typical
sights: signs on the wall advertising financial services and soda,
stores selling water bottles, machines featuring Coke and candy.
But what's that up ahead? Could that be a pile of garbage? A closer
look showed it was not just any garbage but discarded soda cans
and water bottles ingeniously piled into a giant brick, six feet wide,
six feet deep, twelve feet high, held together in a metal cage. In fact,
its producers called it just that, *The Cage*, and warned its visitors

SodaStream *Cage* in South Africa

about the dangers it contained. The cans and bottles had been collected from local garbage dumps and landfills: "5,078 bottles and cans per family, every 3 years." Ouch. Bottles and cans were a modern plague, it seemed to suggest, desecrating the planet in landfills. There had to be a better way.

Displays like this one had appeared not only in South Africa but at thirty different locations around the world, from New Zealand to Times Square, produced not by artists or activists but by a for-profit company traded on Wall Street: SodaStream, the largest manufacturer of home soda makers in the world. In 2002, when the Israeli company's products first arrived in the United States, they often framed the SodaStream as a seltzer solution. "Americans need to kick their bottled soft drink habit," argued one press release, "and make their soda and seltzer at home."

On June 8, 2012, however, SodaStream had a problem, a problem it welcomed and had partially engineered: South African lawyers representing Coca-Cola delivered a cease and desist order. *The Cage*, it contended, infringed on the registered trademarks of the Coca-Cola company and breached the South African Advertising Standards Authority's Code of Advertising Practice. In other words, those bottles were Coke's, and SodaStream was disparaging them. Coke wanted *The Cage* torn down.

"We think it is absolutely ridiculous," responded SodaStream CEO and Brooklyn boy Daniel Birnbaum in the company's official press release entitled "Coca-Cola Has 'Fizzy Fit' Over SodaStream's *The Cage*." You could practically hear the glee in his voice as he proclaimed to a reporter at *Forbes* magazine, "I'm not complying."

The corporate history of SodaStream is rather long and convoluted. In 1903, the British gin distillers W & A Gilbey Ltd. began selling an "apparatus for aerating liquids" to the upper class. It was not until 1955 that its first machine for home carbonation, the SodaStream, was brought to market. Sold originally in the United Kingdom through its own subsidiary, it soon appeared in Australia, New Zealand, and Germany. Immensely popular in England in the 1970s and 1980s, many today still associate the product with a catchy jingle from the time, "Get busy with the fizzy." (Look it up online.)

Gilbey eventually sold off the SodaStream division. For a number of years it was passed from company to company like an unwanted child. In 1998 it landed safely in the arms of Soda-Club, an Israeli company founded earlier in the decade. Soda-Club rebranded the line, added new machines, and expanded to North America, Australia, New Zealand, South Africa, and Europe. In most countries, the brand was known as Soda-Club, except in America where (due to an international copyright dispute over the term *club soda*) it operated as SodaStream.

When SodaStream entered the US market, few if any Americans had ever heard of it. By the beginning of 2018, SodaStream had over 5.6 million products in 1.7 million American households. Sold in over ten thousand stores (like Walmart, Target, Staples, and Costco), SodaStream's kitchen carbonator took in an annual revenue of $91 million in the United States alone. Even people who didn't own a SodaStream could name at least one person who did.

And along with its explosive growth came an embrace of environmental causes. "Our vision is to create a world free from plastic bottles and cans," read the introduction to the extensive "Earth Friendly" section of the SodaStream website, "making it a better world for our children." SodaStream promoted environmental campaigns, donating money to build water wells in Kenya.[31]

And then, of course, there was *The Cage*.

The first *Cage* was developed as a centerpiece of SodaStream's March 2011 exhibit at the *International Home + Housewares Show* in Chicago. One of the twenty largest trade shows in America, it had in attendance over sixty thousand home goods and housewares professionals. SodaStream wanted to make a splash. *The Cage* was a big success, and efforts were soon under way to replicate it around the world. Occasionally the exhibit garnered some local coverage, but the three-page letter from Coca-Cola delivered in South Africa ignited an explosion of press coverage around the world. The king of carbonators knew Coke had gotten trapped in their *Cage*, which allowed the young company to position itself in a real David versus Goliath story. And the press around the world followed along with headlines like "Coca-Cola Stoops to Corporate Bullying against SodaStream" and "Coca-Cola Cry-Baby."

Coca-Cola, however, was no stranger to public criticism. A few weeks before its run-in with SodaStream, the soda manufacturer was attacked by another potent foe, New York City mayor Michael Bloomberg. Public health had become a top priority for the mayor. In previous years he had led controversial campaigns to ban smoking in public places and artificial trans fats in restaurants, policies that later spread to other cities. On May 31, 2012, the headline of the *New York Times* announced his latest campaign: "Mayor Planning a Ban on Big Sizes of Sugary Drinks."

While SodaStream took Coke to task for being bad for the planet, Bloomberg attacked the soft-drink industry for being a threat to public health. When the mayor announced his new plans, it came on the heels of his administration's $2.8 million public interest advertising campaign. In one ad, a hand emptied a bottle of Coke into a short glass over the text, "Are you pouring on the pounds?" But that's not brown sugar-water in the glass. It looked like fat. Body fat. As if to

assuage any doubts, it admonished: "Don't drink yourself fat." Instead of soda, the ad recommended three alternative drinks: low-fat milk, water . . . and seltzer.

These two themes often ran hand-in-hand: seltzer was better for both the health of your body and the health of the planet. In short, to many of its fans, seltzer meant health.

Historically, seltzer had always walked the line between a medicine and a beverage, accumulating expectations over time that seemed unreasonable only in retrospect but once must have appeared as exciting and hopeful as a fresh glass of sparkling water.

How did these separate strands of seltzer and health become so intertwined?

The natural history of seltzer began back before SodaStream, before seltzer was first siphoned, before spa towns peddled the healing waters to both merchants and tourists. It began back before the earliest days of spa culture, before emerging civilizations polluted their waters, before water even began to bubble up through the earth as it collected a wide assortment of minerals along the way.

It went back, in fact, four billion years, and not on earth at all but rather on thousands of asteroids heading to earth on a collision course with destiny.

WATER: AN ORIGIN STORY

"The next time you pour a glass of mineral water
you may reflect that water and life itself are both ancient immigrants
to Earth. . . . Sating your thirst is to be the latest event this water
has taken in its four-billion-year-old history on Earth."
—Chris Middleton, *The Water Connoisseur*

Would you drink water from outer space?

What if you already were and didn't know it?

One theory about how water emerged on earth—every drop that has ever passed through our bodies, whether carbonated like Perrier or flat from the tap—is that it all came special delivery from outer space. Once upon a time, so the story goes, comets and asteroids were heading toward earth. Not a single Hollywood-sized one that threatened the planet but many smaller ones. How many? Not dozens. Not thousands. But tens of thousands.

These comets and asteroids didn't travel alone. They carried water, were in fact made of enough water to cover the earth, creating an aquatic cauldron in which life could bloom. (At the same time, the moon received a makeover, lending the event its common name, the lunar cataclysm, and the moon its current crateral design.)

Or perhaps not. A strong competing theory posits that water was not added to our molten planet, but was actually part of its initial formation. According to this theory, Earth was formed by some of the smallest objects in our solar system: dust. Dust and minerals condensed into droplets, called chondrules. These tiny chondrules gathered together like a snowball rolling down a hill, building up not speed but gravity, which accelerated the process. This is called accretion. Water in the form of hydrogen and oxygen already existed in our pre-Earth solar system and was wrapped up through accretion into the formation of our baby planet. So, by the time of the lunar cataclysm, water might already have been here, with ringside seats to the show.

Whichever theory wins out, our understanding is the same: the water in our Perrier originated in outer space.

Before looking at how terrestrial water turned into seltzer, recall something taught in elementary school, the water cycle: evaporation, condensation, precipitation, collection. In the hydrologic cycle, the sun heats ocean waters, transforming the liquid into water vapor. The vapor drifts up to the sky to form clouds.

These clouds turn back into water as rain or snow. The rain or snow falls back to the ground, collecting into streams and lakes, and eventually pulled down by gravity back into the oceans, where the process begins all over again: evaporation to condensation and back again. This describes roughly 98 percent of the water reaching the ground, which, for humans and other animals, becomes surface water from which to drink.[32]

As hydrologist Francis H. Chapelle wrote in his excellent overview *Wellsprings: A Natural History of Bottled Spring Waters*, when humans were nomadic, they and their animals could soil their communities as much as they wished. Once the bodily waste accumulated, they could easily move on, leaving their feces and urine-polluted waters behind. However, once humans settled down on farms and in villages, all that waste began to pile up in shallow pits, open sewers, and cesspools fed by humans but also by goats, donkeys, horses, cattle, chickens, geese, mice, and rats. This waste would wash into nearby rivers and streams or seep into the water table underneath their land. Between water's natural tendency to dissolve organic material and humans' propensity to pollute their local waters, drinking, while necessary to survive, was hazardous to one's health.[33]

As Chapelle wrote, "The effects on the populace of this poor water quality varied from being lethal, as happened during the cholera and typhoid fever epidemics that boiled up regularly, to simply causing chronic intestinal upset and dysentery."[34] Most people, most of the time, were either sick from water or fearful of becoming so. Water, the very source of life, was also the carrier of death, transporting the ills of humanity.

As a result, according to Chapelle, only the poorest of the poor drank water, as none but the most desperate and down-and-out would take such risks. "Drinking water—any water," he wrote, "was a sign of desperation, an admission of abject poverty, a last resort."

Yet humans must drink or die. The most common method, throughout much of recorded history, was to get drunk. "There is no question that the daily lives of Egyptians and Mesopotamians," writes Tom Standage in his book *A History of the World in Six Glasses*, "young and old, rich and poor, were steeped in beer."[35] But a beer of a different sort than today's beer; it had a lower alcohol content and was rich in proteins and vitamins, crucial at the time to replace those lost as people moved from hunting to farming, which reduced meat consumption in the process. So beer was not simply a recreational beverage but a necessary food source and, of most interest to us, a purified alternative to fast-polluting lakes and streams, as the water was boiled and thus sterilized in beer's creation.[36]

If only the poor drank water, while the average person—the farmer, the merchant—drank beer, what did the wealthy drink? It turns out they drank water of another sort, water qualitatively different from that drunk or avoided by the hoi polloi. But if they wanted to drink it in large quantities, they had to travel to its source, often spending weeks vacationing at the hotels, restaurants, and entire towns built around it.

In short, they had to go to a spa.

SPA CULTURE

The Greeks were one of the first to appreciate the medicinal virtues of regularly bathing in naturally occurring carbonated waters, aided in part by Hippocrates's *On Airs, Waters, and Places*: "Those persons whose bellies are soft, loose, and pituitous," he advised nearly twenty-five-hundred years ago, "should choose . . . those kinds [of springs] that are most crude and the saltiest, for . . . such waters are adapted for boiling and . . . naturally loosen readily and melt down the bowels."[37]

Hippocrates

The Romans learned from the Greeks, and, as they spread across Europe from Italy and Germany to Belgium and England, they also spread knowledge about the medicinal properties of the springs they encountered along the way. In 77 CE, for example, Pliny the Elder, a Roman historian, visited and detailed the sites in Italy in his *Remedies Derived from the Aquatic Production.*

The Roman conquerors were not the only ones to spread what had once been local knowledge. Religious proselytizers played their part as well. According to Chapelle, "virtually all the early Christian evangelists in Ireland and Britain are associated with miraculous dealings with springs and wells." For example, Saint Columba, the first Christian to evangelize Scotland, converted one town of pagans by "banishing" the evil spirit polluting their local well, proving his worth by drinking the water and living to tell the tale. "Over the years," Chapelle wrote, "as numerous saints roamed the landscape, blessing wells and springs as they went, traditions of holy and healing wells accumulated in Great Britain."

Whether ascribed to the gods, one God, or simply appreciated for its demonstrable medicinal effects, societies learned to distinguish the good water from the bad. Yet it was one thing to have healing water bubble up from the ground and another to build a phalanx of hotels, restaurants, and resorts around it and charge for access. Once that began, the age of spas had arrived.

What exactly is a spa? An 1838 review of German spas attempted to define the term: "a mineral source at which people assemble, to drink as well as to bathe in the waters, and at which gas-baths and mud-baths are also administered." The central focus of the spas was the naturally occurring flow of deep water, purified and, most often, mineralized enough to contain the power to heal.

So, what's so special about naturally occurring seltzer? For much of human history water was dirty and often deadly. So how did seltzer get knocked out of this polluted hydrologic system to enter, instead, an alternative cycle, one that left it both purified and infused with the perceived power to save lives?

Recall that about 98 percent of water from the sky entered rivers and streams, but most of those accessible sources turned deadly (by quite literally passing through the bowels of civilization).[38] The remaining 2 percent, however, joined the groundwater but didn't remain there for long, connecting with bodies of water that brought it right back to the surface.

A tiny percentage of water, however, took a different route, avoiding rivers and streams altogether, sinking past shallow surface water to go down, deep down, into vast aquifers. Flowing as little as one foot per year, this slow seep purified the water of any organic matter, sediment, or microorganisms that it might be carrying. Eventually, some of this water was tapped for wells or emerged through natural springs, offering nature-filtered water. As a result, naturally occurring spring waters could be healthier than regular surface water.

However, something else happened as well. The cleansing filtration was often just the first step along the route to a spa's healing water. If this water passed through rocks, as was often the case, trace amounts of the rocks dissolved, and in the right proportions, its minerals changed the water from something not just less dangerous to something actually health promoting, offering medicinal properties and crafting taste sensations unique to that very source. And finally, if this mineral water happened to combine with water saturated with carbon dioxide produced in deep volcanic aquifers, the result was health-providing, carbonated, free-of-human-pollutants water. And this kind of water attracted and supported an entire industry.

A spa was what emerged when a natural spring met a capitalist. "The homes of these waters have become from time to time immensely popular," reported the *National Bottlers' Gazette* in 1883, "for, as doctors were in the habit of sending their patients to 'drink the waters' as the waters could not be brought to the patients, each town became in turn the centre of a little world of invalids."

Invalids, however, were not created equal. Chapelle noted that while "visiting springs to take advantage of the healthy, clean water became part of the established medical practice, it also became fashionable." And it was fashionable precisely because the associated costs and efforts marked it an activity for the elite, as all but the richest and most affluent members of society were excluded. "Being 'seen' at the springs was a statement of economic and social status," Chapelle wrote. "So it is no mystery that the fashion of 'taking the waters' came to be associated with wealth and sophistication."

One of the most famous spas in Europe, Niederselters, Germany, supported visitors to their healing waters for centuries; it was known as much for its welcoming spas and hotels as for its clay jugs that transported its sparkling, healing waters around the world.

A TOWN CALLED SELTZER

The Bay of Gdańsk, in the Baltic Sea, has been in active use since the Middle Ages and took its name from the Polish port city of the same name. Over the centuries, ships had come and ships had gone, but some just disappeared, down into the dark waters below.

For over fifty years, the underwater archeology department of the National Maritime Museum in Gdańsk sent marine archaeologists down to investigate shipwrecks, some dating back as far as the late fourteenth century. Their mission: to document and protect the cultural and technological maritime heritage of the region.

On June 27, 2014, the museum's website announced that it had just made an unusual discovery. "Starting today," it proclaimed with great enthusiasm, "the National Maritime Museum in Gdańsk has become a part of the legend of the finest mineral water from Selters."[39]

Its marine archaeologists had been exploring an unidentified vessel designated with the technical name F-53-31. The explorers, however, gave it the more colorful name Głazik, from the Polish word for the ship's main cargo: stones.

Clad head to toe in black diving suits, with only their hands exposed, twin tanks of oxygen strapped to each of their backs, the scientists swam down forty feet in Gdańsk Bay. They spread out long yellow rulers to take measurements and sketched out the wreck and its dimensions. At the same time, they took more than seven thousand photos that would be stitched together to create a digital 3D model of the wreck. "It's absolutely pioneering work," said Tomasz Bednarz, one of the archaeologists who worked on the wreck, "a revolution in underwater archaeological documentation."

Back aboard their research vessel, the brown wooden deck covered in ropes, tubes, and containers, the scientists hauled up their finds in mesh bags. There were ceramic pieces, a small bowl, and even a few pieces of dinnerware. But the most valuable treasure was a simple, brown clay bottle, cork still in place. Thirty centimeters tall, the container was believed to be one of the world's oldest bottles of seltzer water.

The bottle was easy to identify due to the maker's seal pressed into the top proudly proclaiming its spring of origin, Selters (short for Niederselters), the small German town from which modern seltzer water takes its name. The bottle was believed to have been manufactured between 1806 and 1830 due to the initials printed above the town's name, *H* and *N*, topped by a crown. The initials stand for "Herzogthum Nassau," which means the Duchy of Nassau, an old section of western Germany where, for hundreds of years, the town of Selters was a popular spa. Those who could travel were welcomed to Selters to take in its healing waters. Those who could not travel would seek out Selters water in their local pharmacy or market, bottled in clay jugs, like the one brought up from Gdańsk Bay, with a short neck designed to maintain carbonation during its world travels.

When the first images of the clay bottle landed in the English-language press, online readers had a field day. One reader on Gizmodo wrote, "Now they are looking for a 200-year-old stain to see if [the seltzer] can really get it out," while another wondered, "I can't even imagine what this would go for on the clown market."[40]

"We are very pleased to have gained such a valuable piece for the museum's collection."

Niederselters, 1870

"We have not opened the bottle," Bednarz reported to the press. It could be the original water from Selters. Or it just as easily could have been refilled with something else, like wine. Whatever the lab tests reveal, one thing is certain: This seltzer bottle, once a common trade item, just one bottle among millions, was now a prized cultural treasure with a grand new home. "We are very pleased to have gained such a valuable piece for the museum's collection," Bednarz announced.[41]

For centuries, the water beneath Niederselters were famous throughout Europe, its purpose as clear as the town's name, a derivation of *seltrisa*, meaning "salty water." Travelers often wrote of the waters. For example, William Saunder, a physician, described it in 1805 as "perfectly clear and pellucid, and sparkles much when poured into a glass." And as to the taste, "It is somewhat pungent, but much less so than might be supposed from its mere appearance, and has a gently saline and decidedly alkaline taste." More important than how it looked and tasted was, ultimately, how it made you feel. "The effects of this water, when drank in moderate doses, are to raise the spirits" and offer "an exhilarating effect." Because the water becomes "strongly fetid in a very short time when exposed to the air," it "requires therefore to be kept closely corked, and the mouth of the bottles covered with a cement, to prevent the escape of the carbonic acid, for as long as this antiseptic acid remains, the water continues perfectly sweet."

The entire town found employment through the spring, a five-square-foot hole in the ground positioned under a large circular shed with a slated roof. The German *Mineralwasserversand*, or "spring water packaging operation," was built around the hole, eight acres surrounded by a high stone wall supporting what was an orderly yet time-consuming process.[42]

The objective of the *Mineralwasserversand* was to bottle the water to survive transportation and maintain carbonation through tight sealing—no small feat in a time before scientific designs, mass production, or even mass-produced glass bottles. As carbonation, or carbonic acid, is only maintained under high pressure, the slightest crack in storage containers destroyed the batch. Local potters handcrafted the earthenware *Krüges*, or "jugs," each designed to hold about three pints. But not all *Krüges* were created equal. To test their ability to preserve carbonation, new jugs were filled with water toward the close of business then left overnight. If by morning the water remained at the original level, the jug would survive. Otherwise, each morning, an officer called a Brüchlingszähler (literally, "broken jug counter"), brandishing a thin, long-handled little hammer, wandered the orderly rows, swiping away and smashing all jugs displaying diminished content, a sure sign of cracks or porousness.

Then, teams of women in full-length dresses and head wraps cleaned each surviving *Krug* in a vat of water. (The shards from the broken jugs, meanwhile, were used to pave the streets, which meant pedestrians literally traversed the town across the remains of failed seltzer bottles.) Men with sleeves rolled to the elbows worked at filling machines, empty jugs resting at the end of spokes splayed out from a small center wheel. The men would inject the water into the jugs, then cork them tightly to hold back the carbonation bursting to escape. Other men made the seals airtight by applying tar, after which they packaged the sealed *Krüges* in crates. Assuming they could avoid the bands of roaming robbers stalking common trade routes, the crates eventually arrived via horse and wagon at ports on the Lahn and Rhine Rivers.

Other residents of Selters were engaged in serving those fortunate enough to be able to afford a "water

The Niederselters crest

cure," catering to clients in the pubs, restaurants, and small hotels throughout town.

Niederselters wore its pride on its sleeve, its crest a red shield framing an angled, yellow water jug, its contents pouring out with generosity. In fact, a traveler, Sir Francis Bond Head, suggested that, more than anything, life in town was defined less by the water than the bottles that contained them. From three in the morning until seven at night, townspeople toiled away bottling the waters;

"The townspeople toiled away bottling the waters."

at the close of business an army of local children lined up to claim a portion for their homes. "The children really looked as if they were made of bottles," he wrote. "Some wore a pyramid of them in baskets on their heads. Some were laden with them hanging over their shoulders before and behind. Some carried them strapped round their middle. All had their hands full." Even the youngest had a role to play. "Little urchins that could scarcely walk were advancing, each hugging in its arms one single bottle."

Townspeople were delineated by their relationship to the bottles. An infant was defined as one not yet able to carry a jug. Puberty and manhood were expressed by the ability to carry an increasingly heavy load. Old age arrived with the inability to carry bottles anymore. "Life, they say, is a sound bottle, and death a cracked one," wrote the traveler. "No writer can possibly do justice to that place unless every line of his description contains, at least once, the word *bottle*."

At first Selters exported its waters within Germany and later, after frequent reports of its curative powers, to locations around Europe and the globe.

As it traveled far and wide, from India to the West Indies, the waters occasionally took on modified names, such as *seltz suyu* in Turkey, *selterskaja* in Russia, and *eau de seltz* in France.

Within the young United States of America, it was known simply as *seltzer*.

AMERICA GETS A SPA

By the turn of the nineteenth century, Americans wanted in on the spa action.

Fort Saratoga was built by the British in 1691 on the Hudson River, with a settlement soon following. In 1767, an injured British soldier was taken by Native American friends about ten miles west of the village to a natural spring that was believed to provide healing assistance. Within nine years a permanent settlement would form around that spring and other springs around it, aptly named, in collective, Saratoga Springs.

Saratoga Springs lay atop a geological fault line and a solid layer of shale, beneath which deep limestone beds produced naturally carbonated, filtered, and mineralized waters. The town's fame expanded when a noted doctor, Simon Baruch, who had traveled to European spas, began advocating for Saratoga Springs to convert from a local attraction to the first great American spa. With names like Big Red Spring and High Rock Spring, the nearly two dozen springs around Saratoga became famous, in part for how distinct one spring was from another—some waters were clear, some salty, some tasted of the different minerals infused in their waters. All were carbonated. Within a short time many hotels were built, like the United States Hotel, including the one called the largest in the word, the Grand Union Hotel, with four hundred rooms, a banqueting room accommodating twelve hundred guests, and a sixteen-hundred-seat opera house. Each hotel provided its own version of therapeutic activities (including gambling).

While wealth was required to attend the spa, doing so was still far from easy. As Chapelle reported, "Traveling to springs was an expensive, exhausting, and time-consuming endeavor." Milo Linus North, a physician who spent two years in Saratoga Springs, argued in his 1840 study "The Invalid of Saratoga" that "the healthy, the fashionable, and the pleasure-seeking cannot appreciate, at all, the sacrifices and painful efforts that are often made by those whom they meet at the springs."

> To the Invalid, whom infirmities have depressed, whom pains have harassed, and whose hopes of regaining health have hitherto proved elusive, the enquiry "Shall I Visit Saratoga?" is one of no ordinary moment. Home must

be abandoned—toil and exposure encountered—the
supervision of domestic concerns and of business sus-
pended—expense incurred—strange faces and scenes
met—new lodgings, new accommodations, new reciprocities
established; and, often, what is most painful of all, a beloved
and trusted family physician exchanged for a stranger.[43]

In spite of these "sacrifices," North felt that the alternative
was clearly worse. "Yet what is toil, what estrangement from
home, what a few days of pain or trouble among strangers, what
the loss of money, what a few weeks of pilgrimage even, if death
can be averted, if pains can be chased away, strength, appetite
and spirits restored, and all the delightful sensations of health
revisit the sufferer?"[44]

North was, however, concerned about how often the "valetudinarian," the diseased wanderer, misused the waters, returning home
"with increased infirmities and cutting disappointment." It pained
him greatly to see "these excellent medicines which flow from the
hand of nature . . . so misapplied as to become undeniable evil."[45]
North was one of many physicians who authored spa guides, which
greatly expanded the mythology of healing waters. He directed his
readers in the proper techniques for both "internal uses," that is to
say, drinking the waters, and "external use," that is, bathing in it.

As to internal uses, he helped spa visitors answer such questions
as: How shall I take the waters? Which springs? In what quantities and at what hours? He offered a range of advice on external
uses as well: a bath of about ninety degrees, for example, can be
"pleasant and soothing, like a pleasant ride or the society of a long
absent friend." But when should a cold bath be used in place of hot?
"Wherever the lancet is called for," he wrote, "there also will the
cold and shower bath be suitable; and where the lancet would be
injurious, there should the hot bath be used."[46]

During her return trip from Saratoga aboard the steamboat *Erie* on August 26, 1839, "valetudinarian" R.G.W. wrote a letter to a local paper. After three weeks at the spa, she reported, "I can now walk two or three miles without much fatigue." Referencing a popular medicine of the time, the writer continued, "Many seem to think that these waters are the 'Matchless Sanative' for almost every disease that affects the human race. Their medicinal properties are indeed wonderful, and many of the cures which they effect border nearly on the miraculous."[47]

While ostensibly a cough medicine, the Matchless Sanative promised to cure everything under the sun. So, too, did Saratoga Springs.

Yet the Matchless Sanative, it would later be revealed, was pure water and nothing more. Sold in small vials at an exorbitant price, it made suckers of the nation. According to one report, "many a poor widow was drained of her last farthing to obtain this worthless stuff."[48] Were the spas and the carbonated waters they bottled and sold another hoax perpetrated on an ignorant and desperate population seeking effective medical treatment? To find an answer, we must first look at the claims.

MATERIA MEDICA

Some of seltzer's health claims were indistinguishable from marketing. According to the first seltzer bottler in England, Schweppes, seltzer could reduce fever, ease "biliousness" (indigestion), and address nervous afflictions and "the debilitating consequences of hard living." Perrier, whose spring water originated in Les Bouillens springs in southern France and was first bottled in 1898, claimed that "drinking Perrier in the morning . . . awakens your senses and jump-starts your day." Poland Spring is a bit more specific. First bottled in Maine in 1844, it was originally sold as a cure for kidney ailments. Other claims associated miraculous occurrences with

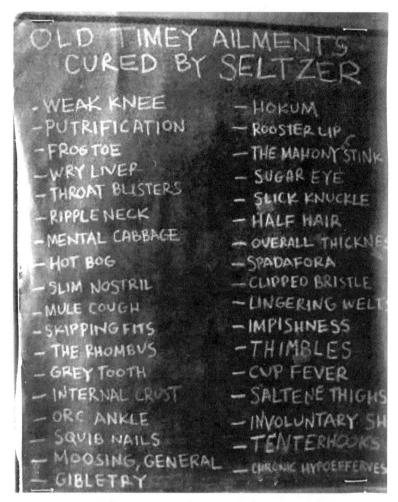

**A creative interpretation of seltzer's mysterious properties
(by students at Carnegie Mellon University, circa 2015)**

this or that spring. The specific infirmity or injury being healed may have been lost in the telling, but the essential message got through: these waters heal.

Doctors agreed. For example, Saratoga Springs was reviewed in 1806 by a Dr. Stoddard, who said its waters provided "tone and strength to the stomach, and improves the condition of the blood by increasing the number of red blood corpuscles."[49] But Stoddard was just getting started. The springs also aided in the fight against liver and kidney difficulties, dyspepsia (indigestion), chronic constipation, gout, and rheumatism. Reports like these could go on for pages, as many did in these books of old.

In 1800, Dr. William Saunders, in *A Treatise on the Chemical History and Medical Powers of Some of the Most Celebrated Mineral Waters*, offered an entire section on "Seltzer water."[50] He contended that "few mineral waters have acquired a higher reputation than that of Seltzer" due to "the real medical virtues which it possesses" and "the variety of disorders to which it is applicable." Saunders took the reader on a veritable tour of the human body, inside and out.

First the lungs: "It is particularly serviceable in relieving some of the symptoms that indicate a morbid affection of the lungs."

Next the skin: "This water often brings considerable relief . . . in those exanthematous eruptions of the skin."

The alimentary canal follows: "Foulness of stomach, bilious vomiting, acidity and heartburn, spasmodic pains in any part of the alimentary canal, and bloody or highly offensive stools, are the symptoms for which this medicine brings the greatest relief."

But that's not all. Those suffering from venereal diseases like gonorrhea and even those voicing "hypochondriac complaints and their attendant symptoms" could find relief through drinking "the Seltzer waters freely for a month or more."

Medical properties aside, seltzer had one advantage over all others: taste. "The circumstance of agreeable flavor is no small recommendation with patients," Saunders wrote, "who . . . have conceived an utter aversion to any of the numerous class of tonics and stimulants that stand on the list of the Materia Medica," the Latin term for "medicines."

Apparently, there was little seltzer was not called upon to address. Which was a problem. In 1817, former President Thomas

Jefferson expressed concern in a letter that "the medical effects of the different springs are now so little known that they are used at random." As a result of being unable to distinguish the health properties of one spring from another, he continued, "patients" act as if they "should take something of everything in his Apothecary's shop, by way of making sure of what will hit his case." In other words, the waters became a cure-all for the simple fact that the infirm lacked the information required to use it in a more discerning, and efficacious, manner.

To contemporary ears, an apothecary might seem preferable to a trip to a spa. However, according to Chapelle, historians debated whether the infirm were better off avoiding doctors altogether. "Fear of doctors was common and often justified," he wrote. "For this reason, many people opted to medicate themselves." Healing waters were just one of multiple options peddled for consumption.

While the various incarnations of natural seltzer had no labels indicating which types helped which illnesses, today we can see that many historic sources cited examples that detailed the medicinal properties of seltzer in a means that would satisfy a discerning modern doctor. Someone suffering from anemia could find comfort in a pool with a high concentration of iron. Those requiring a laxative could drink waters with sulfate and magnesium. Goiters could be cured with iodine-laced water. Sour stomach could be addressed through a good dose of water infused with bicarbonate of soda, the very substance from which "soda water" got its name.

Whether or not patients found relief at the spas, they benefited just from drinking clean water, a message that has filtered down to us today and motivates so many to drink bottled water, carbonated or otherwise.

"It is no wonder that spring waters were considered to be healing," wrote Chapelle. Sure, he admitted, on some occasions trace minerals might offer a cure or alleviate symptoms. But the bottom line was that they were clean. "Upon arriving at a spring and ingesting for a day or two water that was free of fecal bacteria, the effects on the digestive tract would be striking. The more-or-less chronic digestive upset, the loose bowels, the unpleasant gas would disappear." The pains of civilization were alleviated, to be replaced with a deep and lasting appreciation for the waters that returned them to health, and an association between the two, everlasting.

Today, the association grows even deeper. Seltzer aficionados believe seltzer is not only good for the body. It's good for the planet.

THE SELTZER WARS: CAGE BATTLES, PART 2

"You know that awkward moment when you try to stop something but instead wind up drawing more attention to it?" asked Rick Aristotle Munarriz, a blogger for the investment site Motley Fool. "Coca-Cola's doing exactly that with SodaStream's *Cage* exhibit." The June 2012 post was titled "This Week's 5 Dumbest Stock Moves," and Coke's held the top spot. Usually the corporation was so smart, he argued, but the more Coke responded, the more attention it gave to SodaStream's environmentalist message. "It's understandable why Coke wouldn't want to see its crushed cans and bottles displayed that way," sympathized Munarriz, "but there's no way SodaStream isn't going to milk this new publicity."

And milk it they did, sounding increasingly defiant with every interview. "No one's going to shut us up with a lawyer's letter," Daniel Birnbaum, chief executive officer of SodaStream, told Bloomberg News. "Not in South Africa or anywhere." When speaking to *Forbes*, Birnbaum clicked the rhetoric up a notch. "We find it incredulous that Coke is now re-claiming ownership of the billions of bottles and cans that litter the planet with their trademarks,"

Birnbaum claimed. "In that case, they should be sued in the World Court for all of the damage their garbage is causing."

Perhaps Coke had learned its lesson that the only way to win this game was to sit it out. It did not respond to Birnbaum's aggressive criticism, which threatened to sound shrill in the absence of new harassment from Coke. Coke did not respond to David Birnbaum's aggressive criticism, nor did it need to. It was busy in Brazil at the United Nations Conference on Sustainable Development (known as Rio+20), attended by more than forty-five thousand participants and 188 diplomatic delegations. There it joined with PepsiCo to set targets on factory water efficiency and pledged $3.5 million toward sustainability efforts in Africa.

Then, will little fanfare, SodaStream's South African *Cage* was dismantled and removed from Johannesburg's international airport. "Our *Cage* eco-exhibit was scheduled to be taken down on 8 July," confirmed SodaStream's general manager in South Africa at the time, Francois Dippenaar, "and that is what we did last night." But SodaStream wasn't done: they reported plans for at least thirty new sites in thirty countries. "The threat is real," Dippenaar concluded, "and we will continue telling the story that plastic is destroying our planet."

CHANGE IN US BEVERAGE CONSUMPTION, 2009–2014

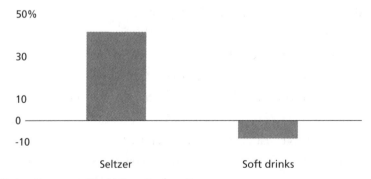

Data: Beverage Marketing Corporation.

The story of seltzer involved more than just plastic, however. It reflected themes that went back to humanity's earliest associations with liquid sustenance. And, at the same time, SodaStream took that story to a new level, moving beyond personal health to the health of the planet. Seltzer was seen as good for both your mother and Mother Earth. While SodaStream focused its energy on how reusable home carbonators reduced plastic pollution, new seltzer drinkers from around the nation were finding additional motivation to drink seltzer.

Take the reasons shared by Brooklyn filmmaker and festival producer David Holbrooke, the client of Brooklyn seltzer man Eli Miller. "We try to be on the fringe of consumer culture in the way that we shop," he explained. "The disposable culture that we have—Eli is certainly not a part of that." David continued without the least hint of sanctimony, "It's like everything else: farmers' market tomatoes, fresh seltzer. You know where it's coming from. It makes a lot more sense." With home-delivered seltzer, David combined an ecological drive to reduce waste, an anti-consumerist desire to lower his carbon footprint, and support for local food to reduce the distance from food production to his table, all while helping a small business. While each reason might be distinct, together they painted the same picture: drinking seltzer was a lifestyle choice, a way to live your values through consumer decisions.

That made perfect sense to Kenny Gomberg, whose seltzer works kept Eli in seltzer. He explained why bottled seltzer was such a green product: "There's no waste involved. The vessel itself is reusable and recyclable." The only thing not green about seltzer was that it was still delivered by car or truck. "The carbon footprint is in the delivery," Kenny said, before adding tongue-in-cheek, "until we can pump it directly into the homes."

Meanwhile, on the West Coast, Kathryn Renz of the Seltzer Sisters also saw a lot of the new growth coming from the organic food movement. Most Bay Area residents had no idea what it was like growing up in Brooklyn or other seltzer spots and felt no palpable absence of seltzer. But they knew organic food. "There's a company based out of Santa Cruz," Kathryn said, by way of example, "and they go around the country and put on events out in the farm." They set up kitchens and pull together whatever is in season, cooking dinner for up to one hundred people. "Talk about your farm movement!" While diners enjoy the fresh, local, organic, seasonal cuisine, their eating is enhanced with Kathryn's seltzer.

"And so that's where we pick up a lot of customers," she explained. "The organic farming movement really has brought us a whole new chapter of 'foodies,' as they say, you know, people that . . . " She paused to consider how to describe them and what drove them to both organic food and seltzer. "Everything is so instant now. But everyone wants something that's traditional in some sense, and this kind of fills the need."

The reasons change over time—from healing a goiter to healing the planet—but one thing remains constant: seltzer promises to better our lives.

As the New York City Department of Health and Mental Hygiene warned: "Don't drink yourself fat."

No, don't do that. Instead, drink yourself seltzer.

6

HOW SELTZER GOT TASTY

In which seltzer transitions from prescribed
medicine to an effervescent treat.

THE RISE OF SODA FOUNTAINS

When Elias Durand left war-torn Europe, he was one of many
prominent pharmacists to set his sights on Philadelphia. At the age
of nineteen he had joined the medical corps of Napoleon's army.
After many battles, he resigned his commission in order to become
an apothecary, but after two years of work and Napoleon's downfall, he was suspected of having "Napoleonic tendencies," which
curtailed his freedoms and led him to seek a home more appreciative of his expertise. After spending some time in Boston he moved
to Philadelphia, the largest US city at the time and its scientific
center. It was the perfect place for him to establish his drugstore
and employ many of the most eminent physicians of the day.

But this is not another story of seltzer's association with health.
Rather, this is about what happened when all that began to change.

In 1825, Durand opened his apothecary on the corner of Sixth and Chestnut. But his was unlike other drugstores of the time. At great expense, Durand designed his shop with French glassware, porcelain jars, mahogany drawers, and marble counters. He also added a new innovation: a machine for making carbonated water. Before long, his pharmacy had become a gathering point for local scientists, specifically botanists, specifically at his soda fountain.[51]

And thus the drugstore soda fountain was born, although it took some time for Durand to be recognized as the father of the American soda fountain. Before long, no pharmacy could be without a marble counter designed for customers to socialize and the seltzer to bring them together. Now the affluent and nonaffluent alike could buy seltzer waters for medicinal purposes without the need to travel to a spa. Seltzer no longer required the infirm to leave business, family, and friends behind. The democratization of seltzer had begun.

Seltzer's transition from medicine to refreshment is generally recognized as an American innovation, resulting from pharmacists responding to the needs of their customers. Gradually, imperceptibly, pharmacists removed harsh-tasting medicinal elements, like bicarbonate of soda for indigestion, and added flavors like lemon and strawberry. The measure of good seltzer shifted from its therapeutic power to its taste, from long-term health to short-term pleasure.

And thus we come to the second reason people drink seltzer: for refreshment.

In fact, new terms came into use that avoided seltzer's medicinal connotations. For example, after Prohibition was repealed at the end of 1933 and people went to elegant supper clubs or private clubs, they often found "seltzer" had been replaced with the new term "club soda," even though there was little or no difference between the two.

A seltzer bottle from a deli doesn't require a prescription. It's certainly not covered by health insurance. When most people today think of a place to drink seltzer, they might picture a bar or a restaurant. For an older generation, however, something else might come to mind: the soda fountain at their local candy shop or pharmacy, and its associations with fabulous drinks mixed on the spot, like the egg cream.

FOR 2¢ PLAIN

Seltzer's transition from medicinal aid to refreshing drink supported a new type of establishment, one quite distinct from the pharmacies of old: the corner candy shop with its popular soda fountain. The intense competition among these new establishments fueled culinary creativity for decades.

Take for example the Lower East Side of New York City, where at the turn of the century there were no fewer than seventy-three soda fountains located within its one-third-square-mile area. This intense concentration of seltzer sites would be memorialized a half century later in a book titled *For 2¢ Plain*, penned by Harry Golden, recounting tales from his youth. It shot to the top of the *New York Times* Best Sellers list when it appeared in 1958 and opened with the following anecdote:

> I remembered in this story how the entire East Side Civilization was addicted to seltzer and of the great variety of sweet drinks mixed with seltzer. You bought a drink from a man behind a marble counter at any of the hundreds of soda-water stands scattered through the sections. A small glass cost a penny—"Give me a small plain." No syrup. Syrup cost another penny. For a large glass you said, "Give me for two cents plain." As the man filled the glass,

you said casually, still holding tightly to your two pennies, "Put a little on the top." You wanted syrup, of course, but you didn't want to pay the third penny.

A 1905 soda fountain manual described the distinctive features of the best soda fountains:

> . . . the matchless beauty, the perfect sanitation, the extreme durability, the ice-saving qualities, the faultless mechanical construction, the tasteful blending of exquisitely shaded variegated onyx, the clean and sanitary white porcelain syrup containers and hard rubber syrup cocks, the magnificent large beveled French plate mirrors, the rich and massive quartered oak and mahogany woodwork, the rare statuettes, the artistically decorative electroliers and candelabra.[52]

The Palace Soda Fountain, circa 1925, Tampa, Florida

How could patrons not come to love the soda fountain?

This same 1905 manual offered a wide range of advice to budding soda jerks, the people who operated the soda fountain: "Do not get confused." "Do not shake a beverage containing carbonated water." "Be careful that drinks served do not contain specks; these are often mistaken for insects." Other advice made the guide feel like a book of manners: "When you are tired don't lean on the counter." "Always offer a carnation to the ladies." "Don't stand and watch a customer drink."[53]

Lorri Trachtman, a retired public-school administrator, enthusiastically recalled the counter owned by her aunt and uncle at 921 Holmes Street in the Bronx.[54] Until she was sixteen she worked there as a soda jerk. She smiled when talking about the ladies she served, sitting in chairs outside the front door, gossiping away in their European and Yiddish accents. "The old ladies at the time would order plain seltzer." These were first-generation immigrants struggling to get their children educated and do better for themselves. "It was a very big treat," Lorri explained. Paying two cents was sometimes very hard for them. "You have to remember, these were the times when someone was only earning thirty or forty dollars a week, so spending two cents on seltzer was sometimes seen as taking it away from their children."

According to David Fox, CEO of the family business that produced the line of U-Bet syrups used by generations of soda jerks, people who grew up in the Bronx, Brooklyn, or Queens might have had as many as three different candy stores on their block, five in a two-block area, each with its own distinct clientele.[55] And David certainly had his favorite store. "I remember, as a kid, working in a candy store. I was all of thirteen years old and I learned how to make sodas and how to pump syrup."

The candy store was instrumental in giving seltzer new meaning. "Seltzer will always be by itself," David asserted, but as a result of soda shops and candy stores, syrup became intimately connected with seltzer. Yes, people had been drinking seltzer at pharmacies for years, but these new soda fountains offered endless opportunities for sweet sensations. The syrups originally came in bottles with metal caps. David explained that the caps were used to measure the syrup: the soda jerk took off the cap, poured the syrup to a specified level in the cap before pouring it into the customer's drink, then charged a penny more for mixing the drink.

As syrup companies got in on the action, the list of flavor combinations seemed endless. "Once that happened," David insisted, "there was an evolution."

Lorri Trachtman listed the menu in her relatives' shop. "We had lemon and lime. We had vanilla—it was like cream soda, but we called it vanilla—strawberry, raspberry, cherry. You could have whatever you wanted."

Elaborate displays evolved for advertising and pumping out the syrup, which turned the consumption of these drinks from a taste to an experience. Some fancy pumps, sold now as antiques for tens of thousands of dollars, cost nothing to the candy store owners at the time. "The syrup manufacturers would supply many of these outlets," David recalled, "specifically these candy stores." But not just the syrup pumps; they would supply neon signs, fudge warmers, scoops for the ice cream, dishes, malted machines—the list went on and on. "The ice cream guy didn't supply anything. They made the syrup guy supply it. And they were so competitive because they wanted the business."

This fierce competition led to the most interesting concoctions—even the slightest advantage could determine the survival of a soda jerk in the most popular shops. Drinks came and went at a dizzying pace. Recipes called for a variety of syrups, milk and eggs, and crushed fruit. The Fuzzy Flip would replace the Red Banana, which was pushed aside by the Kola Phosphate.

PHROSO.
Ready-made Syr. Ginger.....oz. 1
"Liquid Fruit" Lemon........oz. 1
Jamaica Rum ....dash, 1
Angostura Bitters ....dash, 1
Egg 1
Acid Phosphate to suit.
Shaved Ice.
  Shake well together, strain, add
fine stream and serve with nutmeg
and straws.

CLARET FLIP.
Ready-made "Liquid Fruit"
  Claret ....oz. 2
Ready-made "Liquid Fruit"
  Lemon ....oz. ½
Egg 1
Shaved Ice ....oz. 2
  · Shake well, and strain into 12-
oz. tumbler; fill with the coarse
and fine stream of carbonated wa-
ter and cover top with ½ inch
claret wine.

MANHATTAN FLIP.
Ready-made "Liquid Fruit"
  Lemon Syrup ....oz. 2
Jamaica Rum ....dashes, 3
Egg 1
Ice Cream ....teaspoonful, 1
Sweet Cream ....oz. 2
  Ice, shake and add soda. Strain
into bell shaped glass.

CHOCOLATE CREAM.
Chocolate Syrup ....oz. 2
Cream ....oz. 1
Egg 1
  Shake well, as directed for all
egg drinks, and fill glass with car-
bonated water, using fine stream.
Serve in 12-oz. glass with whipped
or ice cream, and spoon.

CHAMPAGNE FLIP.
Ready-made Catawba Syr..oz. 1
Ready-made "Liquid Fruit"
  Orange ....oz. ½
Egg 1
Sweet Cream ....oz. 2
Angostura Bitters .....dashes, 2
  Shake, ice and add soda. Strain
into a glass.

PINK PUNCH.
Yolk of Egg................. 1
Ready-made "Liquid Fruit"
  Raspberry ....oz. 2
N. E. Rum..................oz. ⅓
Shaved Ice ....oz. 2
Milk enough to fill 12-oz. glass.
  Shake well, strain and fill glass
with fine stream of carbonated
water.

KOLA MINT FIZZ.
  Into a 12-oz. tumbler draw 1 oz.
of Kola Mint Syrup. Add a dash
of sweet cream, 1 egg; half fill
with cracked ice. Shake all together, pour off into a tumbler
and fill with carbonated water.

CHERRY PUNCH.
Ready-made "Liquid Fruit"
  Cherry ....oz. 2
Ready-made "Liquid Fruit"
  Lemon ....oz. ⅓
Egg 1
Shaved Ice ....oz. 2
Milk enough to fill 12-oz. glass.
  Shake well, fill glass with
fine stream of carbonated water,
and grate over top a small amount
of nutmeg.

WHITE PLUME.
Ready-made "Liquid Fruit"
  Catawba ....oz. 1
Shaved Ice ....oz. 2
White of one Egg.
Milk enough to fill glass.
  Shake well, strain into 12-oz.
glass, and serve with whipped
cream and a spoon.

NAVEL FLIP.
Ready-made "Liquid Fruit"
  Orange ....oz. 1½
Ready-made "Liquid Fruit"
  Pineapple ....oz. ½
Egg 1
Ice Cream ....spoonful, 1
Shaved or Cracked Ice.....oz. 2
  Stir well together, strain into
12-oz. tumbler, nearly fill the lat-
ter with coarse stream of carbon-
ated water, and complete with
fine stream.

HOT EGG CHOCOLATE.
Ready-made Chocolate Syrup
  oz. 1
Egg 1
Cream ....oz. ½
Hot Water enough to fill 8-oz.
  mug.

HOT EGG LEMONADE.
Ready-made "Liquid Fruit"
  Lemon ....oz. 1
Egg 1
Fruit Acid ....dashes, 2
Hot Water enough to fill 8-oz.
  mug.

EGG AND MILK.
  To 1 egg add 1 ounce Ready-
made "Liquid Fruit" Catawba, 2
teaspoonfuls of ice. Milk to fill
glass. Shake and strain.

51

One popular type of drink was known as the egg phosphate, a mixture of raw egg, seltzer, phosphate, and a syrup, like orange or chocolate. An 1896 account of the theatrics involved appears in a recent book, *Sundae Best: A History of Soda Fountains*, by Anne Cooper Funderburg:

> The dispenser began by breaking the egg with a flourish, pouring all the ingredients into a silver-plated cocktail shaker, covering the shaker with a glass tumbler, and thoroughly shaking the mixture. When he judged that it had been adequately mixed, he removed the tumbler, held the shaker with his right hand at arm's length above his shoulder, and poured the beverage into a tumbler, which he held several feet away in his left hand. An alternative method was to pour the liquid back and forth, several times, holding the shaker and the glass farther apart each time. . . . Then, for the finishing touch, he sprinkled grated nutmeg on top, with a showy flourish.[56]

Soda jerks and their marble fountains are largely a thing of the past. Sometimes an old-fashioned soda fountain can still be found in a small town or on a city block. A few recipes, however, live on around the country at the average diner or ice cream shop, where a lucky customer might still find a lime rickey, a cream soda, or a black and white.

One particular marriage of syrup and seltzer, however, has managed to survive the passing of a thousand Fuzzy Flips and Kola Phosphates. By outlasting them all, it's in a class of its own. That drink, of course, is the egg cream, and the current debate over its legacy illuminates some of the fascinating sights that mark the route to Seltzertopia.

THE EGG CREAM MAFIA

Little Stanley Auster was terrified when the mobster insisted he follow him to the back of the store. "Oh, my God," he thought. "I'm dead." It just wasn't fair. He wasn't even supposed to be managing his grandfather's candy store at the time, at least not on his own. And he was only thirteen. But what he realized next gave him courage: "I don't think anybody has ever been shot by someone who had an egg cream in his hand."[57]

Like most of his friends on the Jewish Lower East Side, Stanley had become a bar mitzvah earlier in the year. But he felt he truly came of age a few months later, when a family crisis forced him to learn his grandfather's recipe for the egg cream. Not "an" egg cream, but "the" egg cream, as Stanley and others would later argue; the Auster egg cream is the original, its recipe still a family secret, locked in a vault and never shared outside the family, even to this day.

Stanley's grandfather, Louis Auster, had arrived in the United States, in New York City, in 1890. The diminutive man was a dapper dresser: suit, white dress shirt, a diamond stickpin in his tie, and a suit. He was described as a "tough little bastard" who ran numbers and possibly sold illegal liquors. With no particular trade or profession to speak of, he eventually opened his first candy store on Stanton and Cannon, then continued to open one for each of his six sons, each more successful than the last. The largest, in the heart of the Yiddish theater district, was at Second Avenue and Seventh Street. To meet theatergoer demands, the candy store featured a 125-seat ice cream parlor in the back. Like other candy stores of the era, it sold cigarettes and cigars, but 98 percent of their business was egg creams.

As Stanley recounted in Jeff Kisseloff's 1989 oral history of Manhattan, *You Must Remember This: An Oral History of Manhattan from the 1890s to World War II*, egg creams began when Louis Auster grew dissatisfied with the sodas he was selling. He

A contemporary chocolate egg cream from Farmacy, in Brooklyn, New York

began to fool around, mixing water and cocoa and sugar. "And somehow or other, eureka, he hit on something which seemed to be just perfect for him." There was never any egg and never any cream, and the original reason the drink was called "egg cream" has been lost to history. "There were milk products but not cream, although it looked and tasted creamy," Stanley admitted, "because we also made a delicious chocolate syrup, which was the base drink." They used a unique cocoa, a bittersweet chocolate, and what he described as a "certain substitute type of dairy product." It made their syrup smooth, pouring "like the water of a lake." Made daily, the syrup had a shelf life of less than half a week and produced a lot of foam when three ounces were mixed in a glass with seven ounces of seltzer. "We made the seltzer so alive that if you put down the glass, you could watch it from the side and see the bubbles bouncing up in the air like a little geyser for five or ten minutes."

Everyone wanted to know the secret of the Auster egg cream—not just customers but competitors as well, with at least one willing to spend upward of twenty-thousand dollars for the exclusive rights. The Austers sealed off the back part of the store where the syrup was made and even painted the windows brown to protect their secret. "They used to study our deliveries to figure out what ingredients we used," Stanley reported. While its contents were unknown, its impact was clear. On an average warm day, one location would report sales of six to twelve thousand egg creams.

At the start of one summer, young Stanley got the call he had been waiting for. "Stanley," his uncle Milton said, guiding him behind the brown-painted windows, "I'm gonna show you how to make the egg cream." Stanley's father had recently taken ill and would need to rest for the season. To keep the recipe in the family, it was time for Stanley to enter the elite circle of egg cream experts. "I came of age suddenly that summer," he explained. "Like my bar mitzvah: today I am a man." That afternoon he learned, and soon mastered, the family secret. "I cooked the syrup and managed the store with my mother and two hired people the whole summer. I'm still very proud of that."

Stanley offered more than just a drink. The candy store was a bustling social club composed of a motley assortment of out-of-work men, many of whom were evading (even breaking) the law, with names like Shpuggie, Swindler, and Bumblenose.[58] Drinking an egg cream "was like a reason for coming down to mix socially," recalled Stanley. "It seemed preposterous that people would travel so far for a drink, but the egg cream was tantalizing. It was like marijuana. They needed it."

While most patrons were harmless, just a bunch of kibitzers standing around chatting, the store also attracted the Jewish mafia. Before Bugsy Siegel would visit, three of his men, big like wrestlers, would drive up and check out the store like the Secret Service, then make everyone leave. Upon receiving the all clear, three more men outside would halt pedestrian traffic, opening a path for a man arriving in a second car. Surrounded by two additional men, in walked Bugsy for his egg cream. When he was ready to leave, Louis Auster would refuse to let him pay.

Stanley recalled a different mobster, more of a lone wolf than a leader, always full of smiles and warmth and fondness. But that was only for his friends, it turned out. He was psychopathic, Stanley learned, and would later be machine-gunned in the street. But years before his demise, this mobster made Stanley fear for his life. At the time, thirteen-year-old Stanley was alone in the store. The gangster came in, walking very quietly. "Hello, Stanley," he said with that same sweet smile. "Can I see you in the back for a moment?" Stanley was petrified. Two days earlier he had thrown the gangster's brother-in-law out on the street for refusing to stop harassing some female patrons.

"I give him his egg cream," Stanley recalled. "He takes it and walks to the back."

The mobster tried to confirm what he had heard, that Stanley had had a shoving match with his brother-in-law.

What could Stanley say? Lying was not an option so he tried to downplay it. "It was nothing," he insisted, "really nothing."

The mobster would have none of it. They went back and forth a few times, the mobster looking for confirmation, Stanley insisting it was nothing.

"Well, I want you to know," the mobster finally explained to the young soda jerk, "you won't have any trouble with him." The mobster had broken the brother-in-law's arm and put him in the hospital. "He'll never bother you again," he repeated. The mobster wasn't there for revenge; it was just his form of an apology, over an Auster egg cream.

A few years later, Stanley's grandfather stopped working at the store. In 1955, at ninety-seven years of age, Louis Auster passed away. "Very few people came to the funeral," Stanley would lament to Jeff Kisseloff in his oral history. By then everything had changed. "It just became an ordinary candy store after a while." And the egg cream just an ordinary drink, no longer worthy of such feverish devotion. Absent the colorful and vibrant social scene that once supported it, "just having an egg cream alone today is not the full flavor of it," Stanley complained. "Those days are long gone."[59]

The stores might be closed, the egg cream camaraderie behind him, but one thing remained for Stanley: his family's egg cream recipe. "I'm the only one alive who knows the formula," he often said with pride. "I'll probably carry it into my grave."

It would be tempting to leave it at that, to credit Louis Auster with inventing and popularizing the egg cream. But that would mean ignoring one nagging problem that undermines any such grand claim: if the Austers never shared the recipe, what have the rest of us been drinking all of these years?

Many people still mix the drink at home and in restaurants around the country. They may debate whose recipe is the most authentic. But all agree on one ingredient: Fox's U-Bet chocolate syrup.

Well, all agree except Stanley. "We didn't use U-Bet and milk and seltzer, like they do today," he once said. "I can't even drink that."

U-BET IT'S GOOD

"Psychologically," Mel Brooks explained in a February 1975 interview with *Playboy*, "it is the opposite of circumcision. It pleasurably reaffirms your Jewishness."[60] The *it* Brooks referred to was the egg cream. Promoting the release of *Young Frankenstein*, *Playboy* had given

Brooks the royal treatment, a rambling, uproarious interview covering everything from his Jewish childhood in Depression-era Brooklyn, to writing for *Your Show of Shows*, to the joy of flatulent cowboys.

When Brooks raised the topic of egg creams, the magazine asked him to explain how they are made.

"First," Brooks began, "you got to get a can of Fox's U-Bet Chocolate Syrup." Then he laid out the details:

Take a big glass and fill one fifth of it with U-Bet syrup. Then add about half a shot glass of milk. And you gotta have a seltzer spout with two speeds. One son-of-a-bitch bastard that comes out like bullets and scares you; one normal, regular-person speed that comes out nice and soft and foamy. So hit the tough bastard, the bullets of seltzer, first. Smash through the milk into the chocolate and chase the chocolate furiously all around the glass. Then, when the mixture is halfway up the glass, you turn on the gentle stream and you fill the glass with seltzer, all the time mixing with a spoon. Then taste it. But sit down first, because you might swoon with ecstasy.

When that *Playboy* promoting U-Bet came out, David Fox bought copies for everyone he knew. And then he wrote a letter to Brooks, asking if he could send him a case.

Before the month was out, David received his reply. "Money, diamonds, jewels I could refuse," Brooks wrote, "but never a couple of jars of U-Bet Chocolate. Send it to me quick. Milk and seltzer are waiting."

David Fox worked in a nondescript office at the back of the U-Bet factory in Brownsville, Brooklyn, that his family had owned for the past century, manufacturing not just chocolate syrup but a wide variety of flavors for institutions and retailers. In the winter of

2010, just like every winter for the past hundred years, Fox's had to prepare the plant to produce that spring's Passover batch of flavored syrups. The thirty-six-thousand-square-foot factory produced two thousand crates, each containing a dozen bottles, on a good day. But kashering syrup, preparing it under strict kosher guidelines, was no small task. First the ingredients had to be changed, namely the sweetener. Corn syrup went against the dietary restrictions of the

"Take a big glass and fill one fifth of it with U-Bet syrup."

holiday. Only real sugar would do, producing something a bit sweeter but maintaining the smooth, round taste that distinguishes U-Bet syrup from other brands. Real sugar, however, is expensive. "The cost factor is humongously higher," David said. "Dramatically higher. Yet we don't charge more." Why not? "We just don't think it's the right thing to do."

Next, the vessels in which the syrup was made needed to be kashered, the whole processing line from beginning to end: everything was sanitized, sterilized, and boiled. It took an entire day to prepare, a lost day of production. "We drain the boiler, starting with new steam," David said with the pride of a job done right. "Everything."

And of course, U-Bet needed a rabbi to oversee it all. And David has had a problem with his rabbi. It's not a new problem—it just wouldn't go away. The rabbi had been with the company for forty-five years. "He's not in the OU," David explains, referring to the Orthodox Union, one of the oldest Orthodox organizations in

the country and best known for its kosher certification services, "but he is extraordinarily versed." Fox's rabbi, however, is not the problem. It's everyone else, David says. It's a society whose values are far removed from the world in which U-Bet was first born.

H. Fox and Company was founded in 1900 by David Fox's grandfather, who cooked syrup in his Brooklyn tenement house. But he was more than a syrup entrepreneur. He was also a gambler. One day he traveled to Texas with an eye on an oil well investment. The well was dry. Although he failed to pick up a fortune there, he did pick up a phrase used about town: you bet it's good! David's grandfather may have left his money in Texas, but he returned with a new name for his chocolate syrup: Fox's U-Bet It's Good. The "It's Good" came off and it became simply Fox's U-Bet.

As David Fox approached his sixty-ninth birthday, he was running one of the two or three syrup companies left in the New York metropolitan region. His son, Kelly, joined the business. "The experience of saying that I am working with my son, that there is continuity. . . . It's awesome."

But it was a different time than when David first worked professionally within the company and there were three to four *dozen* competitors down the block. "You barely had television. What was a computer?" The speed of life felt slower, simpler. "Everyone wore a hat—a homburg or a fedora," David said. "No one wears a hat anymore." And a rabbi's word was all that was needed to assure consumers a product was kosher.

"Now we're used to rushing around, getting things done, getting there quickly," he explained. "I didn't live in the 1800s, and I wouldn't trade what I have, but I think there are pieces from every era that we need to look back on and ask, 'Are we going in the right direction?'"

So, when some people—not most, but some—heard that Fox's U-Bet's rabbi was not with the OU, preventing the syrup from carrying a more stringent kosher certification, they inevitably asked why U-Bet wouldn't make a change. "Because we've been working with a man who has been with us almost fifty years," David responded. His business ethics—how and why he does business—go back to the values he attributed to his youth: caring about people, building relationships, and knowing what your word meant. "You don't just write people off like throwing away a fountain pen," he explained before mocking current sensibilities: "Why should I get a refill when I can

H. Fox and Company's first fruit and syrup delivery truck, 1925

throw it away and get another one?" That's not David. That's not what he wants to pass on to his children, employees, or customers. "Relationships are not supposed to be disposable."

David loved that his product made people happy. But with egg creams, "I don't think it's only a taste sensation." It is something more, much more. "I think the concept of going in and ordering an egg cream brings back a lot of memories. It puts them back into a different time."

Every bottle of U-Bet syrup purchased is more than history made liquid. Every egg cream mixed with U-Bet supports a company that embodies a way of being in the world held over from an earlier era, maintaining a family-run business that proudly stands against the tide of history, refusing to fire its rabbi. "At the end of the day," David asserted, "when you die, all you're left with is your name, your name and what it represents."

REINVENTING THE EGG CREAM

How did something as unrefined and pedestrian as an egg cream end up on the menu of a high-end restaurant? A visitor to the fancy Eleven Madison Park in New York City (researching, it turns out, a book on seltzer) decided to find out for himself.

The maître d', dressed in a jacket and tie, ushered me into a collection of high-back chairs and benches composed of subdued brown woods marked with silver silhouettes of abstract tree leaves. The sound of well-dressed lunch patrons bounced off the high ceiling and around the marble walls and floor like an indoor pool. The low hum was pleasant, cut occasionally by the sharp clang of utensils on plates.

After honing his skills in European restaurants, executive chef Daniel Humm's career took him first to San Francisco then, in 2006, at age twenty-nine, to Eleven Madison Park. But what possessed him to consider egg creams as a midcourse palate cleanser?

"It's called an egg cream, which makes it sound heavy," Humm conceded, "but, you know, there is no cream and no eggs and it's done with the seltzer water, which is very sparkly." At dinner or lunch every patron receives an egg cream, made on a small cart wheeled to the table just for the occasion. "It is actually a really refreshing little drink you have after your main course and before your cheese or dessert." Who knew an egg cream could be so refined?

When Humm and his staff first decided to add egg creams to the dining experience, they were challenged to pick the right recipe. "People who grew up in Brooklyn believe it was invented in Brooklyn," he said, "and people who grew up in Manhattan believe it was invented in Manhattan." Ultimately, as a fine dining restaurant, they needed to be more . . . creative. That creative license ultimately led seltzer traditionalists to go ballistic. Were their concerns misplaced or on the mark?

A waiter in a blue suit and red tie arrived, pushing a beautiful cart. The key items were perfectly arranged on the top shelf, as if in a still life: two carafes, one caramel brown, the second white; a yellow olive-oil cruet; and two small glasses. Set apart from these, towering above them all, was a clear and classic seltzer siphon ready for duty. Hidden from sight, on the waiter's side, was a white cloth napkin and a long spoon.

Humm narrated as the server prepared the drinks. "Now he's pouring the vanilla malt syrup," he described as the thick caramel liquid curled out of the carafe into one glass then the other, "which also has some sea salt in it." Why malt instead of chocolate? "Malt has always had this childhood memory," he explained, when as a boy in Switzerland it was commonly mixed with milk, "and I think it's similar here, because you see malted milkshakes, and I think people associate it with their childhood."

The server replaced the brown carafe and raised the white. "And now the milk," Humm said as the server placed a long spoon in the first glass, its bowl curving in. The server poured the milk not into the malt but onto the spoon, from which it spilled down to the syrup below. He did the same with the other glass. The milk was brought in from an upstate creamery. "Now, some olive oil." The server splashed six, seven, eight dashes or so into each of the two glasses. "The olive oil adds a creaminess," Humm explained, "and the sea salt, because there's also sugar, it's sweet and a little salty. . . . I think it's great."

The server picked up the siphon and held the spoon inside the glass. "Now the seltzer." As the siphon sprayed with high force, mixing together the milk and syrup, the spoon stirred all three together, causing a foam to form. "Ideally it comes slightly over the top," Humm explained. "Yes, that's perfect." The server repeated the performance with the second glass. Then, in one swoop, he lifted both drinks onto his hidden napkin, cleansing the overspill underneath with a flick of his wrists, and served them.

"Enjoy," said Humm, followed by, "Cheers."

The taste and texture came as a surprise. It was thick. And rich. Creamy and sweet, without the light feel of the seltzer. Perhaps that was by design. Perhaps the server stirred with too much vigor, destroying the carbonation. The flavors were complex, orchestrated across the tongue. Most importantly, it was fun. Audacious and bold.

However, many detractors had posted comments in an online debate on the topic for the *Forward*.

"The person who came up with that egg cream they serve at Eleven Madison Park," wrote one critic, referring to Humm, "should be whipped with fifty of Goodman's egg noodles (extra wide)." He added for good measure, "Just reading the ingredients made me sick to my stomach."

Blogger Jeremiah Moss, chronicler of a vanishing New York City, launched a more impassioned call to arms, fighting not just for a recipe but a way of life:

This trend of dressing up the egg cream and slapping a big price tag on it is part of a larger trend in which foodies take the ordinary food of ordinary New Yorkers, like hotdogs and pizza, and upscale them for a more affluent and "discerning" clientele. It's not unlike the movement of the wealthy into poor and working-class neighborhoods. The new egg cream becomes "artisanal" and "exclusive," just like the new real estate across the Lower East Side. So you could call this the gentrification of the egg cream. It's a hostile takeover.[61]

When told about these detractors, Humm shifted and laughed. "I mean, you know, you can look at things from different ways," he said. "The real traditional in everything has its place, but also there has to be an evolution." He turned to the city for inspiration and guidance. "New York is a constantly evolving city. Its cuisine evolves as well." Humm was not against the traditional egg cream—in fact, he said he loved it and called it "almost an art form"—but what he loved more was that his New York allowed him to re-create the original. "And that's what cooking is all about: finding inspiration from somewhere and then using your creativity to make it your own." Humm returned once again to the dynamic spirit of New York. "I know that it is hard to accept change, but in a city of constant forward movement, we must embrace it!"

Humm cautioned his guest not to think he would disrespect the past. "Sometimes I like to go to a place where nothing has changed," he shared. But still, things have to change. "If they get reinvented it gives a new life to the classic one, you know? I think it's important." Save the past by translating it for the future. "If they don't evolve, maybe they also disappear."

Humm didn't want to gentrify egg creams. He was not interested in displacing one recipe for another. He had higher expectations for egg creams and its fans. He believed there was room for both the classic and the nouveau.

The waiter removed the empty glasses. What was in the future for Humm's egg creams? "We've done malted strawberry before," he said, referring to an earlier approach to the egg cream. "That I also really liked." And for the approaching fall season? "We're working on a hibiscus right now." Yes, that's what he said: a hibiscus egg cream. "The flavor combination, it's endless."

In cities like New York, you might be lucky and find a place that still serves a classic egg cream. But as U-Bet's David Fox had said, it was all about the egg cream experience, and that era came to an end with the decline of the candy shop, even with our nouveau entrepreneurs. "By the 1960s they started to wane," David explained. "By the '70s they were closing up." Diners became dominant, along with McDonald's and other fast-food venues. "Candy stores had too much competition." As old-fashioned candy stores disappeared, so too did the ubiquity of the egg cream.

Nowadays, most egg creams are made in the privacy of one's home, with store-bought seltzer and a bottle of Fox's U-Bet chocolate syrup. Only a handful remain who can fashion one in a shop the traditional way, mixing it up with Mel Brooks's "bullets of seltzer." In New York City, a traditional egg cream could be found at Famous Sammy's Roumanian Steakhouse, Junior's, Eisenberg's Sandwich Shop, Gem Spa, the 2nd Ave Deli, or at any of a handful of other Jewish delis.

And thanks to John Seekings keeping the Pittsburgh Seltzer Works active, the people of Pittsburgh, Pennsylvania, shared in that rare distinction and could enjoy a real egg cream mixed with their own seltzer siphon. "Just in time for summer," John posted on May 11, 2010, to their Facebook page, "We now carry Fox's U-Bet Chocolate and Vanilla Syrups," garnering numerous "Likes" from his clients on the social media site.

But the question remained: Was a new egg cream era taking the place of the original one? Was the egg cream destined to be forever mired in stagnant nostalgia until it faded from memory, or was it changing with time, transforming into something barely recognizable? Were new concoctions like those offered by Eleven Madison Park a revelation or an abomination?

Maybe the best way to settle the debate is at a nice marble counter over a freshly mixed concoction of milk, seltzer, and chocolate syrup (with a nice pretzel stick on the side).

7

HOW SELTZER GOT RELIGION

In which we see the affinity of Jewish Americans for seltzer and how its Jewish origins launched us all into the golden age of Seltzertopia.

SUNDAY AT THE BRUNCH WITH SELTZER

Jim Rogal, John Seekings's silent partner in the Pittsburgh Seltzer Works, felt the Jewish connection to seltzer deep down in his cultural DNA. Among his fellow Jewish Americans, long since emigrated from Eastern Europe, it was more like an understanding. It was not something anyone ever thought about. It was just common sense. Plain and simple: Jews drank seltzer.

But for his non-Jewish partner, John, Pittsburgh Seltzer Works was an unfamiliar world, no less so because it ran counter to everything he knew: advertising. He understood how to spend money to build brand awareness, but the Works had no advertising budget for cute radio ads or sharp magazine placements. The most surprising thing was that seltzer didn't need marketing for customers to find them; seltzer spread on its own, like an overflowing river.

"It's almost like a family tree now," John said, "where a friend told a friend and these neighborhoods start to grow." One neighbor received a delivery, and friends saw it and asked what it was all about. After speaking with John, the potential clients would try it out at their holiday party. Afterward, not only did they become regular customers, so did a number of their guests. "It starts with one person," John explained, "and all of a sudden you've got this pocket, all neighbors of neighbors."

The seltzer sold itself.

Perhaps that steady demand always made customer acquisition and coordination somewhat of a slapdash affair. The team who sold John the Works did the best they could. They passed on a card system, one card for every customer, their delivery history captured through the collection of stapled receipts. And that was quite a step up from what little they had received from Sam Edelmann: a list of customers collected on a scroll of fax paper. Back then delivery was concentrated in the Hill District, where Jewish immigrants first lived, and then the Squirrel Hill neighborhood when the community settled in. They called it the East End, and that's where the seltzer sold. They used to joke, "Our customers were either gay or Jewish." And, occasionally, both.

But times had changed by the summer of 2011. "There isn't just one person that is the standard consumer," John said. "They range in age from ninety-eight to twenty-one." And everyone had a different reason to order seltzer from the Works. "Some it's environmental. Some it's taking them back to when they were a child. Some because it just really tastes good, or they're going to mix it with Fox's Chocolate Syrup, or put it with bourbon."

Whatever the reason, they were all absolutely committed. And that was good enough for John Seekings; his path to seltzer had been accidental, from left field. He was ultimately a seltzer outsider who "went native." Not so for his partner, Jim Rogal, who brought to the Works his long personal and communal history with the drink. Jim always loved seltzer, considering it his drink of choice for as long as he could recall. Seltzer was always in his childhood home and in the homes of his friends. "The adults mixed it with alcohol," he said, "and the kids drank it with ice."

When Jim bought the seltzer plant he wanted to know more about his customers. As he reviewed the inherited customer list, reading their names, learning where they lived, the numbers forced him to think about the culture of seltzer for the first time, moving from anecdotes to statistics. While less than 5 percent of the city's residents were Jewish, Jim saw right away that the vast majority of the Work's customers lived in the East End, an area heavily popu-lated with Jews. "If I had to guess—and it's a pure guess—I'd say at least 50 percent of our home-delivery customers were Jewish." In other words, Jews didn't just drink seltzer, it turned out. A lot of Jews drink a lot of seltzer. Jim was amazed by just how popular seltzer actually was among his local Jewish community.

Soon after purchasing the Pittsburgh Seltzer Works, Jim and his wife had John and his family over for Sunday brunch. It was a beautiful and warm morning as they sat around a table in Jim's backyard. Like all their Sunday brunches, the Rogals shared a feast of bagels, cream cheese, and lox with a dozen or so friends, kids, and neighbors, including a rabbi, Aaron Bisno, who lived next door. Of course, something new had joined the table. No more store-bought seltzer, just authentic siphons, bottled in his own plant. And as Jim spritzed a glass for the rabbi, telling him all about the Works, a question formed in his mind, as if it had been waiting his whole life for just this moment, suddenly rising like a bubble escaping a tall glass and bursting out: Why do Jews drink seltzer?

Not everyone sees the seltzer/Semitic connection. When asked, some Jews (and Gentiles, too) profess ignorance about the "Jewish Champagne." Others reframe the issue, perhaps concerned about providing fodder to would-be bigots. Harry Golden, for example, in his collection *For 2¢ Plain*, suggests that many Jewish practices were simply a result of the insular nature of life in the ghetto. "On the Lower East Side of New York there were many traditions which we associated with the Jewish Civilization," Golden wrote, "until some of us began to read the literature of the world." Liberated from the ghetto mentality, Golden found that "many things were not 'Jewish' at all, but they were part of the tradition of all mankind." What at first seems specific is really universal.

But a direct look at the subject undeniably showed a connection. The fact that John, Jim's partner, was not Jewish served as the exception that proved the rule. Jim was Jewish. The three friends who sold him the Works were Jewish, as was Sam Edelmann, who had sold it to them. Kathryn of the Seltzer Sisters in San Francisco was Jewish. Kenny Gomberg, the third-generation seltzer supplier in Brooklyn, was Jewish, as were Eli, Walter and almost all of the delivery men he supported. One could go on and on.

In the world of books, "seltzer" is often a code word for "Jewish." In fact, the most popular books with seltzer in their titles are not about seltzer at all but about the Jews who drank it. Undoubtedly, the most famous seltzer-titled book, *For 2¢ Plain*, is not actually about ordering seltzer from the corner soda shop but about Harry Golden's boyhood in the Jewish community of the Lower East Side. *Up from Seltzer: A Handy Guide to 4 Jewish Generations* by Peter Hockstein, illustrated by Sandy Hoffman, an early-1980s cartoon collection, is a meditation on several generations of Jewish Americans. Seltzer becomes an emblem, a marker for the Jewish content within.

Seltzer is Semitic. Jews effervesce. But the question still remained: Why?

Eating their bagels that day, Jim explained to his neighbor, the rabbi, that he was curious to learn if there was some religious basis for the connection. "For example," Jim said, "is there something in the liturgy that says, 'Thou shalt drink seltzer water?'"

It was an interesting question, thought Rabbi Bisno. He was not surprised to learn that so many within his congregation were on Jim's customer list. He recalled his grandparents, second-generation Americans, making their own seltzer in the kitchen, preparing egg creams and chocolate sodas. Had they been motivated by the liturgy, some Hebrew word that could be read in more than one way, leading to an affinity for seltzer?

No, not that he could imagine. "I suspect it has to do with Jews adapting themselves to American society and making it their own," the rabbi said. Judaism is at once both a religion and a culture, the two strands tightly interwoven. If religious practice is not the direct source of Jews' seltzer affection, then it must be cultural. Maybe, he suggested, "it became part of the ways Jews would celebrate, or self-medicate, or adopt certain mores and means of integrating themselves into American society." On one point, however, he had no doubt. "I am not aware of any liturgical connection that would leave them to favor seltzer over any other libation."

Jim got the message loud and clear: it's purely cultural. But this simply passed the buck from one domain to another, leaving him with the question: what is the cultural source of this time-honored habit?

As it turned out, many before Jim had already pondered this question. There are three common reasons given for the Semitic/seltzer connection.

The first explanation is the significant presence of Jews in the seltzer trade. William B. Keller, who for decades through his

National Bottlers' Gazette had his eye on all aspects of the industry, noted the emergence of Jews at the turn of the century. And it was hard not to miss—while in 1880 there were only two Jewish-owned soda-water companies, a generation later there were over one hundred.[62]

In July 1903, Keller penned a rather unusual editorial for his periodical, sandwiched between a piece on the temperance movement and the importance of stamina in businessmen. It was entitled "The Jew in the Bottling Business." It was unusual because Keller was never one to focus on any particular ethnicity, nationality, or race. "Lest we be misunderstood," he began, "in reference to the 'Jews' in the bottling business, we desire to say that we use this term advisedly, as a descriptive appellation, to distinguish a certain class of industrious and energetic men, who are finding the business of bottling beverages an attractive vocation." Keller wrote that "there can be no mistake in the statement when we say that the Jews are learning the business in large numbers" and have become "a very respectable minority" in cities like New York, Newark, Philadelphia, Boston, and Chicago. After challenging them not to create a rival bottlers association, Keller's pet cause, he concluded by commending the Jewish bottlers and declaring: "These remarks and close observation lead us to say that the Jew is no doubt in the bottling trade—'for keeps.'"[63]

Within a few years it became evident that Jewish seltzer bottlers were not only on the rise as owners but among the wage workers as well. The *Jewish Daily Forward*, an avowedly socialist paper of the time, dutifully covered labor conflicts within their growing community. On November 3, 1906, as the seltzer industry tried to unionize, the *Forward* wrote: "Despite hunger, exhaustion, and beatings of employees at the hands of gangs hired by their bosses the ongoing strike of the Union of Mineral Water Workers is holding fast and is as strong as iron." Until the "bosses and shops

. . . simply accept the union and allow their workers to join it," wrote the paper, always ready to wave its partisan flag, "the *Forward* requests that its readers not drink any seltzer," unless of course it has the union label on the bottle. "Without the union label," the *Forward* exhorted, "you'll be drinking bloody seltzer!"

Walter Backerman, seltzer man extraordinaire, had bristled at the notion that his profession was somehow connected to his family's Jewish roots. "Let's analyze it if you want to go realistically, okay? In New York, Europeans came in, and, like anything else, you bring your interests from your former home. And seltzer was part of it, part of the culture."

Walter asked rhetorically, "Why did my grandfather, Jake, become a seltzer man?" It wasn't an ethnic thing, he explained. It wasn't because being Jewish gave him some inherent understanding of seltzer. To Walter it all came down to nepotism, what he likes to call the "winky dink," one person identifying with another and wanting to help him out. Walter explained, "Because he had a relative in the business, when he came he also became a seltzer man." Same with his dad. "The fact that my father was a Jewish seltzer man was mainly because he was introduced to the seltzer business by my grandfather." That's just how it was. "It follows lines of ethnicity, because when most people find a way to make money, they take care of their own."

Undoubtedly, Jews played a significant role in the development of the seltzer industry. Seltzer's role as a "family business" within the Jewish community certainly might have affirmed an affinity between Jews and the product. However, this argument fails to satisfy, as it leaves unanswered one key question: which came first, the job or the affinity? That is, did Jews learn to love seltzer by immersing themselves in the industry, or did Jews enter the industry due to their existing skills and interests? If Jews were new to seltzer, which seems unlikely, it is not clear why they chose this trade over others.

If Jews already had an affinity for the syrupless soda, then their industrial role cannot be the source of that affection. In either case, this argument, while interesting, ultimately falls flat.

The second explanation has to do with Jewish dietary habits or, to be more blunt, Jewish digestion. Eastern European Jewish cooking can be what we might call "heavy." This assertion is made, for example, in the two-paragraph entry on "Seltzer" in *The Encyclopedia of New York City*. Seltzer, it tells us, "was popular among Jews because it complemented rich foods included in kosher diets." In other words, it is no coincidence that the Yiddish word most often associated with seltzer, *greps*, means "to burp." The *New York Times* took a less delicate tone when it wrote that "seltzer, along with chicken soup, constitutes the powerful one-two punch of Jewish home medicine. While chicken soup was applied to colds and the like, seltzer combated stomach ailments, brought on by overdoses of pastrami or leaden matzoth balls."[64] Rabbi Bisno saw the logic as well. "It would settle your stomach," he said. "We still do

Matzah ball soup

that. If someone has an upset stomach we might offer them Sprite or something with some carbonation, a sort of home remedy."

The problem with this theory is that Jews are not unique in their consumption of heavy food. The Irish, for example, are known for corned beef, but they are no more associated with seltzer than they are with keeping a kosher kitchen.

This provides a natural segue to the third frequent explanation: kosher restrictions. Mark Epstein is a retired bottler who once ran Ferriss, a seltzer company.[65] "It might have nothing to do with taste preferences," he explained when asked why Jews liked seltzer. "It may turn out because seltzer was kosher. There were hardly many national franchises with kosher products." That logic resonated with Rabbi Bisno. "Arguably, that could be right," he considered. "If those early sodas didn't have a *hechsher*," the mark designating a food as kosher, "or you didn't know where it was bottled, maybe that could be a reason to favor seltzer."

These theories run the gamut—that Jews drink seltzer because it is in the family, it is medicinal, or they can drink little else—but all three have one thing in common: they have nothing to do with the magnificent taste sensation touted by its fans. If suitors professed their love with the same weak arguments—you settled their stomach, brought in the bucks, or, frankly, the one they really wanted was unavailable—how quickly would they be turned down?

It turns out the question is backward. It should not be, Why do Jews drink seltzer? Instead, the question should be, Why doesn't everyone else?

MINERAL WATER, AMERICAN-STYLE

In the early 1800s, American drinking habits were similar to those of the Europeans to whom they looked for "culture." Europeans tended to distinguish only between uncarbonated ("flat") water and carbonated mineral water ("water with gas"), which they continue to do today. In other words, seltzer back then *was* mineral water. They were essentially the same thing. So when nineteenth-century Americans weren't buying imported (mineralized) seltzer from European springs like Niederselters or Apollinaris, they searched for local mineralized sources or added minerals to filtered water in factories.

Before the century was over, however, American tastes changed. By 1900, an American who ordered seltzer expected carbonated water sans minerals. What happened? How did American tastes break from the European canonical definition of seltzer?

Chapelle, author of *Wellsprings*, noted the importance of this change.[66] In fact, he called the 1880s' popularity of unmineralized water (carbonated or flat) "the first predominantly American water fashion," one that "stands in stark contrast to the European custom of preferring mineral waters." In the end, it did not come down to taste but to notions of purity. Recall that back then, seltzer's medicinal value still rivaled, and perhaps trumped, what it offered as a beverage. This value arose from the water's unique combination of minerals. Thus, the presence of minerals chemically signified the very health-giving properties of the seltzer. However, as modern science began to understand the true nature of seltzer's healing power and more and more popular attention was given to debunking the hucksters and quacks selling home remedies, American's notion of purity changed. Minerals no longer signaled health benefits as much as pure water signaled purity. The first popular water brand to sell that purity, the first non-mineral water, bubbled up from a little spring in Maine named Poland.

In 1844, Hiram Ricker's chronic case of dyspepsia was relieved at last. Hiram credited the waters from Poland Spring, originally purchased by his grandfather, Jabez Ricker. The Rickers developed a profitable inn and resort around the spring, encouraging those like

Hiram to "take the waters."[67] The following year the Ricker family opened a bottling plant and delivered the waters in three-gallon clay jugs for five cents a gallon to local groceries by horse-drawn wagons. They also sold water in barrels to sea captains and travelers on the strength of its purported health benefits. By 1860, physicians were prescribing Poland Spring for kidney and bladder diseases, while a new Boston-based office coordinated agents selling the waters in the Deep South and Far West. By the mid-1880s a depot was established in New York City for national distribution.[68]

The natural mineral water of Saratoga Springs was once the American ideal; by the turn of the century, that honor was held by Poland Spring, "not much more mineralized than rainwater." And this new American preference became the new orthodoxy.

Chapelle documented Poland Spring's rise to glory, with successive public awards further cleaving American tastes from European. "By the 1880s," he wrote, "Poland Spring bottled water was enough of a fixture in Maine that it was included in the central exhibit at the World's Columbian Exposition in Chicago, where it was awarded a Medal of Excellence." In 1904, after competing against all the best-known waters in the country at the St. Louis World's Fair, the United States Geological Survey designated Poland Spring the "best spring water in the country," not due to taste or medicinal power but due to "purity." A century later Poland Spring still reigned supreme: in 2016, Poland Spring was one of the top bottled-water brands, with annual revenue for its current owner, Nestlé, of $1.146 billion.[69]

As American's water tastes underwent a radical change, the country experienced another, even more profound, change: the absorption of millions of immigrants, most of whom carried with them the traditions and tastes of old Europe. The United States at the time was a giant assimilation machine, using public schools and other civic institutions to guide its new residents into becoming model American citizens. But as Michael Pollan explained in his book *The Omnivore's Dilemma*, few things are more change resistant and less likely to be assimilated than habits pertaining to food and drink.

The common phrase "We are what we eat" usually referred to the nutrients people chose to ingest. But to Pollan, the key here was the word *chose*. A koala bear does not choose to eat eucalyptus leaves; it eats leaves because that is all it can eat. But as omnivores, humans must make a choice again and again and again: What shall I eat today? So, to Pollan, "We are what we eat," is really, "We are what we choose to eat." The staying power of these choices is strong. "The immigrant's refrigerator is the very last place to look for signs of assimilation," he argued, as, historically, national cuisines were "remarkably stable and resistant to change."[70]

People choose not only what to eat but with whom. "Taste . . . brings people together . . . as communities," argued Pollan, since "a community's food preferences—the strikingly short list of foods and preparations it regards as good to eat and drink—represent one of the strongest social glues we have."[71]

In the beginning the social glues that held Jews together were the Bible and the accumulation of religious practices, such as food restrictions and Passover seders. Later came more modern cultural practices, such as the unifying power of Yiddish, bagels, and, eventually, seltzer.

Some practices, like seltzer, were fetishized, essentialized, as if they had always been central to Jewish culture and not a new twist in modern times. As assimilating immigrants turned toward "pure" water (and then sodas) and away from mineral water, immigrant Jews used seltzer as a new cultural glue to strengthen their community in the United States. It was the inversion of Harry Golden's quote in *For 2¢ Plain*. Recall that to Golden many of the Jewish-associated traditions with which he grew up turned out not to be strictly Jewish at all, but rather universal. With seltzer, however, what was once universal suddenly became Jewish. What began as a popular habit grew increasingly ethnically Jewish.

"Jewish tastes in America were becoming Jewish American tastes," wrote Maria Balinska in *The Bagel: The Surprising History of a Modest Bread*. "By the late 1920s, it was estimated that sixty percent of the bread consumed in Jewish neighborhoods was white and 'non-Jewish.'"[72] As Jewish people moved from the tenements to the suburbs, many had to say farewell to their seltzer delivery men and corner soda shops. As seltzer became more of a fond memory than a daily presence, it began to represent an entire way of life that had been left behind, both capitalized upon and crystallized in popular consciousness by Golden's best-selling books. As the wheel of assimilation turned, that nostalgia turned, in some corners, to embarrassment. To Balinska, shifts in bread-eating habits were a "modest but concrete indication of the cultural assimilation that was taking place." These shifts in Jewish seltzer-drinking habits tell a similar tale, tracing both Jewish attitudes toward seltzer and, more important, their own role within American society. This tale can be easily decoded from the 1981 cartoon book referenced earlier called *Up from Seltzer*.

Each of the one hundred or so pages in this tiny, square book is split into a two-by-two grid, with each of the four cells featuring a portrait of a cartoon couple. The grid of four couples repeats on every page throughout the book as the four generations of Jews in America are contrasted with each other in response to each page's topic. The topics include such significant cultural markers as "What I made at camp," "How to order lox," and "Where grandma lives."

In the book, the first generation of Jewish Americans, a stereotypical Orthodox couple dress like they have just left the shtetl. The man's face is framed by a traditional fuzzy hat and religious sidelocks (*payos*), a mustache tracing the arc of a stern frown. The babushka wears her hair in a conservative scarf and looks like she has just heard the Cossacks were riding back into town. According to information later in the book, they live in a "hovel on the Lower East Side." Each successive generation pictured seems marginally happier. The second-generation couple have begun to assimilate, leaving behind their impoverished roots by moving to the suburbs. The third generation, in a Beverly Hills condo high-rise, looks little different from non-Jewish Americans; their only remaining ethnic identifier is the gold *chai*, symbolizing life, around the man's neck. The fourth generation, the one who wrote this book, are happy hippies living in a tent on an all-organic commune in Vermont. They sport identical exploding Jewfros and dark sunglasses; no signs remain of their immigrant, impoverished, Jewish roots. They are thoroughly delighted to have left behind everything their great-grandparents represented. And what would that be, exactly? The book summed it up in one word, at the end of the title: seltzer.

The opening phrase "Up from" suggests Jews in America have been on an upward trend since they first arrived, their assimilation

bringing both financial and emotional well-being, with little of value lost along the way. But those ethnic elements, carried from Europe to the Lower East Side, bottled in siphons and nostalgized beyond recognition by the second and third generations, are rejected, page after page, all in the name of good humor.

The book documents only four generations, but the fifth generation, the one emerging in the 1980s as *Up from Seltzer* went to print, had the last laugh in the end. They rejected the rejection, they disdained the disdain, and they learned, along with so many other groups of the era, to "embrace the hyphen," to be both Jewish and American at the same time, to reclaim their past but rework it for a new age. And it all started with a little bottle of French water: Perrier.

BEFORE PERRIER . . .

In 1981, the *Pittsburgh Post-Gazette* published an article about the Pittsburgh Seltzer Works, focused on owner Sam Edelmann. The piece opened with a phrase that perfectly captured the shifting role of seltzer within the Jewish community: "Before Perrier, there was seltzer."[73] This moment was captured as well in *Up from Seltzer*. Under "Jewish beverage of choice," the first generation drank "Seltzer water (Fer two cents plain)" while the fourth generation preferred "Perrier water (Fer two dollars, fancy)." The book even calls modern Jews the "Perrier generation." How did the overnight sensation of Perrier force a whole generation of Jews to reconsider its own relationship with bubbly water and, ultimately, themselves?

While Perrier did not hit the United States until the 1970s,[74] it had been pleasing the tastes of Europeans since 218 BCE, according to legend. The soldiers of Julius Caesar's army in 58 BCE were the first to erect buildings and a stone basin at the site of the spring in southern France. By the mid-nineteenth century the site had become an active spa, and water was bottled there. In 1898, the spring was leased to a doctor, Louis Perrier, whose name would forever be associated with its waters.

An Englishman, William Albert St. John Harmsworth, bought the spring soon after and shipped Perrier throughout the British Empire—to India, Afghanistan, and Africa—as a healthier alternative to local waters. In 1976, crossing the Atlantic against the prevailing headwinds of American tastes, Perrier opened its first US office in New York City and launched a nationwide, five-million-dollar ad campaign.[75]

Perrier's rapid rise to US fame was remarkable. At the time, single-serving bottles of water were unheard of, and American tastes still favored the mineral-free variety. But in just a dozen years, Americans were buying 300 million bottles of Perrier each year.[76] Perrier dominated the imported water market, with 80 percent of the share. Poland Spring fought back with an anti-Perrier campaign. "For an American to be healthy, is it necessary to get the water from Europe?" challenged the ad. "That's like sending your laundry to Europe."[77] Perrier's response? It acquired Poland Spring.

Perrier's rise to prominence was driven, in no small part, by the emergence of a new class of young urban professionals, or yuppies, flooding New York City. Amid concerns about the quality of the city's tap water, yuppies demonstrated their power—through their spending and the cachet they brought to their conspicuous consumption. They were attracted to Perrier's overseas pedigree; drinking mineralized water distinguished them from those who drank flat water. Chapelle wrote that Perrier's timing could not have been better. "It was all the things yuppies wanted in a lifestyle-defining product." Perrier's unique green glass bottles, designed after Indian exercise clubs, offered something that was "cool, it was sophisticated, it was European, it was expensive." It was also the wedge that broke open American drinking habits. Not only did it return a certain prestige to mineral and carbonated waters, it opened the door to single-serving drinks at places like convenience stores.

With bottled water now ubiquitous and Perrier in demand, could Jews still think of seltzer as a mere anachronism? Like seltzer, Perrier traced its nineteenth-century roots to Europe but was now a must-have—for the health conscious and for people of all backgrounds—and enjoyed its own distinct cultural heritage. So, if Perrier was now popular, could the same be said of seltzer?

Google Ngram Viewer provided one set of evidence. This web-based tool, launched in 2010, searches words or phrases within Google Books—their project to digitize all books and periodicals. In other words, Ngram is used to track the frequency of the word *seltzer* over time, which obscures details but reveals larger trends like seltzer's fall and rise.

USE OF *SELTZER* IN BOOKS IN THE UNITED STATES

The above chart shows the percentage during any given period of the appearance of the word *seltzer* among all books written in American English and published in the United States. Seltzer enters the chart in 1803, the all-time low for *seltzer* (after entering the lexicon in the late 1700s), and ends in 2008 because Ngram doesn't search through the present. (To reproduce this chart, visit books.google.com/ngrams, select "American English," and set smoothing to "5.")

In brief, seltzer's popularity rose during the post–Civil War industrial boom, peaking first in the 1880s, dipping and then rising again with the new tide of immigrants from Eastern Europe, and reaching its all-time peak just after the turn of the century. From there the only direction was down, down, down, over seven decades, until the search term *seltzer* hit rock bottom in 1971. But in the second half of the decade, something rather remarkable happened: a return to interest in seltzer. This initial bump, the "Perrier effect," doesn't explain what happened next: interest in seltzer continued to rise and never stopped.

The above chart ends in 2008, but a second chart picks up this trending topic and brings it to the present:

USE OF "SELTZER" IN US GOOGLE SEARCHES

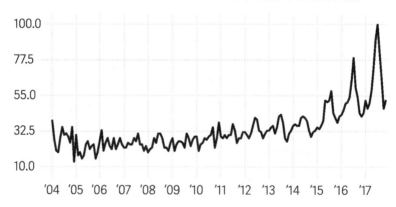

This Google Trends chart shows the relative frequency during any given month of the word "seltzer" used in a Google search over a given period of time. In other words, between 2004 to the end of 2017, the average rate of searches for "seltzer" grew and grew.

(To reproduce this chart, visit trends.google.com, select "United States," "Food and Drink," and "Web searches.")

Perhaps the decisions made with our wallets are even more enlightening.

US SELTZER SALES BY VOLUME

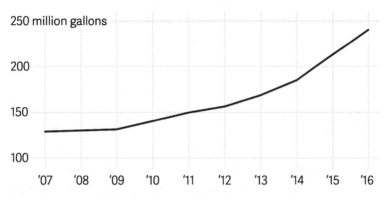

Data: **Beverage Marketing Corporation**

This chart shows seltzer sales in the millions of gallons from 2007 through 2016. In 2007 nearly 129 million gallons of seltzer were sold in the United States; in 2016, more than 240 million gallons of seltzer were sold in the United States, an 86 percent increase in nine years, with almost half of that increase in just the last two years. Not only is seltzer still on the rise, it appears to be escalating.

Right now, in America, seltzer might just be experiencing a popularity that surpasses anything seen in the past.

The late 1970s and early 1980s marked a turning point, initiating seltzer's gradual return to prominence after decades of decline. For many Jews, particularly young Jews, all this public interest in Perrier led to a rediscovery of seltzer. This is nicely summed up in the title of that Pittsburgh article on Sam Edelmann: "For Him a Shot of the Bubbly Means a Spritz of

Seltzer." In 1979 the *New York Times* noted the return of seltzer, calling it "A Renaissance in Fizz."

> At a time when the *haut monde* has turned to Perrier and other sparkling waters in its relentless effort to inject all life with effervescence, a coincidence of nostalgia and the desire for unadulterated products and calorie-less treats has focused attention on the city's ineradicable and thriving seltzer underground.[78]

Seltzer was back, and with it an old-way-made-new for Jews to publicly take pride in their heritage. Jewish Americans, more comfortable than ever being both Jewish and American, looked back at their own traditions and discovered they didn't need this Perrier newcomer. They harbored their own tradition of effervescence, and it was once again something they could be proud to call part of their past. This time its popularity was shared with millions of people from *every* walk of life, who integrated seltzer into both their daily routines and their very identity.

Seltzer, ultimately, was a hybrid, a natural by-product of both its European mineral water source and the American preference for clear spring water. Seltzer was a perfect mix of old world tradition and American modernity. Kind of like the modern Jew. Kind of like Jim Rogal.

"There's this vectoring of my own personal experience with this much bigger cultural history," Jim said upon reflection after his Sunday brunch, "and it makes me smile." Perhaps the most important thing for Jim was that, through the Pittsburgh Seltzer Works, his private, personal tastes for seltzer water connected him with the deeper legacy of his people. He had always loved seltzer as a kid. "Whether that was genetic or not, I don't know." And now he's a seltzer man. "It's funny that I always had a taste for it, which I think is neat, and it fits with everything I've done and known with my life." But Jim hesitated to make too much out of it. "I don't look at it too cosmically or spiritually. Right now, it's a business that I am trying to kinda figure out, along with John."

In the end, it's only seltzer.

8

HOW SELTZER GOT FUNNY

In which the common association between seltzer siphons and humor
helps answer the question: Why is seltzer funny?

THE CARBONATED COMEDY OF THE THREE STOOGES

After seltzer's associations with health, refreshment, and ethnic identity, there is one final, pervasive association: comedy. And not just any kind of comedy, but one marked by a certain level of aggressive intimacy. In fact, in the history of slapstick, few images are more iconic than a seltzer siphon spritzed in the face. Whether sprayed by the Three Stooges or famous clowns like Clarabell, Chuckles, or Krusty, the pressure released from a depressed valve causes chaos, tickling our funny bones and easing the tensions of the day.

For many fans, the Three Stooges—bossy Moe, third banana Larry, and nyuk-nyuk Curly—still remain the indelible link between seltzer and humor. "You know, I'd seen them when I was a kid; I've seen them in the movies," John Seekings responded when asked if he had seen siphons as a boy. "I have memories of seeing those seltzer siphon bottles, the old TV with Larry, Moe, and Curly spraying each other."

Among the Three Stooges' movie shorts, TV appearances, and feature-length movies, the team's best-known work is comprised of their roughly eight shorts a year produced during the 1930s and early '40s. Contracted by Columbia Pictures, these years are now known as their Columbia period.

Ted Okuda and Edward Watz, historians of the Stooges and their peers, marveled in their book *The Columbia Comedy Shorts* about the vast gap between the poor critical reception of the Three Stooges' work and their ability to strike the public's funny bone.[79] "Aesthetically, the Stooges violated every rule that constitutes 'good' comedic style," the authors argued. "Their characters lacked the emotional depth of Charlie Chaplin and Harry Langdon; they were never as witty or subtle as Buster Keaton." Furthermore, they lacked discipline to sustain lengthy scenes. They never missed

The Three Stooges in *Three Little Pigskins*, 1934

an opportunity to suspend the narrative structure if a gratuitous joke could be stuffed in. "And yet, in spite of the overwhelming artistic odds against them, they were responsible for some of the finest comedies ever made." At its core, the historians describe the humor of the Stooges as "the most undistilled form of low comedy," which was to say, "as quick laugh practitioners, they place second to none." And the Stooges understood that one of the best ways to get a quick laugh was a seltzer spritz in the face.

One of the earliest Three Stooges shorts to feature seltzer was the 1934 *Three Little Pigskins*. Within a short two-minute sequence, they pack in everything one can possibly do with a siphon. Like most Stooges films, the setup is irrelevant, a mere excuse to position the three for high jinks and shenanigans. The scene begins with the Stooges lounging in the parlor with their three new wives. "Step over to the bar, boys," one wife suggests, unaware of what is about to be unleashed. "Make yourself a drink."

Moe saunters over to the well-stocked bar, picks up a siphon, taps Curly's shoulder for no discernible reason (beyond their eternal feuding), and asks, "Say, you like some sparkling water with your liquors?"

"Always," responds Curly, walking into Moe's trap.

And with that, the seltzer sprays. First Moe sprays Curly in the face. When Moe leans over, Curly's retaliation misses its mark, striking Larry instead. When Moe stands up, Larry's retaliation hits him instead. Now all three are wet.

The humor derives as much from the rapid "who's on top?" switcheroos as the percussive beats of the siphon squirts, a seltzer symphony so to speak, with carefully crafted pregnant pauses in between.

"Just a minute," the wives demand. "This has gone far enough. Don't you know there are ladies present?" You can probably guess what happens next. After a fine dousing, one suspects that by the time the actresses yelled through their giggles, "Okay! Okay! Okay!" they had long since dropped character. Few could keep it together in the face of such a sustained seltzer attack, an audience of Stooge fans included.

In other shorts, seltzer was both subject of and emphasis for a punchline. In the 1939 *Yes, We Have No Bonanza*, the Stooges worked in a saloon in the Wild West. At one point Moe watches with increasing disgust as Curly mixes a drink. First, he sprays seltzer into a glass goblet, humming along. Then, wielding an oversized ice prong large enough to grab a melon, he adds a tiny ice cube. After one final spritz, and a self-satisfied, "Nyuk, nyuk, nyuk," Curly raises the glass to sniff the fine aroma.

"Hey," Moe demands, "what kind of a drink is that?"

"That's my own brand," Curly replies. "A Western Surprise."

Inspecting the glass, Moe insists, "There's no liquor in that."

Curly responds, "That's the surprise."

Moe's response, however, comes as a surprise to no one and is shouted in sprays of seltzer.

The Stooges continued to wring humor from seltzer over the coming years, in shorts like *No Dough Boys* (1944), *Three Loan Wolves* (1946), and *Love at First Bite* (1950). Siphons were props in their continuous efforts to rough one another up. But occasionally they would find a new use. In *No Dough Boys*, the Stooges accidentally stumbled into a swanky New York City apartment filled with Japanese soldiers and German spies. As Moe attacks the Germans with pie in hand, Larry and Curly use siphons to take on the Japanese. Before the end of this comedic short, one of the soldiers is taken out by a prolonged seltzer burst. The seltzer flows into his mouth from Curly's siphon then exits, like a fountain, out of his ears. Rarely has seltzer been put to such patriotic use.

This is all well and good but begs the question: why is seltzer funny? Perhaps it is because slapstick often relies on building anticipation for a moment of unbridled release. The audience recognizes the potential for chaos, then waits in sheer delight for that moment to arrive. It relies on the dramatic principle known as "Chekhov's gun," in reference to the Russian playwright Anton Chekhov, who once asserted, "One must not put a loaded rifle on the stage if no one is thinking of firing it." When a table of pies is on-screen, someone must get it in the face. When there's a seltzer siphon, someone must get wet. In the hands of the Stooges and their contemporaries, a seltzer siphon became no more and no less than slapstick in a bottle, compressed tension awaiting release.

Steve Zimmerman and Ken Weiss, authors of *Food in the Movies*, also gave the subject considerable thought. They reframed the question, asking, "Why is playing with food funny?" First, they asserted, we are all intimately familiar with food and the rituals surrounding its preparations and consumption. "Anything that disrupts or mocks the social customs and decorum surrounding food—or that defies natural laws, probability, and all conventions—seems to strike us as funny."[80] Second, comedians like the Three Stooges were childlike or simpleminded characters. "In other words," they said, "these were grown men acting in many respects like children, so it seems natural for them to play with their food."[81] Finally, in the earliest days of cinema, flying food was a special effect that all viewers could appreciate. "When people went to the movies during the silent era—and this included many immigrants who couldn't speak or read English—sight gags of all sorts got laughs in any language."[82] Especially when the target was a figure of authority, the antisocial behavior was recognized and appreciated.

On January 18, 1952, Curly died. His antics with Larry and Moe, however, earned them a new generation of fans as their films were repackaged in 1958 for the new medium sweeping the nation: television. But times had changed. Siphons became less common within the households tuning in. After World War II, urban residents had flocked to the suburbs, soda shops were threatened by diners, and Coca-Cola was the big player in town. Seltzer, while still around, was becoming an anachronism. "As opposed to just a pump machine dispensing water," explained Mel Gordon, a professor of theater arts at the University of California, Berkeley, "seltzer now represented the Golden Age of Comedy."[83] And that was when siphons literally changed hands, from post-vaudeville film comedians like the Three Stooges to an entirely new class of comedian: clowns. "I think when seltzer stopped appearing in normal households," Gordon contended, "then it became a clown device, because then it seemed something weird and old-fashioned."

NO CLOWNING AROUND

Modern clowns still use seltzer siphons, but some have translated them into a twenty-first-century idiom: emoji. On web-based clown discussion boards, rather than end their posts with emoticons simulating winks and laughter—;-) and LOL—they end with :pie: and :seltzer:—signifying a pie in the face, followed by a well-placed spritz. A welcome email from one such board painted the following picture of heaven for clowns: "Thanks for registering at Clown Forum! We have hot and cold running seltzer, fields of squirting flowers, and acres and acres of custard pies."

Clowns commiserated over the same challenges everyone faced in our post-9/11 world, but perhaps with a little twist. "I did the Fantasy Flight event at Dulles Airport at the beginning of December," wrote a clown named Sir Toony Van Dukes. "Let me say that getting through security in a clown costume can be a challenge with the current state of TSA screenings." "I imagine it would be difficult nowadays," replied a clown named Bingle. "Where does one find a three-ounce seltzer bottle?"

The carbonated craziness of clowns goes back many decades. As television in the 1950s kept the Stooges alive, it also gave birth to one of the most famous clowns to ever wield a seltzer siphon: Howdy Doody's Clarabell the Clown.

The *Howdy Doody Show* first aired in December 1947, when only a handful of viewers could tune in. It would go on to be the first children's show to last more than a thousand episodes, and it was NBC's first regularly scheduled show to be broadcast in color. It featured Howdy Doody, a marionette, and Buffalo Bob Smith, the show host and voice of Howdy Doody, along with a cast of both human and puppet characters. Clarabell the Clown was Howdy Doody's best-known sidekick. "Well, his feet are big, his tummy's stout, but we could never do without," sang Buffalo Bob and the kids of the Peanut Gallery in Clarabell's honor. Appearing in a baggy, striped costume, Clarabell never spoke, communicating à la Harpo Marx via twin bicycle horns mounted on a box. And inside that box? A seltzer siphon. According to his obituary in the *New York Times*, "Clarabell the Clown made his feelings known by spraying Buffalo Bob with seltzer." A horn might communicate "yes" or "no," but apparently seltzer was required to bring out the love.

While the man behind the makeup changed over the years, the first to play Clarabell was Bob Keeshan, who started out managing

Clarabell the Clown showering Buffalo Bob Smith with carbonated affection on *The Howdy Doody Show*

the children in the Peanut Gallery. A producer saw Keeshan on-screen and felt he would fit better into the show's circus scene if he were dressed as a clown. Keeshan's Clarabell was aggressive and, echoing Steve Zimmerman's analysis of the Stooges, often acted like a small child. Many an episode included Keeshan chasing Buffalo Bob around under threat of a seltzer spritz. Children loved it. Some parents complained, however, saying Clarabell's seltzer antics were working their kids into an inappropriate pre-bedtime frenzy. Keeshan left, replaced by Bobby Nicholson.

Nicholson's Clarabell was gentle and shy, and while parents might have preferred him, children did not. So Keeshan and the seltzer-powered Clarabell returned, but not for long. Due to a salary dispute, Keeshan and three of his coworkers were let go. While Keeshan would go on to become Captain Kangaroo (starring in his own beloved children's show with a remarkable run, from 1955 until 1984), Clarabell's aggressive antics continued with a new performer, Lew Anderson, and a generation of children would grow up learning about the comedic perfection of a well-timed seltzer spray.

In 1970, a new children's show clown was introduced to the viewing public: Chuckles the Clown, on *The Mary Tyler Moore Show*. Chuckles, however, while often referenced, rarely appeared on the show. He was as much a comedic prop as a seltzer siphon, less a clown than a commentary *on* clowns. In the end, Chuckles is most famous not for how he lived but how he died.

"Chuckles Bites the Dust," broadcast on October 25, 1975, struck a chord that would reverberate for decades and would go on to rank near the top of *TV Guide*'s "100 Greatest Episodes of All-Time" list, winning an Emmy for its writer, David Lloyd. Lloyd, a budding sitcom writer, would later write for *The Bob Newhart Show*, *Cheers*, *Taxi*, and *Frasier*. But despite all his future accomplishments, it was this singular episode that would define his work.

And that episode, Lloyd's sensibility, and perhaps the entire history of seltzer and comedy can be summed up by its now-famous carbonated catchphrase: *A little song, a little dance, a little seltzer down your pants.*

When Mary and company learn that Chuckles has been crushed by an elephant while dressed as Peter Peanut, Mary is beside herself as her colleagues make sport of Chuckles's improbable demise.

And then something almost imperceptibly shifts. As the reverend begins to eulogize the deceased clown, Mary's colleagues finally grow serious. Mary, however, confronted with the absurd solemnity of a clown's funeral, can no longer hold it together. With each new reference to some comedic aspect of Chuckles's past—the silly names of his characters, his goofy sound effects—she struggles not to break out laughing.

The reverend reflects on the hardships encountered by Chuckles's characters, constantly beaten down by his comedic enemies, and commends him for always responding with such bravery and honesty. "And what did Chuckles ask in return?" he ponders. "Not much—in his own words—'A little song, a little dance, a little seltzer down your pants.'"

With that, Mary loses it, laughing uproariously. The reverend asks her to rise, not to reprimand her but to affirm Chuckles's credo. "You feel like laughing, don't you?" he asks. But rather than ask her to stop, he tells her to go ahead, to laugh. What better way to honor Chuckles the Clown?

In response, Mary, being Mary, bursts into tears. Confronted by Chuckles's lifelong commitment to spreading joy, epitomized by a well-placed burst of self-deprecating seltzer, she finally completes the arc of mourning: from anger, to denial, to acceptance.

This episode not only metaphorically killed off children's television clowns but also brought new depth to seltzer, imbuing it with a clown's deep philosophy on how to live life, for crying until you laughed and laughing until you cried, for finding humor in even the most unlikely, or inappropriate, of places.

Those places would become even more inappropriate fifteen years later when the memory of Chuckles was replaced with an even more outlandish clown: Krusty.

His name could not be more fitting. One of the many side characters on the animated show *The Simpsons*, Krusty the Clown inverts every positive image of clowns and exploits every possible fear. Krusty was a children's show clown who abhorred kids, hated life, and was addicted to alcohol, cigarettes, gambling, and pornography (not to mention Percodan, Pepto-Bismol, and Xanax). As host of his eponymous children's show, he brutalized Stageshow Bob, his sidekick, not with seltzer bottles but flying axes. (Bob later took his revenge by framing Krusty for armed robbery.)

Krusty never appeared without his clown makeup, even when off-camera, as if he were not even human but some monstrous aberration. Krusty was, in essence, the anti-Clown—he was just not funny—and when *The Simpsons* launched in the deconstructionist 1990s, nothing could have been funnier.

Krusty, however, predated the series. He was introduced on January 15, 1989, when *The Simpsons* was no more than a comedic short developed by cartoonist Matt Groening for *The Tracey Ullman Show*. Krusty was Homer in clown makeup, with crazy green hair, blue bowtie, traditional red clown nose, and oversized shoes. As originally conceived, *The Simpsons* was about "a kid who had no respect for his father, but worshiped a clown who looked exactly like his father," said Groening. As Krusty became one of the most commonly featured characters on the Simpsons, it was clear that he deserved an appropriately deep and twisted backstory, a story, it would turn out, in which seltzer played a crucial role.

The October 24, 1991, episode, "Like Father, Like Clown," explained that Krusty's real name was Herschel Shmoikel Pinchas

Yerucham Krustofski. Son of Rabbi Hyman Krustofski, voiced by Jackie Mason, Herschel rebelled against his father's intentions to send him to yeshiva. Instead, he pursued his secret desire to make people laugh.

Krusty's illicit attraction to humor as a boy is demonstrated in a scene parodying a classic moment in Philip Roth's novel *Portnoy's Complaint*. Young Herschel has locked himself in the bathroom while Rabbi Krustofski pounds on the door with his fist. Forcing the door open, his father is shocked and horrified to find that his son has locked himself in the bathroom to play with his . . . seltzer siphon. As the bottle spritzes his face, Herschel bows his head in shame.

As an adult, Herschel's path to comedy takes him to a Talmudic conference in the Catskills. He folds balloons not into animals but Stars of David and Hanukkah menorahs. The rabbis in the audience eat it up, even Rabbi Krustofski, unaware that the clown on the stage is his son. Behind the clown make-up, he might have fooled them all, if not for a rabbi in the audience who approaches the stage with a loaded siphon. The audience laughs as the spray hits Krusty but then gasps as the clown makeup comes off and they realize he is Krustofski's son. Krustofski rises to decry the shame that has been brought upon their family and declare that he never wants to see him again. And Krusty never saw his father again (that is, of course, until Bart and Lisa Simpson reconcile the two).

For Krusty, seltzer was an object of illicit desire that represented his repressed comedic longings, leading him literally to hide behind the clown makeup, like a superhero behind a mask protecting his identity. Little Hershel was no more. Krusty was forever. Yet, ironically, it was that same seltzer that exposed his true identity and hit him where he was most vulnerable.

Seltzer giveth and seltzer taketh away.

BADCHANS, HIGH JINKS, AND THE SPREAD OF AGGRESSIVE LOVE

It's hard to imagine the rise of Hollywood and television without seltzer's comedic punch, that brutal carbonic love, that aggressive hitting where it hurt. But how did seltzer become an intrinsic part of the comedic DNA of American life?

Mel Gordon, theater arts professor at Berkeley, explained that seltzer was identified with comedians rather early. There was another characteristic identified with many early comedians: Judaism.

First, Gordon explained, siphons were almost a sort of plaything found in every Jewish home in New York during World War I and the decades that followed. Second, as with the silent comedies of the time, siphons "had endless aggressive possibilities: squirting, and making a big mess, and it looked great, and so forth." Third, seltzer was funny because "it's from a folk culture—Eastern and central European—but it's also sort of a children's delight." And finally, "it's also an apparatus, in places like [the movie] *The Thin Man*, of sophisticated drinking."

With Jews into both seltzer and comedy, it was natural that someone would eventually combine the two. Gordon argued in an essay called "The Farblondjet Superhero and His Cultural Origins" (within the book *Funnyman*) that Jews dominated American comedy. He reported that in 1978 a psychology professor at the University of Pennsylvania calculated that Jewish Americans, at the time only 2.5 percent of the population, made up more than 82 percent of the top comedians in the country.[84] Comedy, however, was more than just a professional skill among Jews. It was a desired and highly valued trait. For example, according to Gordon, Jews were nearly five times more likely to advertise in personal ads that they had a sense of humor.

Beginning in the mid-eighteenth century, one style of Jewish performer started to dominate Jewish humor in Europe, the badchan. The word *badchan* is of Aramaic origin and first appeared in the Babylonian Talmud, circa 900 CE. It originally referred to a sort of ghost who imitated, according to Gordon, "the worst qualities of unsavory individuals" after death. By the late 1500s, the term referred to just one among a variety of Jewish entertainers. This particular type of entertainer had one primary goal, wrote Gordon: "To disrupt or overturn the established social order."[85] To achieve this end, no rules of propriety could hold him back. "A talented [badchan] could juggle references to drooping breasts, oversized buttocks, small penises, and gaseous excretions into an evening of raucous laughter." As a result, the badchan "stimulates a different way of thinking about what is funny and where humor belongs in the culture."

The badchans were on their way out, a dying tradition, when a new and original American art form was created, one drawing heavily from that strain of humor and eventually defining American comedy in the twentieth century: vaudeville. And it was here and then that seltzer siphons were adapted by the comedians inventing a modern version of this traditional humor.

The Three Stooges were best known for their film work, but their comedy began on the vaudeville stage. Some of their most popular routines came right from the badchan playbook. Verbal jousting. Eye-poking. Heavy objects smashed over heads.

And then came Hollywood with its voracious appetite for stage talent, with studios regularly scouting New York theaters in their efforts to transfer the vaudeville stage to the silver screen. And Hollywood was just one example among many of how vaudeville impacted the American entertainment industry, spreading seltzer's aggressive love one comedic spritz at a time. Vaudeville, wrote Henry Jenkins in his book on the topic, *What Made Pistachio Nuts?*, "provided a training ground for Broadway, Hollywood, nightclubs, radio, and television," and as a result, "its impact on popular culture could be felt for years after its demise as an institution,"[86] bringing a "particular style of performance characteristic of the vaudeville tradition."[87] That tradition, Gordon argued, was essentially that of the badchan made modern.

"It goes all the way to the 1950s," Gordon contended, "where *Esquire* magazine talks about the Yiddish invasion of American humor." This humor was the dominant form of comedy after World War II, nurtured and intensified at the hundreds of Jewish bungalow colonies and resorts in New York's Catskill Mountains, in the Borscht Belt, where it grew increasingly scatological and aggressive, where it was transferred back into nightclubs and later to Hollywood by comedians like Danny Kaye, Mel Brooks, and Jerry Lewis. Eventually it would move to magazines, books, and, perhaps most influential of all, television. But not just by Jews. "Jewish humor is no longer limited to Jews any more than jazz is limited to African Americans," Gordon explains. "It's a way of thinking, an aggressive notion toward the audience."

This aggressive style of comedy that seltzer and Jews once helped spread across America is alive and well but nowadays requires the participation of neither.

SELTZER VERSUS SALSA

Nostalgia for the old days of seltzer siphons and television clowns has long since faded in today's comedy routines. The cultural references are mentioned no more. "Seltzer was used in vaudeville and the old circus," one contemporary clown reflected, "but today, with a lawsuit-happy country, it sort of went out of style."

Perhaps the last great moment in seltzer comedy came through the wildly successful "sitcom about nothing," *Seinfeld*, a show whose embittered humor is a strong demonstration that badchanism is alive and well.

"The Pitch (Part 1)" ran in the fourth season of *Seinfeld*, in September 1992. In it, Jerry Seinfeld was invited by an NBC executive to pitch a new television series. (The audience was well aware that the fictional series referred to the very show it was watching.) Jerry, however, did not know where to start. A fresh idea was nowhere to be found. And then came seltzer.

Jerry and his friend George are eating at their regular hangout, Tom's Restaurant. George, apropos of nothing, complains that they don't have salsa on their table. Then an idea hits him: it must be impossible, he tells Jerry, for a person with a Spanish accent to order seltzer and NOT get salsa.

The two then riff back and forth in an increasingly absurd manner about the comedic similarities between the two words: salsa and seltzer.

And that's when inspiration hits. Their conversation, George tells Jerry, is the show they should pitch.

Jerry thought they were just talking. What would the show actually be about?

It would be about nothing, George replies with obvious glee. Over the rest of that season, that show about nothing was exactly what Jerry and his friends set out to produce, turning seltzer and salsa into the muses that inspire the creation of Seinfeld, one of the most popular television comedies of all time (albeit, just the fictional version).

Most telling about this moment in seltzer history: it did not actually involve any real seltzer, not even a seltzer siphon. It was just about the *idea* of seltzer as a drink one might commonly find in a diner or restaurant, contrasted with the idea of salsa as a condiment. Both signified cultural contributions from an assimilating immigrant group, and both pointed to items ethnically identified but available to all, making each thoroughly American.

In many ways, this *Seinfeld* scene demonstrated how seltzer had outgrown the metaphorical siphon that separated it from the rest of mainstream culture, a tension that once upon a time had kept it charged with the potential for aggressive love.

Until seltzer humor enjoys a fresh burst of effervescence, John Seekings and the rest of America have the Three Stooges to keep us laughing, reminding us of the time when seltzer played an important role translating a 350-year comedic history into a modern idiom and forever changed the face of comedy in America, one carbonated kiss at a time.

○ ○ ○

Whether he knew it or not, John Seekings's Pittsburgh Seltzer Works was built upon these four common seltzer associations. His customers wanted seltzer because it made them feel healthy and it tasted good, on its own or mixed with syrups. For some, it spoke to their nostalgia for classic comedy; for others it reaffirmed their ethnic identity. Each of these connections was at least a century in the making. Yet a new reason for people to drink seltzer was bubbling to the surface, one that more than anything would drive Seekings's immediate success and drive America closer to a state of Seltzertopia: the new perception that seltzer had become, most unexpectedly, hip.

The full story of the person who started it all, Randy Miller, has never been told. Until now.

Some of Richie Strell's favorite siphons

PART THREE

Seltzertopia

And now we enter the effervescent age.
Seltzer is widely available in plastic bottles,
in supermarkets and corner stores, in a
wide range of flavors.
Discover seltzer's global appeal,
then revisit John Seekings, now a seltzer
master in an emerging generation of
new seltzer professionals.

"As [seltzer] was present almost everywhere,
it deserved a cultic role in our lives that was due
to its magic simplicity, power of usefulness and
extraordinary vitality. It is a great feeling to
meet it, craving for it or being enslaved to it—
it is your decision."

—*Soda Water: A Cult Drink*
(a Hungarian Seltzer Museum exhibit catalog)

9

HOW SELTZER GOT ITS GROOVE BACK

In which seltzer is redefined for the modern age by Randy Miller,
who rejuvenates seltzer in the 1980s by successfully marketing
a new type of bottled beverage: flavored seltzer.

THE RISE OF ORIGINAL NEW YORK SELTZER

In 1987, Randy Miller sat on top of a carbonated empire that stretched across the country, with recent expansions around the globe into Saudi Arabia, Great Britain, Japan, and the Philippines, garnering annual sales of $100 million. This was far from where the twenty-three-year-old envisioned himself when he began driving the streets of the west side of Los Angeles in his dad's 1968 Mustang convertible, hawking this new drink called Original New York Seltzer (ONYS).

Six years earlier Randy had been a senior at Beverly Hills High, heading nowhere after graduation, which was right around the corner. At least that's what his dad, Alan Miller, an accomplished aerospace engineer, saw with concern. His son was kind of wild, doing poorly academically; college was certainly not in the cards. On the side, Randy had been going to stunt school, an attractive option for a boy growing up in Hollywood's shadow. Concerned about Randy's future, Alan wanted to help his son learn responsibility and give his life some focus. Before Randy turned eighteen, they created Original New York Seltzer.

Alan first had the idea on a trip to New York for a wedding. Chatting with his uncles who still lived in the city, he realized a good New York drink could do well on the West Coast, where Alan was raising his family. Alan knew little about the beverage industry—he was trained as an engineer and had a PhD in psychology—but seltzer ran in his blood. His grandfather, Jack Miller, was the first relative to get into the seltzer business, back in the horse and buggy days. Alan's father, Frank Miller, inherited the business and drove a truck around Brooklyn. He shared the business with his two brothers and together they sold seltzer and flavored syrups. Eventually, they replaced seltzer with beer and soda and turned their business into a cash and carry warehouse, as did many other New York seltzer men.

Alan's crazy idea was to turn back the clock, but with a twist: take his father's old business to a new level, selling not just seltzer *and* syrups but seltzer *with* syrups. Could Alan and Randy, without any direct experience, revive the family business? Alan returned to California driven to create this opportunity for his son. The plant could be located back in New York and managed by family members. Truckloads of bottles could travel the country to arrive for sale in the local Los Angeles market. Randy received the news with excitement, and in 1982 the company was born. Alan, of course, still worked full-time. So the company's success depended upon Randy, fresh out of high school, and his indomitable spirit.

Randy was responsible for arranging the transport of the product from his great-uncles' plant back in Brooklyn and storing the bottles in a small warehouse when they arrived on the West Coast. He worked out of his parents' garage but spent the vast majority of his time out on the streets, picking up accounts and delivering bottles. He learned early on it was all about the distribution; the key to selling seltzer was getting good business accounts and getting their cute little bottles up on the store shelves.

Randy would overload the Mustang with forty to fifty cases per trip for distribution to stores around Los Angeles, enough weight to require replacement of the suspension system three times. "I was working my tail off driving 150 or 200 miles a day," sometimes for as long as fifteen hours at a time, he reported a few years later.[88] The Mustang was soon replaced with a more practical vehicle, a Jeep, which could hold seventy cases.

Alan picked the first accounts for his son. "I think my father knew those guys," Randy explained. "And then he showed me how to do it." Randy learned fast. He raised selling seltzer to an art form. And he was unstoppable.

Randy knew he had only one shot to impress a store manager. He would go from location to location toting a cooler filled with their best flavors, never giving up until the proprietor had at least one taste. He would bring in his own plastic cup, open a fresh bottle (usually black cherry seltzer), then pour a glass. "I would pour it right in front of them and stick it in their hand. I wanted them to try it." In most cases, they did. "And once they tried it, I had their ear." The product would sell itself and Randy just had to manage the new accounts. With each new account, Randy's confidence grew and it became easier to pick up new accounts; the virtuous cycle was up and running. "When you believe in a product—and this was mine—you're selling part of yourself."[89]

Eventually business was good enough for Randy to move into an actual office. Alan came in a few times a month, but otherwise he was only involved via telephone. Back in his high school days, Randy often fought with his dad. Collaborating on their business brought them closer together, even though his dad, a perfectionist, drove Randy hard. "I had a lot of energy though and I worked long hours," he shared upon reflection, "so it did work out, you know?" The new headquarters were located outside Los Angeles in Walnut, California, combining an eighty-thousand-square-foot warehouse with an ultra-modern office. Randy designed everything he could, from the office layout to the accounting system.

The squat ten-ounce ONYS bottles would become iconic, not simply because of their mascots—those adorable marching bottles sporting running shoes, white gloves, and colorful bandanas—but because of how they stood out from the pack. Originally, ONYS came in bottles and cans of all shapes and sizes. "We ended up in one-liter plastics and cans," Randy explained, "but that ten-ounce was our flagship package"—Randy called it a "sexy package." With that small bottle they were able to get six-packs into supermarkets. Before long ONYS became the number one purchaser of those little bottles. "In fact," Randy recalls, "the plants had to reopen glass lines to keep up with our demand."

Alan designed the label for their plastic shield, inspired by New Yorker magazine covers. Alan also worked with his uncles on the flavors. They started with lemon-lime and orange, flavors they would never drop. Plain seltzer, however, didn't sell and was soon replaced by other flavors, like raspberry and black cherry, which soon grew dominant. Then clear root beer joined the flavor family; the clear color was one of their selling points. Through experimentation they learned that some flavors worked better than others, and all that learning went back into the product. "The orange flavors, with the lower pH and high acid levels, don't spoil, you know?" This informed ONYS's growth—new bottlers had to be willing to deal with a new, low-volume drink that required a higher level of cleanliness so it could stay natural and avoid preservatives.

In the early years, Randy followed every possible lead. Restaurants. Lunch spots. Gyms. He wasn't actively targeting upscale locations at first; he just happened to be starting with the communities he knew: West Hollywood, then Beverly Hills. "Those areas you're going to have high-end accounts," Randy explained, "you know, nice lunch spots, nice health food stores, nice gyms—everything was nice." As the drink became popular over a few years, Randy was able to get into big restaurants and independent supermarkets.

So that's where the first ONYS route started. "It develops an upscale image because it was available in all these nice places and had a great case, you know?"

Revenue was coming in, just not at the speed Randy needed. It took three months to sell their first batch of sixteen hundred cases. When it was time to produce more, the payments for that first load had yet to be collected. They were having a hard time keeping up with expenses. "We were in a bad position," Randy recalled. "No money. Glass bills piled up. Lots of products in accounts receivable. We had to decide whether to quit or to mortgage the house."

The bank offered Alan a fifty-thousand-dollar loan as a second mortgage. It would be a big risk, doubling down on their seltzer gamble. "We decided to go balls out," Randy said, "and hope to God we would do it."

It was a big gamble for sure, but it paid off. They had a product that tasted great, appealed to those with an interest in natural foods and healthy lifestyles, and was selling in upscale locations. "It was about time somebody combined what used to be big, clunky seltzer-water bottles and containers of syrup," Alan said at the time, "into a nice little bottle that you can open and drink right away."[90] Their strategy worked, for a time. Seltzer was selling. But then they saturated their market. Randy needed a new way to distribute. He needed new landscapes to conquer.

"I got really aggressive and started talking up other drink distributors," Randy explained. He tried not to let his youth—and apparent inexperience—get in the way. "In the first two minutes, they think, 'He's young. He has long hair.' After five minutes, they see I know about the business, and in ten minutes they might learn something."[91] Hansen Juice was the first distributor he convinced.

With a distributor who had his back, Randy didn't have to go door to door—the distributor did it for him. But still, juice, soda, and water all competed for the same limited shelf space. Looking for more distributors, Randy discovered Sunset Beverages through an existing account. He called them up and arranged a meeting.

By this point everyone in town knew the ONYS brand and was following it. It was selling well all over—not only in Hollywood and Beverly Hills, but also in Santa Monica and areas like Hermosa Beach and Manhattan Beach. "They wanted it right away," Randy recalled, referring to Sunset Beverages, "and we started sending them truckloads." But that wasn't all. "They offered to introduce me to some of their friends, some of the beer distributorships" that ran in the same area.

Randy grabbed those reins and, as history shows, rode across the world.

Beer was often sold at the same locations as other beverages, but in a different section and by its own distributors. And these distributors were hurting. Nationwide beer sales were slumping, and they needed something that would sell, even something as untraditional as seltzer. This created opportunities for ONYS to go national through beer distributors. "That's how I started with three or four of them in Southern California. It was by just luck," Randy said. "We didn't realize that beer distributors were looking for something new." Alan, however, could see how perfect it was. "This was the logical place . . . to snare new markets."[92]

One was a Budweiser distributor whose dad owned two big Anheuser-Busch distributorships. They spearheaded the development of a network in Southern California carrying ONYS. At the same time, Randy made a deal with another entrepreneur who took on distribution in Northern California. Then there were two more Anheuser-Busch distributors, brothers in Oregon, who took on the whole state, and the biggest beer distributors at that time in Washington joined on as well. Going up and down the coast, Randy was setting up a network of brokers, each of whom would be responsible for his own territory.

ONYS hired a national sales director (a guy from Anheuser-Busch, who knew beer) to push distribution east. In the next eighteen months, ONYS did, supported by six hundred beer distributors. "And I met with every single one of them," Randy recalled. He helped their salespeople launch the brand, talking with them about all the success ONYS was having and how much everyone loved their drinks. During this period, Randy celebrated his twentieth birthday, still too young to legally drink beer.

ONYS reached into all corners of the country. For example, the local paper in Boise, Idaho, interviewed a New York transplant, Blossom Turk, principal of Boise High School, on the arrival of ONYS. "I remember the adults used to drink it," she said, recalling seltzer as a child, "mostly because it was healthy and aided digestion." She'd tried ONYS and liked it. "The flavor is similar, but because it is actually flavored, it makes it more fun."[93]

It was time for a new bottling solution. Randy knew they needed state-of-the-art bottling lines, but they could never afford to build their own. Again, luck blew their way. Just as Randy could not have known how much beer bottlers needed ONYS to solve their problems, soda companies were tackling their own challenges. ONYS could once again provide the solution. As bottling plants around the country found their Coke, Pepsi, and 7Up products moving into cans, their glass-bottling lines were lying fallow. The big soda-bottling plants gladly took on the production of ONYS as contract packing, even though they would be creating competing products. "That's how we were able to pack it clean," Randy explained, "with minimal microorganisms, yeast, and bacteria, so the brand had a good shelf life."

Randy then hired salespeople for ONYS who helped the beer distributors start their own nonalcoholic divisions, with their own sales force focused on the brand. The salespeople helped distributors figure out, for example, that some ONYS clients might not appreciate a delivery from a beer-branded truck; schools and hospitals preferred a truck with a cute ONYS logo on the side. "So, all of a sudden, they're hitting a lot of accounts that they never stopped at before because all they had was beer products." The more ONYS distributors paid attention to these nonalcoholic accounts, the more they ended up building their network. It was a symbiotic relationship— ONYS needed the beer distributors to expand their distribution, and the beer distributors were learning how to diversify their businesses.

Randy and his dad built ONYS from a small LA-based route that defined the brand as delicious, upscale, and a rising star. The one-two punch of the national beer distribution network and the big soda-bottling plants followed, transforming ONYS into a $100 million company in just a few years, growing from three thousand cases sold in 1982 to over thirteen million cases in 1987.

"These are not novelty items," argued Larry Jabbonsky, editor of *Beverage World* magazine, to his readers. "It's a new category. It's redefining the traditional soft-drink market as we know it."[94] The problem, of course, was that ONYS's success brought attention to their distribution magic as others sought to compete in this new category. New brands modeled themselves on ONYS, came into production, and went after the same distributors. "We paved the way," Randy said. "Alan and I were the pioneers of what they were calling us: the new age beverage category. We were living like rock stars."

Randy and his dad lived in the newly reopened Mondrian Hotel. "Mondrian was where you're seeing all the stars who were big back in the '80s," Randy recalled. Late night talk shows kept their guests there. Rock stars stayed there. Some even lived there, like David Coverdale of Whitesnake. The Millers grew close with the hotel owner and the famous guests, and before long, ONYS sponsored celebrity-heavy parties to promote their flavored seltzers. "We would sponsor some of the big Oscar and Emmy parties. . . . There were lots of celebrities showing up with their awards." An expanded events division of ONYS planned and ran the parties. "We made sure New York Seltzer was prominent throughout."

By this point in 1987 and 1988, Randy's grandfather Frank, the inspiration for so much of ONYS, wasn't well. He suffered from Parkinson's and had to be taken around in a wheelchair. Before he passed, he attended at least one of these parties. There he saw recent Oscar winners holding their statues and drinking seltzer. And he was amazed. "Frank never thought it would work," Randy explained, referring to taking seltzer upscale, "because, you know, to him seltzer was cheap . . . 'two cents plain' cheap." Once upon a time, seltzer had a low-end image; now, in part thanks to his son and grandson, it was the drink of choice of the Hollywood elite.

AT THE TOP

Buoyed by the rise of Original New York Seltzer, Randy could afford to get whatever he wanted, and what he wanted often made the news. His eccentric and conspicuous consumption— including wild animals and race cars—attracted the media less interested in a seltzer company and more interested in the outlandish habits of its CEO.

Randy was even featured on an episode of *Lifestyles of the Rich and Famous*. "Randy Miller!" the segment shouted, with "Sultan of Seltzer" at the bottom of the screen. "He'll do just about anything to convince you his soda is the drink you'll fall for," referencing the first ONYS commercial that redefined what seltzer could mean to American consumers.

That first Original New York Seltzer commercial was only thirty-seconds long, but designed exclusively for MTV, with rapid quick cuts and a rock-and-roll soundtrack, it really packed a punch. In fact, back in 1986 one might be forgiven for confusing it with a new video for Whitesnake, whose lead singer, David Coverdale, belted out the commercial's original theme song:

> There is nothing in the world . . .
> There is nothing in the world . . .
> There is nothing in the world . . .
> There is nothing in the world just like New York Seltzer!
> It's the original.
> There is nothing in the world . . .
> There is nothing in the world tastes like New York Seltzer!
> No seltzer ever tasted so good!
>
> (*spoken*) The Original New York Seltzer. Now available, everywhere![95]

The theme song played over thirteen shots, starting with a young man looking down from a ledge as his shoes hung over the edge, ten stories above ground. One hand held the balcony railing, the other a bottle of seltzer. A California blonde on the ground looked up as the man leaned forward, arms spread like a

"He'll do just about anything to convince you his soda is the drink you'll fall for."

diver pre-belly flop, as she and the camera followed his downward descent as he held his seltzer.

She whipped her hair behind her shoulder and shot a seductive gaze toward the camera, presenting a bottle of black cherry seltzer to the young man, who had landed and now walked toward her with a leashed tiger and a wall of paparazzi behind him. The camera zoomed in on a ten-ounce bottle of vanilla cream seltzer, then, closer to the label, blueberry seltzer. Closer still, raspberry seltzer.

Then a close-up of the tiger licking its chops. Then, pouring seltzer on his own head, the man who jumped (an unnamed Randy, in fact) stood next to the blonde at center stage while another man pointed up to the balcony. Then a quick cut showed a ten-ounce bottle of cola berry seltzer and, closer, orange seltzer. Closer still: black raspberry seltzer. Then a flashback montage to his jump, this time shot from a second angle, and a third angle, then a fourth, each time the camera following the downward descent, until . . . shot twelve: an airbag viewed from above, with the jumping man landing on the final musical beat.

Shot thirteen summed it up: a crowd lingering outside the hotel and the animated appearance of the ONYS logo.

The round ONYS logo was adapted for Randy's "Original New York Seltzer presents Alphy's Soda Pop Club," which arranged child-celebrity parties hosted by Randy with his friend Alphy Hoffman and Alphy's dad, a casting agent for child celebrities. The ONYS mascot was seated on top, arms held wide and welcoming.

The publicity just rolled in. "We have the top celebrity kids at the time drinking New York Seltzer, posing with it wearing our clothes, even the kids that had Coca-Cola contracts." A typical group shot in magazines like *Teen Beat* would feature the party's hosts surrounded by young stars like Alyssa Milano, Tori Spelling, and Christina Applegate. Often mixed somewhere in between was someone called "the Seltzer lady," a smiling ONYS employee dressed in a giant seltzer bottle (raspberry-flavored, in case you wondered).[96]

So when it came time to shoot the ONYS ad and they needed people to cheer Randy on as he jumped, the call went out to members of Alphy's Soda Pop Club, who showed up at the Mondrian in droves.

In high school, Randy had explored life as a stunt man, learning how to jump from heights as high as fifty feet. Now the owner of a multimillion dollar company, Randy had phoned his old teacher Kim Kahana and told him he needed training to jump from double that height. He was literally putting his life in Kim's hands.

Standing on the ledge, he held a one-liter bottle of black cherry seltzer. The larger bottle was used to ensure it could be seen by the cameras on the ground. The flavor was black cherry because he knew its magenta label would really pop.

In the middle of the airbag on the ground was a bull's-eye. Randy landed right next to it. "I basically hit my mark," he said, "and it felt really good."

Then he opened the seltzer he had carried down ten stories and poured it all over his head.

Meanwhile, the crowd went crazy. And it wasn't just the Soda Pop Club regulars. The hotel, as always, was full of celebrities. One of those celebrities was comedian Rodney Dangerfield, in his mid-60s, riding high after a string of successful films, from *Caddyshack* to *Back to School*. After Randy landed, Dangerfield was heard to say, quite loudly, "I wonder what this kid would do for a real drink."

USA Today covered the jump and announced the upcoming ad a week before it aired. Readers of *Teen Beat* saw, alongside images of celebrity teens, a photo of a man jumping off a building holding a seltzer bottle. *People* magazine ran an article titled "Fizz-biz Whiz Randy Miller Leaps into High-Rise Hype."[97] "Alan Miller didn't exactly approve of his son's stunt," the article reported, "but says, 'Dissuading Randy from leaping from my hotel was impossible. The guy lives on the edge.'"

After the first commercial aired, Randy looked forward to doing some kind of stunt every few months, turning each into its own commercial. "But after the first one, even though I was holding a bottle of our water, the focus shifted from the product to the stunt." So, Randy's first New York Seltzer stunt was also his last: "We want to keep the public awareness of our products at the forefront, because, after all, we should never forget that the real star of the show is the product itself."[98]

Unfortunately for Randy, that star was about to fall, and there was no airbag waiting to catch it. His "seltzer sultanate" was about to come under attack.

THE COMPETITION

Randy was on the plane with his dad flying to St. Louis. They were traveling to meet with Anheuser-Busch. Many of their first distributors were affiliated with Anheuser-Busch. Now, the giant beer company was interested in buying out the Millers. Anheuser-Busch wanted to own ONYS. Randy saw how much money was on the line and finally realized what was actually going on—Original New York Seltzer was becoming big!

Anheuser-Busch, however, wasn't the only one interested in the flavored-seltzer market; some companies were more interested in joining the competition. "Seltzer's going crazy," began one report from the *California Beverage Hotline*, an industry newsletter. "High prices not scaring anyone away."[99] It was turning into a new gold rush, with lower California once again at the center.

Sundance, Clearly Canadian, 5th Avenue Seltzer, Old San Francisco Seltzer, and Old Chicago Seltzer all offered flavored seltzers. *Entrepreneur* magazine wrote that while once ONYS had no competition, now they were forced to "battle with nearly 100 regional and national soft-drink companies."[100] Randy, however, showed little concern. "They got as close as they could to ours," Randy argued, "but we always had the best tasting one." Still, inside he felt it. "It's like an itch,"[101] Randy told a reporter.

"They've created a completely new type of drink," Andrew Calvin, editor of *Beverage World* magazine, said at the time.[102] "The word 'seltzer' now has a lot of consumer appeal," argued Bob

Coleman in an article titled "Future of Seltzer Drinks Sparkles."[103] Branded by the press as new age beverages, these new drinks were seen as still holding a boutique position within the marketplace. "But if they take hold," suggested the publisher of *Beverage Digest* magazine, "the giants will move in."[104]

Among the explosion of next-generation seltzer companies, ONYS was indisputably the king. *California Beverage Hotline* wrote in amazement, "For a soft drink company to make big things happen, as NYSeltzer did in CA this summer, is highly unusual if not downright unprecedented since the early days of Coke and Pepsi— and the stuff of which aspiring entrepreneurs' fondest dreams are made of." Then, in a final parenthetical observation, *California Beverage Hotline* added, "A rumor that A-B also is discussing a takeover of NYSeltzer has been denied by both companies."[105]

Behind the scenes, Randy and his dad had spent six months negotiating with Anheuser-Busch as the "giant" decided whether and how they might move in. But in the end, the purchase didn't go through. Randy just didn't trust how they wanted to change their product. "They didn't like a long name, you know?" They wanted a shorter name, something catchy, like "Bud." Maybe "ONYS" rather than Original New York Seltzer? It wasn't clear. What was clear was that the deal was based on performance, and both Randy and Alan were concerned that the changes would undermine the success of the company. "And that's what ultimately killed the deal."

Before parting ways, Anheuser-Busch revealed their plan B: Zeltzer Seltzer. If Anheuser-Busch couldn't buy ONYS and distribute it, they would make and sell their own. They already had the distribution system in place. "The Anheuser-Busch distributors didn't want it but they took it," Randy explained. "The same distributors that we had."

Zeltzer Seltzer released six flavors: raspberry, peach, blueberry, black cherry, vanilla creme, and cola-berry. Terry P. Poulos, head of Anheuser's beverage division, reported that sales of flavored seltzer—one percent of the $30 billion soft-drink market—had topped $260 million in 1986 and was expected to double in 1987. Clearly, they wanted a piece of that action. One article touting Zeltzer Seltzer ran a photo of a seltzer spigot from a local candy shop alongside the caption "Anheuser-Busch is the latest in a string of consumer products to add pre-packaged convenience to that old soda fountain stand-by—syrup and seltzer."[106]

While press coverage was welcoming, customers felt otherwise. Maybe it had something to do with Zeltzer Selzer's ad campaign, which was hard to categorize. The ads were just strange. In one print ad, a tray carrying the squat seltzer bottle (clearly modeled after ONYS's signature shape) was held aloft by a cartoonish 1950s-style waitress. Her name tag reads "Lou," she sports a button reading "Zeltzer Seltzer—something utterly new in the world," and her speech balloon tells the reader, "Drink it and nobody gets hurt." Another print ad had three dinosaurs standing around, each raising a bottle, while one offered the toast: "Here's to our future." What was a consumer to think? Zeltzer Seltzer—the drink for the about-to-be extinct? A radio ad, narrated by Lorenzo Music, the voice for the animated cat Garfield, was even odder, as nearly the entire commercial was delivered in pig latin: "Eltzer-zay eltzer-say—avored-flay oda-say."

Randy made flavored seltzer upscale and hip. Anheuser-Busch threatened to make it simply bizarre.

Three decades later, Randy was quite clear about who took the biggest hit during the seltzer wars: Coke and the other big soda companies. And they didn't take it sitting down. "They came after us," he said. "They had the government on us, you know?"

The government did indeed go after Original New York Seltzer. In the fall of 1987, five years into their meteoric rise, Randy opened his mail to discover an alarming letter from the Food and Drug

Administration (FDA), which was followed by a call from the New York State attorney general. There was nothing wrong with the contents of ONYS, Randy learned. It was still legal to sweeten or flavor carbonated water.

They just could no longer call it seltzer.

In the late 1980s, the FDA's definition of seltzer was remarkably outdated: seltzer still meant carbonated *mineral* water. And that's it. Not salt-free carbonated water. And certainly not sweetened or flavored carbonated water.

It didn't matter to the FDA that for a hundred years carbonated water had been delivered to customers as *seltzer*, by *seltzer* men, in *seltzer* trucks, by *seltzer* companies. Or, inversely, that their mineralized definition meant that Perrier and San Pellegrino were technically seltzer waters, whether they liked it or not. The FDA didn't care. As long as these "seltzer" products met bottled-water requirements and their ingredients were far from soda's, the FDA could focus their efforts on preventing botulism and more important matters.

"There is a lot of confusion," reflected Eugene Leger, an assistant to the director of the FDA's division of regulatory guidance, to the *New York Times*. "My advice is to forget about it."

Randy wished he could. Instead, he had a letter from the FDA requiring ONYS to change their label if they wanted to be in compliance with the law. At the time all ONYS bottles read "Original New York Seltzer. No Sucrose, No Artificial Color, No Artificial Flavor." All of which was true. But the FDA said including "No Sucrose" was misleading and would need to be removed. "Consumers may be misled into thinking that the product contains no sugars," Leger explained.

So ONYS removed the phrase from the next batch of labels. That step was easy. Then the New York State attorney general took things a step farther. Removing "No Sucrose" was not good enough for them. Using the word "seltzer" in and of itself, they argued, suggested the beverage contained no calories. So ONYS was offered two choices—add "soda" to the label or remove the bottles from shelves.

Any bottles for sale in New York State without the change after forty-eight hours would result in a $500 fine. Per bottle.

So, Randy stayed behind as his dad, Alan, got on a plane to meet with New York State attorney general Robert Abrams. Abrams was the chief legal officer of the State of New York and head of the Department of Law. The son of a Bronx candy-store owner, Abrams was no stranger to seltzer. Having built a reputation as an activist and consumer advocate, battling environmental polluters and charity frauds, he was now taking on "so-called seltzer."[107]

We have no record of what happened in that room. One can imagine Abrams or his staff reiterating what had already been written in the letter. According to the FDA, since ONYS wasn't mineral water, it wasn't seltzer. And with all the added sugar, it not only was not seltzer, but it also was soda. So how did ONYS intend to comply?

The attorney general had the law on his side, but the Millers had history, and local history to boot. Alan likely explained that the FDA's definition had no bearing on reality. Who was the FDA to tell New Yorkers that the past century's home delivery of seltzer was a sham? It made no sense. They knew what seltzer was—highly carbonated water. It was as simple as that. And Alan, who had recently left aerospace engineering to become the company's chief financial officer, probably delved into their history as a four-generation seltzer company with deep roots in New York City, where the first few thousand cases bottled in the same Brooklyn plant supplied Jack Miller's seltzer wagon.[108]

Whatever transpired, it was settled in the end: ONYS could keep its name and its association with seltzer. There would be no fines and no need to remove their product from the shelves. But the label would need an upgrade: it would now say "soda" as well.

Randy wasn't happy with the decision—it seemed so unnecessary—but for the moment it saved the business.

The FDA wasn't happy. "We have not agreed that by adding 'soda' . . . to the label that they have been brought into compliance with the law," Leger said at the time. "What they have done is introduce confusion." The FDA still refused to recognize that ONYS sold seltzer, but there was little the FDA was willing to do about it. "We are not prepared to expend limited agency resources to invoke formal regulatory action against the labeling of so-called seltzer." ONYS might have won the seltzer battle, but the FDA wanted to make it clear: the war wasn't over. "Our current unwillingness to act should not be interpreted as sanctioning of this misbranding, nor does it preclude action in the future."

But, in hindsight, the war *was* over. There was no further action. When the furor died down, ONYS quietly removed *soda* from its label. The government had argued for a seltzer rooted in the eighteenth century; the Millers had argued for a seltzer that had ruled most of the twentieth. But through this battle and their success in the marketplace, ONYS and their competitors eventually secured the unexpected emergence of a new branch in an evolutionary seltzer tree: flavored seltzer.

The first generation of seltzer was carbonated mineral water that naturally bubbled up from deep underground in European spa towns like Niederselters. This was followed by the second generation of seltzer, spurred on by Joseph Priestley and the industry that could now artificially re-create and sell spa-like water. The third generation reflected the emergence of America's new interest in pure water, free of minerals, "pure seltzer"—water infused with carbon dioxide and nothing else. So, in short, spa water inspired artificial spa water, from which minerals were removed to become pure seltzer.

When Randy and Alan Miller took on the FDA, the fight was over more than ONYS or consumer safety. The FDA was using a definition for seltzer that was two centuries old, based on the first generation, spa water. Seltzer was defined by the agency as "carbonated mineral water" and mineral water as "water from a natural underground supply." That meant even the second generation of seltzer from the nineteenth century—"artificial spa water"—didn't meet this definition. The Millers responded to the complaints of the FDA using the more common definition of seltzer's third generation, of "pure seltzer," and emerged victorious.

The irony is that ONYS didn't sell pure seltzer. Instead, it popularized a new generation of seltzer, a fourth generation, best described as flavored seltzer. For the first time, people could buy bottled seltzer with the flavor prepacked, not mixed in a cup at a fountain or on a kitchen counter. For some, flavored seltzer meant zero-calorie seltzer with a hint of natural essence. For others it meant something with a hit of calories. In either case, this new type of seltzer, which would rise in popularity until it became ubiquitous and lived alongside pure seltzer, did more than just signal a new type of beverage. With flavored seltzer, branding—always so important for beverages—took precedence over the drink's ingredients. Perception of seltzer trumped the bottle's actual content.

While ONYS continued to disrupt beverage definitions, it did so only by putting a modern twist on an old seltzer habit: adding natural syrups to seltzer. And that was a practice anyone could copy. Although Anheuser-Busch's play in the flavored seltzer market fell flat, local competitors were making an impact, and more competitors were coming. "It seems like I get an announcement on my desk every week about a new seltzer company starting up," Jabbonsky of *Beverage World* enthused to the *Los Angeles Times*.[109] For the first time, Randy had to look over his shoulder, keeping an eye on those trying to pass him, knowing he needed to find new ways to compete. Word of mouth, point-of-purchase displays, and celebrity sponsorship had taken them just so far. They were starting to run out of options.

THE FALL

"Original New York Seltzer had a high-end image," Randy once shared during a wistful moment, "until the end . . ."

When their distributors began to sell the competition's bottles, Original New York Seltzer began to lose its market share. "Our brand starts dropping 20 percent a year," Randy recalled, still frustrated decades later that he couldn't stop it, "every year, and we just couldn't turn it around. We couldn't get it, you know, back up." Because of the competition, they were forced to drop their prices. "We got to a point where we had to sell it really cheap."

Randy learned distributors were not the only ones he could not rely on. There was no loyalty among customers either. "The people drinking New York Seltzer were the same people moving from brand to brand," he came to understand. "That's why they tried us. They were trying new brands and new products." That's one of those things that are obvious, but only in retrospect. "They did it with us, and they did it with brands after us." ONYS might have been the first to discover this new breed of customers, but they were also among the first to feel their rejection. "It cost us our business."

Randy took the downfall of ONYS personally. "As part of my demise, you know, I lost track of what's important." For many years his mind had been elsewhere. Randy knew he was instrumental in building that first route, getting it picked up by small juice and beer distributors, and rolling it out nationwide. "Then we hired management to really run it." That's when Randy began to lose touch with the company. "It's not hard to fall into the money," he recalled, "and it's a hard and fast lifestyle. I definitely fell into it for sure."

Randy shifted gears when he realized he was losing his business. He and Alan did everything they could to save it. They tried introducing new drinks, like Original New York Express Iced Coffee. They put millions into it, gave it to the distributors, and watched it get hidden on the shelves. "It just didn't work." Nothing did. "There was a point where it was just—you know, there wasn't much we could do. I watched ONYS just stop selling."

In 1994, Original New York Seltzer filed for bankruptcy. As he turned thirty, Randy was surprised that the company had fallen apart. "Because it was so popular," he explained. "I mean, it was a high-quality, good-tasting drink. It should have had staying power, you know?"

After Randy lost the company, he had nothing to show for it. His personal savings were wiped out, and not just because of his extravagant lifestyle. "We thought we were investing our money responsibly," he said, referring to both his dad and himself, "and it turned out we were just getting ripped off. So, we lost millions." They made poor real estate investment deals. "We didn't have experience with that kind of money," he explained. "We ended up losing everything."

Randy especially didn't want to lose the fifteen animals he cared for in his animal compound. Ever since he was a little boy, Randy had been fascinated with animals in movies. Once ONYS started having success, Randy started donating money to animal sanctuaries, but he found that wasn't enough. He wanted to care for them. "I had to be around them and learn how to handle them and, you know, that was my thing."

He acquired the necessary permits and started an eighty-acre animal compound outside the city limits. He began with cougars, bobcats, lions, and tigers. Bears would come later. With assistance

from other local animal compounds, he was able to bring in people to care for the animals and work with him so he could gain experience.

Before long, visiting his personal compound wasn't enough. He built an atrium in his house so the cats could visit. He would take them to the ONYS office and to seltzer-related promotional events like the ONYS commercial. He wanted them around all the time. "Of course, at first it can be intimidating to enter the cage with the cats," Randy explained. "Approaching even a relatively small mountain lion can be a chilling experience. After a while, though, the animals become used to you, and they become your buddies."[110]

Randy saw an opportunity and he seized it. The year he filed for bankruptcy he started a new company that he runs to this day. Predators in Action provides wild animals to film shoots. "It was really just to save my animals," he confided. Now Randy had both a new way to make a living and a way to be with his animals all the time. For the last twenty years, Randy has grown Predators in Action, adapting to meet new challenges in the movie business.

Randy even started getting movie stunt roles himself, doubling for a main character locked in mortal combat with one of his "predators." He doubled for Russell Crowe, for example, in *Gladiator's* arena tiger battle. Randy added *Double Team* (in which he doubled for Jean-Claude Van Damme and fought a tiger), *Semi-Pro* (in which he doubled for Will Ferrell and fought a bear), and even *Transformers: Revenge of the Fallen* to his resume. In many of these films the fights didn't go exactly as planned, and Randy, bloodied yet bandaged, would return for another take.[111] For the first time Randy was building a life on his own, away from seltzer, apart from his father. Whenever Randy added a new animal to his stable of performers, he would put its picture on the wall and tell himself, "Okay, these animals are going to be stars someday." And then each day he'd wake up and get to work.

THE RESURGENCE

After seven decades of decline followed by four decades on the rise, seltzer returned with a vengeance. And 2015 was the year the news media finally noticed.

While ONYS and other flavored seltzer in the 1980s may have attracted positive headlines, they were mere blips in the universally negative coverage predicting seltzer's imminent demise. The *New York Times* ran the following headline: "Seltzer Keeps Bubbling, But the Business Has Gone Flat." And the *Atlantic* ran this one: "The

Last of the Seltzer Men." The former was from 1974, the latter from 2010. The dates, however, are irrelevant, as the gloomy tone of the articles remained unchanged in the intervening three-dozen years.

Then, in June of 2015, it took just one piece in the *Wall Street Journal* to turn the tide: "Seltzer's Fizz Is Back."[112] In the weeks that followed, newspapers around the country began reporting on their new discovery: sugary soda was dropping in sales, and waters like seltzer were taking their place. Again, the story can be told through headlines: *The Fiscal Times*: "How Seltzer Became the Hot New Drink";[113] *The Washington Post*: "How Seltzer Water Became Cooler than Coke";[114] *The Chicago Tribune*: "How Something as Tasteless as Seltzer Water Won America's Heart."[115]

In summary, here's the news: Seltzer is hot! Seltzer is cool! Seltzer is tasteless!

CBS News soon translated this coverage from print to television, airing the report "Sparkling Success: Why Seltzer Is Seeing a Boom in Sales." By the end of the story, the anchor exclaims with surprise. "Who'd have expected it? Seltzer's resurgent."

Of the many seltzer brands driving this "resurgence," one, Polar Seltzer, attracted fans as passionate as customers of Original New York Seltzer had been, while a second brand, LaCroix, proved that seltzer had never been more hip.

Twice a year since 2010, Polar Seltzer, based in Worcester, Massachusetts, has released limited-run, seasonal seltzer flavors they produce as gifts to seltzer lovers. Cucumber Melon. Champagne Strawberry. Toasted Coconut Crème. Each flavor makes you think "that sounds interesting" and conveys a sense of whimsy. Their release often leads to runs on grocery stores by devotees and a stream of social media posts full of photos of can-filled carts and bottle-stuffed trunks. One headline in the *Boston Globe* from 2015 summed up the scene: "The Cult of Polar Seltzer: Why One Brand of Carbonated Water Has New Englanders Obsessed."

Polar Seltzer's flavored drinks were a far cry from the company's origins in selling whiskey. Founded in 1882 by a German immigrant, the originally named J. G. Bieberbach Company changed its name in 1916 to Polar Beverages, adopted a new mascot (a polar bear named Orson), and jettisoned alcohol for carbonated beverages. Polar is still run by family members, and since the release of these limited-edition seltzer flavors, earnings have risen from $275 million in 2005 to $450 million a decade later.[116]

Then Polar did something no one saw coming. In the spring of 2016 they released a flavor of seltzer so absurd one could say it was an act as outrageous as a CEO taking a (stunt) leap off a hotel balcony. The flavor was called "Unicorn Kisses." And the good people of Massachusetts nearly lost their minds.

Anyone could imagine what cucumber-melon seltzer might taste like—for better or worse the flavor of cucumber mixed with the flavor of melon. But what did a unicorn kiss taste like? The packaging was of little help. The background was an array of pastel rainbows. Orson, the polar bear, seemed to have sprouted a unicorn horn. And each bottle came with a playful origin story:

> Once upon a time our great-great-grandfather arrived in New England with a pocket full of rainbows. Each night he searched Wachusett Mountain for a place to hide his treasure. Then, one eve he came upon a unicorn that was crying. He said, Don't be sad, for I will give you my rainbows. In return the creature blew a kiss and filled the man's bottle with a sparkle, called seltzer.[117]

For those still unsure about what unicorn kisses might taste like, the bottle explained: "Tastes like sparkling rainbows." One reporter found a couple who said it tasted like Fruit Stripe gum or the candy SweeTarts.[118] *Bon Appétit* magazine described it as tasting like "a watermelon Jolly Rancher with a bit of strawberry bubblegum aftertaste."[119] With a limited run of five thousand cases, however, few had a chance to find out for themselves, sending prices on eBay as high as one hundred dollars.[120]

A year later, Polar upped their game. Apparently, the unicorns in their seltzer farms were lonely and needed some friends. In the summer of 2017 they launched a limited run of eight-ounce cans called Polar Seltzer Junior, bringing back Unicorn Kisses (with new packaging featuring a unicorn) and introducing three new flavors: Dragon Whispers, Yeti Mischief, and Mermaid Songs. Launched on August 1, employees must have celebrated with high fives when they saw the headlines in the *Boston Globe* the next day: "People are stocking up on the new Polar Seltzer flavors like the apocalypse is coming."[121]

The staff of *Boston Magazine* tried their best to describe the flavors.[122] Yeti Mischief? Like Hawaiian Punch, but less sweet and tangier, with a subtle powdery flavor like that dust on Hubba Bubba gum. Dragon Whispers? It started with the smell of Pixy Stix, followed by the taste of strawberry and maybe pineapple. Mermaid Songs? A cross between Sour Patch Kids and Swedish Fish, with a hint of pine. *Boston Magazine* reviewed the new Unicorn Kisses as well, but their staff arrived at no consensus, suggesting everything from green apple Jolly Ranchers to Bath and Body Works cucumber melon foaming soap.

But this time, customers didn't have to rely on reporters or lucky fans on Facebook—while limited, these mini cans of fun were distributed widely. One Instagrammer nailed the frenzy with her post, a photo showing an ecstatic little girl pointing to her mom's open trunk bursting with hundreds (yes, hundreds) of the tiny cans. The caption read: "This is what happens at 8am when you are a #polarseltzer addict and they release new flavors."

While Polar had national aspirations, its beverages were still primarily enjoyed in New England. LaCroix, however, a regional product of the Midwest, has since gone viral, becoming the taste of a new generation.

Take, for example, the sold-out exhibition at a small art gallery in San Francisco in August of 2017. It featured an unusual subject: cans of seltzer. The artist, a San Francisco-based street and mural artist who used the nom de plume fnnch, described his inspiration as "the beverage of choice of Millennials."

But these weren't portraits of just any seltzer cans. These were cans of LaCroix, a modern take on Andy Warhol's 1962 series *Campbell's Soup Cans*. In fact, fnnch referred to his own series as *Soup Cans for Millennials*, perhaps only half in jest.

9 Cans of LaCroix by fnnch

Positioned in a nine-by-nine grid, the top three paintings were flavored pure, lemon, and cran-raspberry. The bottom three were peach-pear, orange, and berry. In between sat coconut on the left, lime on the right, and in the center of them all LaCroix's most popular flavor (with over one hundred thousand followers on its own dedicated Instagram page), pamplemousse (a.k.a. grapefruit). Each can was depicted in the same contrasting colors as the real cans, with their font so-wrong-it's-right. "The cans are kind of ugly," fnnch told one reporter, "but kind of beautiful."[123]

Followers of fnnch received an email from the artist explaining his LaCroix-themed work: "I'm exploring some of the same cultural and aesthetic territories as Warhol did." He was inspired, in part, by a quote from Warhol, speaking about Coca-Cola: "What's great about this country is that America started the tradition where the richest consumers buy essentially the same things as the poorest." It didn't matter who was drinking it—the president, Liz Taylor, or your mom—everyone drinking it tastes the same Coke. Fnnch believed that times had changed, that LaCroix was now part of the cultural zeitgeist in an era drifting away from syrupy soda. Fnnch concluded: "The billionaires of Silicon Valley do not drink Coke. Movie stars do not drink Coke. But they do drink LaCroix. And you can too. There's something wonderful about that."

LaCroix (their website asks us to pronounce it "LaCroy," cheerfully adding, "It rhymes with 'enjoy'") comes from La Crosse, Wisconsin, a drink born in 1981 at a family-owned brewery. For two decades, it was far from hip, known as the go-to drink for Midwestern soccer moms.[124] Then, in 1996, it was purchased by National Beverage Corp., based in Fort Lauderdale, Florida, which added it to its slate of low-cost drink acquisitions, like Shasta. It would be another decade before a brand redesign would coincide with the emerging social media scene and the rise of what many now consider the "seltzer of choice for millennials."[125]

NATIONAL BEVERAGE CORP. SHARE PRICE

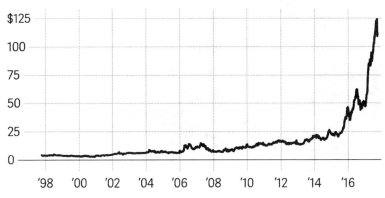

Data: FactSet

To become the drink of a generation LaCroix focused on the medium beloved by its target market of eighteen to twenty-nine-year-olds, Instagram. On the photo-sharing site, LaCroix responded to all of their fans' seltzer selfies and reshared them, filling the internet with images of "attractive young people hoisting a can at pools, beaches and other relaxing places,"[126] as the *Fiscal Times* described in their article "Tiny Bubbles, Big Business."

One fan even turned her post into a side business. Chelsea Steele, like many a twenty-one-year-old, loved LaCroix. "In my house, LaCroix is a part of the family," she shared with a blogger. "If we're out grocery shopping or one of us makes a quick trip to Target, LaCroix is as essential as dish soap or toilet paper." One day the phrase came to her, "LaCroixs Over Boys." She made a handful of shirts for her roommates and shared the photo on Instagram. LaCroix reposted it and asked for shirts for their staff to wear. Before long the shirt was covered in *Bloomberg Businessweek*, Business Insider, and BuzzFeed. Two years later Chelsea still had an active website offering the shirt for twenty-five dollars.

Most LaCroix fans, of course, were not looking to start a business. They were simply delighted when their favorite company gave

lacroixwater ● 　Follow

lacroixwater LaCroix over boys 🐬 (📷 @supchels)

Load more comments

ellabowles YESSS @liz.rock

jrlaz @hunterkarnedy watch out!

carriedawaytocali @k8gritsch

natehills1 @krunk_shox @craig_harvey1

carolinecweeks Where can I get this shirt?!

melsza @nszam my motto!

kristenramirez @cynntthiiaaa you need this shirt

mambonik @lexahemphill

etanmcdonk @gch717

gch717 @coldenchase hahahah why didn't we think to sell these

them a social media megaphone to amplify their passion. They didn't seem to mind that LaCroix relied on their photos to brand their beverages as lifestyle choices. "By visually aligning itself with users who match the colorful, carefree LaCroix brand image," wrote one analyst, "this beverage company has secured a sparkling place in millennial hearts . . . and shopping bags."[127]

In 2017 the gay Chicago rapper Big Dipper released a video for his new single "LaCroix Boi." *Food and Wine* magazine described it as a "90s-style slow jam" that "hits you straight in your LaCroix-loving heart, promising a romantic evening of popping cans of seltzer with your lover."[128] *The Advocate* simply called it "the new song of gay summer."[129]

Big Dipper's lyrics explore the disconnect between the Midwestern soccer moms who kept the brand alive and the millennials who claim it today:

> My mamma use to drink room temp' LaCroix
> As a boy I thought it nasty but now I enjoy
> Carbonated elixir
> It gives me my fix
> Just what I need
> Sweet potion indeed[130]

In the video, after delivering these lines in a car made of LaCroix cans, Big Dipper rolled out on a hoverboard wearing an outrageous jacket composed of empty LaCroix cans (he had already poured seltzer over his head and serenaded us from his throne of, wait for it . . . LaCroix cans).

"It's been around forever," Big Dipper told *New York Magazine*'s food blog *Grub Street*, "so why is it hip now? Why do you pay more money for this water? It's all so silly, but I'm also obsessed."[131]

With an obsession shared across the country, LaCroix is now carrying the torch first lit by Randy Miller. By 2009 sales of LaCroix were reportedly around $58 million; within six years, sales had more than tripled to somewhere between $175 and $226 million a year, becoming the fastest growing seltzer brand in America.[132]

Polar and LaCroix were far from alone in reaping the benefits of this new age of Seltzertopia. In fact, in the summer of 2015, a surprising new headline announced the return of a classic: "Vintage Soda Brand 'Original New York Seltzer' Is Making a Comeback."

"As a kid growing up in the '80s, my family and friends all knew and loved Original New York Seltzer," said Ryan Marsh, new

Rapper Big Dipper on a throne of LaCroix cans, in his "LaCroix Boi" video

president of the reborn Original New York Seltzer. "We're excited to roll out to America again and introduce Original New York Seltzer to a whole new generation."[133]

When Randy and Alan sold off the company, ONYS quickly went off the shelves, leaving behind nostalgic memories of one of the first true "cult" soft drinks. Letter-writing campaigns were organized by ONYS fans, unsuccessfully calling for the drink's revival. "Original New York Seltzer really was ahead of its time [with] no artificial flavors, colors, or preservatives," said Marsh. "Adding color to drinks is just stupid."[134]

They would maintain the aesthetic choices—from the bottle design to the edgy commercials—and increase the focus on being a "natural" drink, with cane sugar as the sweetener. "ONYS never has and never will make boring drinks," Marsh said. "Sparkling waters were a fancy, indulgent thing. We're making that happen all over again."[135]

Randy's rebranding of seltzer from two-cents plain to upscale might have outlasted the original product that introduced it. What was lost during the relaunch, however, was Randy's involvement. "We believe the original owners have moved on to other interests," Marsh reported. "We didn't have any interaction with them during the process."[136]

"We sold forty-eight million cases," Randy said with pride, after being contacted and asked to reflect on ONYS more than two decades after he was forced to fill their last bottle. "That's how many cases we ended up selling over twelve years. That's about three billion bottles. So, we sold quite a bit. I think we introduced, you know, the flavored seltzers to America."

How did he feel about that, as a legacy?

"Feels good," he said. "I wish I had more to show for it, though, in terms, of you know, money. But I'm proud of what we accomplished, for sure, definitely."

Randy also felt deep appreciation for the bold choices his dad had made by helping him start a risky business right out of high school at a time when he felt more like a troubled youth. "He gave me responsibility," he said. "It really straightened out my life."

Randy didn't regret avoiding higher education and taking the quick path into the world of entrepreneurs. "I've got everything to learn here," he said at the time. "Negotiating. Law. Computers. Personnel management. Why go to school?"[137]

Did he ever consider getting back into the business?

"I do miss the soft drink industry," he shared. "I was upset when we went to that bankruptcy and wanted to get away from it but . . ." He seemed to consider the distance from then to now, how time healed wounds, or at least dulled them. "It's been twenty years . . ." he suggested, then trailed off, as if asking whether some debt had been paid.

A few months later when speaking with *The Guardian*, Randy had more to report. "I am still getting animal work, but there's a thought of possibly getting back into the soft-drink business with my father," he said. "There could be an opportunity to come in with a great tasting drink."[138]

It sounds like Randy might be considering taking his next great leap.

10

A PASSION FOR SELTZER

*In which we witness how seltzer is loved around the world, how John
Seekings turns the Pittsburgh Seltzer Works into a successful business, and
how others around the United States develop a similar passion for
old-fashioned seltzer works and bring the bubbly to their own communities.*

A MAGIC SIMPLICITY

While Randy Miller's flavored-seltzer revolution helped fuel the
drink's return to prominence, there were countries outside the
United States where the sparkling elixir had never lost its sway.
Two of the most prominent were Argentina and Hungary.

Gustavo Leiva immigrated to California from Buenos Aires in
1991. He began work as an IT manager doing instrumentations
for refineries, levering his lifelong experience with computers and
electronics. But after two decades, he took a different path—one
reminiscent of both John Seekings and Kathryn Renz—and,
with his wife, Marcela, developed the largest seltzer company in
Southern California: Soda Buenos Aires.

Growing up in Argentina, Gustavo recalls the *sodero* delivering seltzer once a week to his house, carrying the crates of siphons from the back of his horse-drawn, two-wheeled wooden cart. Vans or trucks would eventually replace the carts in the larger cities, but the siphons didn't change. Argentinians love their seltzer.

"Since we were kids," he said, "we were introduced to drinking one little drop of wine full of seltzer," he said. "You think you are drinking wine with the adults. And it gets so into you, since you were a kid. And you maintain your tradition."

These traditions began, Gustavo surmises, with the Italian roots of his country. "Ask them their favorite food, just pick any Italian food, and you'll have what we eat in Argentina. Gnocchi. Cannelloni. Anything Italian." In the first half of the twentieth century, Italian immigrants brought their carbonated predilections to the New World. And while these habits may have faded over time back in the Old World, they found firm purchase in Argentina and followed its citizens wherever they went.

One of those places was Southern California. Gustavo and his wife split the work: Marcela does most of the bottle washing and filling ("she is the manufacturing portion of the process"), while Gustavo dedicates his time to their enormous delivery area: from San Diego in the south to Santa Barbara in the north, covering all points in-between (including this little city called Los Angeles). "I would say that about 50 percent is the Argentinian community," Gustavo explained. "We see the future pretty bright ahead of us. We see ourselves growing big-time."

As popular as seltzer might be in Argentina and among its emigrants, it is perhaps no coincidence that it is Hungary, not Argentina, that boasts the only seltzer museum in the world: Hungary's historic connection with the carbonated drink is part of its national identity.

A fountain in Hungary in the shape of a seltzer siphon

Any visitor to Hungary can't fail to notice the profusion of siphons. Like an infestation of tribbles on *Star Trek*'s *Enterprise*, they are everywhere. At someone's house, a visitor will be offered a spritzer, a combination of wine and seltzer so popular it might as well be the national drink. Mixtures of various proportions are known by different names, such as "minor spritzer" (*kisfröccs*), "major spritzer" (*nagyfröccs*), and "long stride" (*hosszúlépés*), with more than thirty recognized spritzer varieties.

Located in the small city of Szeged, the Soda Water History Museum can be found in Saint Stephen Square, housed within a round, refurbished, historic water tower, filled with artifacts donated by a local, century-old seltzer works. The modest exhibit had once traveled the country before finding a permanent home in this city of seven hundred thousand. The exhibit and its catalog— *Soda Water: A Cult Drink*—paint quite a fascinating portrait of one country's obsession with seltzer.

"Soda water symbolizes sparkling life, activity, and dynamic force and there, deep in our minds, it works like a volcano to erupt," the exhibit declares in both Hungarian and poetic English. "Knowing the maxim that says 'we get identical to what we eat,' we come to love it easily because we ourselves want to be something like that." To say the exhibit's curator liked to wax prosaic would be an understatement:

> [Seltzer offers] recreation and joy, quenching thirst and having a good time to millions of people. It is an accepted companion in our everyday life, by now it has become food of basic importance that could not be missing from the tables of the different social strata. We have already mixed it with wine and syrups, we believed and believe in its medicinal effect, use it for cooking and cleaning. It inspired our greatest artists, it served a model to literary and artistic works. As it was present almost everywhere, it deserved a cultic role in our lives that was due to its magic simplicity, power of usefulness and extraordinary vitality. It is a great feeling to meet it, craving for it or being enslaved to it—it is your decision. We enjoy every drip—all the time and in every way. . . . It has a place at our tables, it has its place in our lives. We get it, we transubstantiate it, and we get transubstantiated ourselves. It quenches our thirsts and makes us burning. It bombards us with bubbles, and cools us down as a waterfall. It breaks in our world and makes peace. It calms down and agitates.

The curved museum walls inside the multistoried water tower support glass cases of beautifully crafted and decorated seltzer siphons, red hand-powered filling machines with majestic round arcs, and historic posters from seltzer's past, which together tell the tale of how Hungary fell in love with seltzer's "magic simplicity."

Hungary's soda-water industry was launched in 1841 when Ányos Jedlik (inventor of the dynamo, an electric generator) opened the country's first seltzer plant. Jedlik developed an inexpensive method for injecting water with carbon dioxide, and the industry exploded. By the turn of the century, his one small plant was in competition with almost five thousand other Hungarian seltzer works.

Meeting the needs of local markets, most seltzer plants were family run and passed down from one generation to the next. But unlike in the United States, Hungary's seltzer industry survived the Great Depression, World War II, and privatization (under the new socialist regime). A family could work hard and make a living through seltzer. The controlled economy kept out the sort of competing forces that in the United States had allowed emerging soda giants, like Coca-Cola, to triumph over the hand-filled siphon industry.

Tibor Bánffi, whose son and daughter-in-law would later spearhead the collection for the exhibit, took action in the mid-1970s, when the restaurant industry was privatized by the government. Before long nearly every restaurant in Szeged served his soda water, with sales totaling upward of 150,000 liters a year. Business boomed, not just for Tibor's Bánffi Soda Limited Partnership but for the other thirty-five hundred seltzer plants around the country.

Then the Berlin Wall fell. The communist era came to a close. A new era was approaching like a tidal wave, shaped by the European Union and its open markets. Seltzer works around Hungary were terrified, sensing the forces of soda giants and their efficiencies of scale massing on the border, preparing to swoop in, capture their markets, and blow their hand-crafted industry into oblivion. Some even feared that seltzer production would be banned, confused by the lack of soda-water regulations within the European Union (EU). Before Hungary joined the EU, something had to be done. They had to prepare to compete. And to compete they had to modernize and take seltzer into the twenty-first century.

The industry developed a new food safety system. They replaced old equipment that had been passed down from generation to generation with modern machinery. They set aside glass siphons and developed reusable, hygienic, and environmentally friendly plastic bottles with steel canisters. And, just to cover all their bases, they successfully lobbied the EU to earn Hungarian soda-water production the classification "Guaranteed Traditional and Special Product," the only one such designated within the country, in case that afforded them additional protections. In 2004, Hungary joined the EU. A decade later, the seltzer industry lived on, with roughly fifteen hundred plants employing ten thousand people.

To save a tradition, they had to change it.

A TRUE SELTZER MAN

Soon after they began talking to customers, John and Jim saw the opportunity for the Pittsburgh Seltzer Works to grow bigger than it had been. Everyone they spoke to about the business came back with the same response: they all thought it was tremendously cool. "Everybody wanted to squirt a bottle," Jim reflected. "Everybody wanted to taste the seltzer." It didn't matter who they were. Young or old. Male or female. Regardless of their socioeconomic background, they would ask, "Can I try it? Can I taste it?" After a few weeks of this, John and Jim looked at each other and shared the thought on each of their minds: "You know, maybe we sort of have something kinda neat here."

Once a week John met with Jim to talk strategy and financials, hiring, and such. Then John would execute their plan. By the end of the first year, December of 2010, they delivered to two hundred residential customers plus half a dozen restaurants. "Let's keep it all in perspective," Jim shared at the time. "This is not Apple computer. It's just gone from a tiny, out-of-your-hip-pocket business to a legitimate, full-time, Pittsburgh-based local business." That in itself was an enormous leap. "Whether it goes beyond that, who knows? I don't have the drive or ambition I once had to turn it into something bigger, even if it could be."

By year's end, as the Works' success grew, John was no longer enough. Two people came on to help John bottle, then two more to help deliver. He went in every day, first thing in the early morning, brewing, getting sprayed with ice cold water, and reveling in it. Then he would change into a professional uniform, tie and all, and go back to his advertising company, as if returning from a world as different as Wonderland.

The delivery base spread from one neighborhood to another. The number of siphons doubled, from thirty-five hundred to seven thousand. They bought a second bottling line from a defunct seltzer works: a carbonator and a four-head bottler as backup. John Seekings spent less and less time at his advertising company and more and more time at the Works until, one day, almost imperceptibly, the ratio flipped and the bulk of his days were spent in jeans and sneakers, soaking wet, wrestling a 110-year-old machine into submission. John Seekings had become a true seltzer man.

"It's so contrary to what I've been doing for so many years," John shared, "which is in an office, on an airplane, in meeting rooms." Recently a seltzer customer dressed in a suit and tie came in from a very affluent part of the city; John wore a pair of ripped jeans and was soaking wet. The man might have been a mirror image of John in his former life. The customer asked him, "How do you like it?" John replied, "I can't even begin to tell you." He still enjoyed his day job, but the Works offered a completely different form of enjoyment.

"I'm always happy when an advertising campaign does well, or an ad looks good, or a TV commercial looks good," he reflected, "but this is something different. This is something you touch, feel, drink." Nothing says, "I just made this!" like a freshly filled crate of siphons.

"At the end of the day I can walk out of there exhausted and tired and sore from moving these things, and that's fine because I can look at the end result of all that hard work and see it. You can look down and see it."

The logo for Pittsburgh Seltzer Works

On top of all that there is the deep satisfaction of a burden carried with pride. "There's not many of these jobs left. There's a certain responsibility I feel and enjoy and kind of embrace, like, 'Hey, we're going to keep this going.'"

Some days, when John would arrive at six in the morning, the sun having barely begun its rise, he might put his hand on the chillers that had been running for twenty-four hours. But now he could tell by feel if the temperature was right. As he'd turn everything on, he'd shift focus to the present moment. He'd no longer wonder if the business was sustainable. He wouldn't think about how to grow it. There was only one thing on his mind: feeding the machine and making the best seltzer. "Everything else is kind of moot."

John's goal was never to turn around and sell the business. "It's inherently inefficient," he said. "You're hand bottling. It's labor intensive." And that's the point, where the beauty comes in. "As long as I can pay the bills to keep the lights on and keep the machinery working, I consider it an absolute success."

"People have actually asked me, 'Knowing what you know now, would you have still bought it? After all the moving, the stitches, and the hospital visits, and blown up bottles and the broken-down machines, broken-down trucks, and everything else?' My answer, absolutely 100 percent, 'Yes!'" John said passionately. "I wouldn't even think twice about it. Great decision. Learning a lot of life lessons having a business license, but I wouldn't think twice about it. Wouldn't even think twice. It was a great thing, and we're fortunate to have it."

Before long, new seltzer men began to crop up around the country, seeking out John for advice on how they, too, could find success through seltzer in their own communities. If John was possibly the last new B.S.S. (Before Sexy Seltzer) entry into the world of seltzer works, the first A.S.S. (After Sexy Seltzer) entries started to seek out Seekings.

SELTZER WORKS: THE NEXT GENERATION

When John first spoke with Ryan Pinnell, the founder of the new Treasure Coast Seltzer Works in Florida, it was like the tables had turned; where once John was the one reaching out for advice, now he was the one whose advice was sought after. John knew how important these calls were when he was starting out. He wanted to be candid and clear.

So he told Ryan to run as far away from creating a seltzer business as he could.

"Why on God's earth would you want to do this?" John asked. And Ryan explained, appreciating that they were so similar, both dot-com kids with smart marketing ideas; both willing to take risks and follow their passion.

John wanted to be sure Ryan understood the workload involved, something that had surprised him in the early days of the Pittsburgh Seltzer Works. He said, "Listen, when we first purchased this [company] with the assets, we had no idea what was going to happen." It was not a money-making venture but a "let's keep this thing going" kind of thing. That was their number-one priority, and everything followed from that.

Beneath the hard work and the pain, Ryan could hear reflections of what John had once heard when initially discouraged by Kenny Gomberg: the pride and the passion. That might just be a treasure worth seeking.

The funny thing is, until just a few years earlier, Ryan had never even seen a siphon. "I hated seltzer," he said, describing his life before the 2012 launch of his works. Yet, in little time, Ryan has become the latest unlikely evangelist preaching the gospel of seltzer.

Ryan's seltzer conversion began on a trip to Szeged with his Hungarian wife Simi. After building and selling a chain of D.C. area tanning salons, Ryan had moved to Florida, gained employment as a vice president of sales at a "green mobility" company; he had every reason to believe he knew just what life held in store. And then Hungary infected him with their passion for seltzer.

Ryan was amazed by the simplicity of the Hungarian approach. He realized Americans were stuck in the past. Hungary had modernized without losing its roots. Could America do the same? If so, what a rich market to exploit. He was charged up to get back home and get things started.

Connecting the dots, he knew he would need contractors and manufacturers to custom build Hungarian-style machines to meet American needs. Luckily, his job entailed finding and managing contractors. The problem was he barely spoke a word of Hungarian. "Not a lick," he said, just enough to order a beer. Fortunately, he knew someone who did speak Hungarian fluently: Simi, his wife.

Simi understood seltzer. She had grown up with it, and it was still an ever-present part of her family back home. She had never expected her husband to care about it, let alone try to convince her there was a niche market they could capture, not just opening a seltzer works but doing it in a whole new way in the United States, using Hungarian know-how.

She was in.

While researching the business, Ryan and Simi had a little boy. And the new business, like their boy, was a merging of two cultures. "It's a kind of a perfect marriage," he said, referring to their business partnership. "When you are sitting across from a major executive there and trying to be some kid from America who thinks he's got his stuff together, trying to cut a deal on some machinery being hand built, it's rather unique when you have to have your wife translate everything for you."

Together they launched Treasure Coast Seltzer Works. The business was named after the area in Florida around West Palm Beach in which gold supposedly was lost when a Spanish fleet sunk in the 1700s. People today still dive off the shore looking for treasure. With Treasure Coast Seltzer Works, Ryan and Simi would embark on their own dive for gold, so to speak, through waters not salty but effervescent.

Ryan and Simi went back to Hungary, as well as to the Czech Republic and Germany. They shared their plans and left local manufacturers intrigued. They returned with new stainless-steel machines. If Ryan's machines ever needed replacement parts, he could simply email the modern manufacturers, unlike the difficulty other seltzer works owners had in finding replacement parts for the one-hundred-year-old machines.

In January 2012, with only limited advertising, Treasure Coast Seltzer Works opened with two dozen customers, just enough to get a feel for things. Then it grew, fast. Within a month a local paper covered the new business, increasing their customers to 150 overnight. "Okay," Ryan said to Simi, as their profits became sustainable, "we've got a real business now."

Treasure Coast was a real mom-and-pop business. As with Gustavo and Marcela in Southern California, Simi filled the bottles and Ryan delivered them. "We're trying to build something to pass on down the line," he said, before adding, "I hope."

While John Seekings might have been surprised when he first heard Ryan's plans for a new type of seltzer works, the move by Alex Gomberg surprised his father, Kenny of Gomberg Seltzer Works, even more. Time and again, Alex had seen his dad interviewed about seltzer for an article here, a documentary there. He knew his family's seltzer history but had shown little interest in the Brooklyn filling station. Yet after he graduated from Amherst during the 2008 recession, Alex looked at his family legacy and at his dad's impressive bottle collection and saw something new: opportunity.

Alex's great-grandfather, Moe, was once a New York City seltzer man; Moe and a group of his peers had shared ownership of a filling machine, a co-op of sorts, and had hired a filler to keep the seltzer flowing. Seltzer men owned their own routes, their own customers, their own trucks.

At some point, Moe decided to put down the back-breaking crates and take ownership of his own machines. In 1953, Gomberg Seltzer Works was born. Back then, seltzer works had to pay their seltzer men a "loyalty" fee, as high as five hundred dollars. But even among the fierce competition, Gomberg Seltzer Works thrived.

Moe eventually passed the business down to his son, who eventually did the same. But by the time Kenny, Alex's dad, took over, the works was out of date; it supported only a handful of seltzer men and was a small side business adjacent to Kenny's beer and soda distribution company. The works was kept alive more to honor tradition and family history than for profits.

Alex Gomberg

After earning his master's degree in higher education adminis-tration, Alex moved back in with his family as he planned his next move. The economy was bad. Alex needed a job. He wished he could help his dad but didn't see a place for himself in the beverage dis-tribution center. Then he thought about the seltzer works and the bottles sitting around unused. So, in 2012, he talked with his dad about starting his own seltzer delivery business. "You don't do any deliveries right now," Alex said, "so why don't we see if we can start?"

"Are you nuts?" Kenny replied. "Are you sure this is some-thing you want to do? You're not going to be making a ton of money right now."

Alex replied he was not going to be making a ton of money anywhere while working in an entry-level position. And he could always lean back on his degree if necessary. "Let's do the seltzer now and see what happens."

Kenny needed more convincing. It is very labor intensive to run a delivery business, he warned his son. The customers needed constant managing. The bottles needed to be fixed, labeled, and maintained. Brand-new boxes would need to be built. There would be a lot to do.

"And this is the time to do it," Alex countered. "I'm living at home. I don't have that many expenses. I don't have children. I have all the time in the world to commit." Kenny knew what this could mean for his son: waking up at 4:30 in the morning and not getting home until dark. Alex argued, "This is the time to put in those types of hours."

"You know what, go for it," Kenny finally agreed. "I get phone calls all the time for new customers and we give them to the seltzer men. Why don't you take those calls and get your own route? Try it and see what happens."

And like that, Alex, at age twenty-five, became the youngest selt-zer man in the country, a new member of the new seltzer generation.

"The bottles needed to be fixed, labeled, and maintained."

Alex's life quickly arced toward running a seltzer works. He wore a blue T-shirt with a modest gold Magen David (Star of David) on a chain tucked inside, faded jeans, a LiveStrong-style wristband, and a baseball cap. Nothing too unusual, but the stories behind them all reflected a theme. "Do you know the Brooklyn Dodgers?" he asked, pointing out the classic embroidered B on the baseball cap. The wristband was for a friend who had died in college of a heart attack. "He was eighteen years old. That was hard." The necklace was once his great-grandmother's. "These are just things I always wear," he explained, his unassuming uniform a walking monument to the past.

In July 2012, Alex made his first delivery, to a woman on Eastern Parkway. Her five-dollar tip, his first as a seltzer man, is pinned to the wall behind his desk. How did it feel getting his first tip for a seltzer delivery, the first in his family in decades? "Good, I guess. I feel like the business should continue," Alex explained. "I don't think it should die. It's been dying for the past twenty-something years. It's always been dying. So, let's do something with it." Alex had an expansive vision for the future of seltzer. "Let's get it into restaurants. Let's get it into bars. Let's do more home delivery. People are into this retro thing now and seltzer is retro."

As he launched Brooklyn Seltzer Boys, a seltzer delivery service for the twenty-first century ("people email me now for delivery; they don't call"), he thought about what success would look like. "All of these three thousand bottles will be in circulation," he said. "That's success." And he would need to find more bottles. "If we need to find more bottles, that's a good problem to have."

Kenny and Alex Gomberg

In 2016 a seltzer man named Tom Vandecott passed away. Alex arranged a deal with Tom's widow to split the route between himself and seltzer man Walter Backerman, who still filled his bottles at Gomberg Seltzer Works. By 2017, Alex had built the business up to around three hundred customers, and that July the *New York Times* announced, "Out of Fizz, Brooklyn's Senior Seltzer Man Passes the Torch." After nearly sixty years, at eighty-four, Eli Miller retired and Alex Gomberg bought him out. Purchasing Eli's route added another eighty to a hundred customers plus two thousand more siphons to Brooklyn Seltzer Boys. Eli could have made more selling those bottles on eBay, but he had a higher goal in mind than mere money. "I wanted to make sure Alex had enough bottles to serve my customers," Eli told the *New York Times*.

"This is a young man's job," Eli reflected. "The fact that I worked this long is miraculous." And Eli was not alone in retiring. In 2017, another seltzer man, Steve Levine, took ill, and Alex took over Steve's handful of clients.

In the summer of 2017 Alex shadowed Eli along his circuitous route, learning from a man who had once filled his seltzer siphons from Alex's great-grandfather Moe. It was all coming full circle.

But Alex Gomberg's entrance into the seltzer business was so much more than just carrying on family tradition. Alex became part of the new seltzer generation reshaping that legacy, transforming a tradition so it could survive into the future. He represented the beginning of a whole new economic model; the rise of online commerce helped produce an appreciation for goods that required a local, human, connection. We might no longer know who delivers our mail, but everyone lucky enough to have one can't fail to know his or her seltzer man.

Eli introduced Alex to his customers while making his farewells. "He's a bright boy," he said of his successor. Eli's clients were sad to see him go, many wanting to know how they could keep in touch. At one building on Eastern Parkway, Eli asked the doorman if his client was home, instructing him what to say in the intercom.

"Tell her the seltzer guy's here."

A COMMUNITY OF SELTZER

In which John Seekings tells his tale of seltzer.

It had been about five years since the great blizzard, since John Seekings had reopened the Pittsburgh Seltzer Works. And his efforts were getting notice. The dinner audience had come to hear from local small business owners, many of whom John had known back in his college days. These Pittsburgh professionals and young entrepreneurs were people whose attention he could hold any day or night if he talked about advertising. And therein lay the problem. He was there to talk about seltzer.

As John rose to speak, he felt apologetic for even taking their time, for sharing the stage with such talented people who were doing so much for his adopted city and the world at large. He was following an award-winning architect, who had followed the owner of a postmodern art gallery. With a siphon bottle in hand and images of the Pittsburgh Seltzer Works on the screen behind him, he began.

"My name is John . . . and we bottle fizzy water."

"My name is John," he said from the podium, "and we bottle fizzy water." He was intentionally self-effacing, but he also was proud of what he did and how hard he worked, and he was not going to miss this chance to spread the gospel of seltzer. "Listen, we work every day 'til two o'clock in the morning. And we make this awesome seltzer."

Despite the aging equipment and an aging customer list, he and his partner Jim had rebuilt the Works into a modern company, maxing out its ability to meet the ever-rising demand. The new generation of customers had come from all corners, with no advertising beyond a Facebook page. They had seen a siphon at a local restaurant or had drunk a glass at a friend's house. Sometimes John increased his customer list by harassing customers at the

Giant Eagle, the local grocery store, if he saw them drinking from a Starbucks seltzer bottle. "I know you don't know me, but what are you doing?" he would ask, with a gentle tap on the shoulder. "Seriously? What are you doing?" Before long he'd have a new customer.

Those potential customers were placed on a one-hundred-person-long wait list with the hope that one day they, too, could join the siphon circuit. The waiting period stood at four months. Despite Ryan Pinnell cajoling him to upgrade, John continued to use the original machines and processes from the turn of the last century. He didn't have the time or money for such a complete upgrade. Still, John received calls all the time from prospective customers from unserved sections of the city. He refused to put them on the waiting list, telling the callers to put their houses up for sale and move closer, or drive to the Works if they wanted a bottle of seltzer. "They always show up," he said. "I don't think they've sold their house, maybe some of them have, but they always show up at the front door."

John even received calls from Whole Foods. "You never want to turn down Whole Foods," he said with regret. He had no choice but to say no. He wanted to get the product in the hands of anybody who asked, so the fact that he couldn't was a constant source of frustration. The business was teetering on the edge of great success, but to get there John needed some help. He just wasn't sure yet from where.

He tried applying for bank loans. He showed them the books of his burgeoning company, ready to go to the next level with a little funding. "They will look at your tax documents," he said, "and give you a pen, which is super nice." But he knew he would never hear from them again. The Pittsburgh Seltzer Works was a unique entity in their business model. Banks just didn't get it.

The dinner audience seemed to get it, though. John noticed a slight shift among the sushi eaters and cocktail sippers. Yes, the speakers before him had done important things and had received the audience's respectful attention, but now they were hearing something unexpected. Seltzer bottling? Did he just say he bottled seltzer water?

"When I purchased the plant with my partner, Jim Rogal, in 2009, we thought it could be a nice little side business." John laughed at the naïveté of his younger self. "Well . . . talk about the tail wagging the dog."

John looked at the siphon in his hand and then back at the crowd. "Let me tell you some stories."

He told them about finding the current location and about the college students he had paid in beer to help him set up the first line. He showed off his scars and spoke about the injuries that came with the job. He described the power of providing a customer with seltzer in siphons that had once been delivered by her own father, a retired seltzer man. And then he told them what he liked to call the July 4th story.

"So, we literally bought the company because we read an article in the paper. That's a smart move to begin with. We have no background in the industry, nothing at all. I am sitting at the seltzer works, it's the Friday of July 4th weekend, my business partner is off, you know, away having a wonderful time, and nothing is working. So, I'm thinking, 'Okay, we are out of business. We had a good run for a few months, but that's it.' Independence Day parties were relying on us.

"So, I called Jim and what do you think he said? 'Call a plumber.' I'm like, I don't think a plumber is the answer here. We brought in mechanical engineering students from CMU and Pitt"—that's Carnegie Mellon University and the University of

Pittsburgh—"and I ask them, 'Why isn't this working? This is the simplest line.' It's just a filler, a carbonator, and a bottler.

"But no one could fix it. No one could figure out what the problem was. We just couldn't keep the pressure up in the carbonator, and the key to good seltzer is really cold water and good pressure. So now it's getting late at night and we're taking stuff apart and hitting things with hammers. Eventually I just lay back and look up and say, 'Somebody, please, we need divine intervention at the Seltzer Works.'

"Then we saw this one part, attached to an old leather washer. It just looked worn out to me. I think, 'This is it, maybe, I don't know.' I start calling around to big-name hardware stores—Lowe's, Home Depot—and they all would say, 'You have a leather what?' They just had no idea. I finally went to a neighborhood hardware store. They were open. I told them I was looking for a leather washer, an inch and a quarter wide. I felt like I was in some '70s sitcom. But instead of laughing, the guy goes down in the basement, comes back, literally blowing dust off this bag, and said, 'You mean, like these?' I said that's exactly what I am looking for. 'How many you want?' he asked. I said, 'I want all of them. I want every single one!' It was the best dollar I ever spent.

"I came back, replaced it, and the line was back up and running twenty minutes later. And these are the types of experiences we've had over the course of the evolution of the company. There's not a lot of people that can appreciate going to a place and buying leather washers for a dollar on a holiday weekend, but I think it's great when we look and say, 'We can't figure this out but we are going to.' And then we do."

When John finished, he received a standing ovation, the first of the night. Which just made him keep talking.

"Wow, thank you," he said, overwhelmed by the response. "Thank you. And it's this kind of appreciation that shows us, you know, how being able to do this in Pittsburgh is so unique, that it's part of the overall landscape of what our city is all about. You can go and get a sandwich with french fries. You can run through a really cool park. You can come and get seltzer out of a bottle from 1912. That's what gets me up at two in the morning to come bottle and that's what, you know, keeps me going."

As he continued to speak, John no longer felt displaced. Just the opposite. He was inviting the audience to join him in appreciating this community of seltzer and its impact on Pittsburgh.

"We take pride in the fact that we know your name, know your secret delivery room, and pet your dog," John explained. "I have got one woman, in Squirrel Hill, who lives on a fixed income. So, when I bring the delivery, she just makes cookies. And you know what?" John paused for effect and looked across the crowd, all eyes on him. "That seems like fair pay to me.

"I am here seven days a week and sometimes late into the night," John said, not complaining, but clearly the years were taking their toll. "And no one appreciates that more than our customers." There's one woman, he says, in her late sixties, and she only orders six crates every three months. That's a lot of siphons sitting around unused. But then one day she said, "If you want me to come in, I can. I would certainly help with anything administrative. I wouldn't charge you." His customers came to him asking what they could do to keep the Works going. "Our customers feel like they are a part of the ownership," he explained. "It's almost like a cooperative." They all believed in the Works and what it meant and wanted to keep it going.

"Two weeks ago, the machines went down. I was at the end of my rope. I am like, I am done! I can't break any more fingers. Done! And it was the customers who called and said, 'What can we do? Can we help? Have you thought about a social media campaign? I will write a check today.'

"This," John concluded, "is the definition of community."

John faced an audience waiting to shake his hand, and the dinner's previous speakers reached out to him first. They told him it was the coolest thing they'd ever heard of, that it was so outside their realm of being they could hardly appreciate it, and to just keep it up and keep it going. And they asked if they could start receiving seltzer deliveries.

"Thanks," he told them. And, "No, but I can put you on the wait list."

In the face of so much interest, John recognized that he had happened to fall into the right place at the right time. It's the product. It's the bottles. It's people moving away from drinking soda. He thinks of the Works as the quiet kid sitting in the back of the classroom, raising his hand, saying, "I am here! I am here!" And now people were finally taking notice.

Maybe too much notice. But that's the kind of problem John liked to have. The pressure is building—to reach more customers, with more product, in more places. Like seltzer in a siphon, something was going to have to give. John likes the siphon-under-pressure metaphor. "That's exactly it," he said. "So, you can hit the siphon trigger and it goes for another hundred years!"

The decisions facing John in the coming years will determine the future of the Pittsburgh Seltzer Works. "Ultimately we are just a simple water company. But at the end of the day I am exhausted," John said. "I think, 'You know what would be great right now? Seltzer, with a little bit of lemon.'"

Appendices

DISCUSSION GUIDE

Your journey to Seltzertopia has just begun! Enhance your reading of Seltzertopia *by bringing it to your book club and exploring the following questions. If you are not part of a book club, gather some friends, read the book together, and discuss. Or join the Seltzertopia community and talk about these questions online at Seltzertopia.org.*

1. *Seltzertopia* uses one simple product, seltzer, to unpack a broad swath of world history. This style of book is often called a microhistory (like Mark Kurlansky's *Salt: A World History*). What do *you* think might be a good focus of a microhistory? What are the limits of historical writing told from the perspective of one tightly constrained filter?

2. John Seekings and Kathryn Renz never expected to become so deeply involved with seltzer. What is something you feel passionately about that seems to have come out of nowhere? Perhaps it's a love of black-and-white cinema, an interest in presidential biographies, or an unexpected talent for making chocolate. Share what it is and describe how you might have acquired it.

3. What role do women play in *Seltzertopia*? Does it pass the Bechdel test, in which at least two women talk to each other about something other than a man? Why do we generally hear about seltzer men but not seltzer women?

4. The chapter "How Seltzer Got Religion" explores the shifting ethnic associations between seltzer and the Jewish people. Is there anything about your background that makes you gravitate toward or away from seltzer? What other culinary habits do you enjoy that come from your ethnic or religious background?

5. Many of the people in *Seltzertopia* leave their careers behind to start their own seltzer works. If you suddenly took on a new occupation, what might it be? (The crazier the better!)

6. Walter Backerman, the seltzer man, often reminisces about the past and wishes things not to change. Others, like Daniel Humm, the chef at Madison Park, seek to modernize seltzer, to make it relevant for the present and survive into the future. Do you tend to put your energy into preserving the past, like maintaining family traditions or collecting old photos, or updating traditions to keep them relevant and creating new ones?

7. Many of the families in *Seltzertopia*, like the Gombergs and the Foxes, pass their business down for many generations. Share the work history of your family as far back as you can go. Do any patterns or themes emerge?

8. Hold a tasting party. Chill a selection of plain seltzers from different brands, pass out paper and pen, and ask each person to rate each one based on taste, fizz, and aftertaste. Or pick a brand of flavored seltzer and buy up to six to sample. Number each flavor before pouring them into numbered paper cups. Ask each person to rate each flavor, describe what it tastes like, and guess which cup contains which flavor.

9. Seltzer is made for drinking. But people use it for all sorts of things, including cooking and cleaning. In what other ways have you used seltzer other than to drink it?

SELTZER DRINK RECIPES

SAM EDELMANN'S EGG CREAM

In the mid-1980s, Sam Edelmann of the Pittsburgh Seltzer Works put out a small brochure of seltzer drink recipes for his customers. The following is his recipe for an egg cream:

1. Put two ounces of milk or half-and-half in a large glass.
2. Fill glass with cold seltzer.
3. Then add two ounces of chocolate syrup.
4. Drink before the foam disappears.

VERY BERRY ADE

Sam's brochure included classic seltzer recipes drawn from 19th-century soda fountain manuals, including this cool drink.

1. Put one ounce of raspberry or strawberry syrup in a glass.
2. Add the juice of one-quarter lemon and two or three crushed ice cubes.
3. Fill glass with seltzer.
4. Stir once and serve.

CLASSIC LIME RICKEY

1. Put ten ounces of seltzer in a large glass.
2. Add two ounces of cherry syrup.
3. Squeeze half of a lime into the glass. Then be sure to add the used lime to the mixture. This is the drink's trademark.
4. Stir briefly and add ice.

BROOKLYN FARMACY & SODA FOUNTAIN EGG CREAM

My favorite egg cream by far comes from Brooklyn Farmacy, a new old-style soda fountain in a beautifully restored 1920s pharmacy in Carroll Gardens, Brooklyn. Their 2014 recipe book *The Soda Fountain* details how you can make your own coffee, maple, blueberry, or orange egg cream. But, for my money, I'd travel any day to drink one of their traditional Brooklyn egg creams.

While many egg cream aficionados offer their own recipe for creating egg creams, their book takes it one step further—they detail *how* to perform what some call the art of the egg cream:

> Pour the milk into an egg cream glass and add seltzer until froth comes up to the top of the glass. Pour the syrup into the center of the glass and then gently push the back of a spoon into the center of the drink. Rock the spoon back and forth, keeping most of the action at the bottom of the glass, to incorporate the syrup without wrecking the froth. Serve immediately.[139]

Many a flat egg cream could be saved by practicing these techniques.

VENA'S FIZZ HOUSE
CHERRY LIME RICKEY

Vena's Fizz House opened in Portland, Maine, in the summer of 2013 as a non-alcholic seltzer-based bar. It was named after the owner's great-grandmother, a member of the Maine Women's Christian Temperance Movement back in the 1920s, who was "committed to curtailing the liquid sins of the day." Although Vena's Fizz House has since added liquor to the menu, they continue to specialize in seltzer drinks both old and new.

The Cherry Lime Rickey is a true classic, and might even pre-date the Egg Cream. There's nothing more refreshing on a hot summer day. Here's how the proprietors of Vena's Fizz House, Johanna & Steve Corman, recommend making it at home:

- 1 ounce tart cherry juice (they use Trader Joe's)
- 1 ounce squeezed lime juice
- 1.5 ounces simple syurp
- 3 drops Owl & Whale Cherry Bitters
- ice, and seltzer

Mix it all up in a 16-ounce mason jar.

VENA'S FIZZ HOUSE
LUMBER JACK LOVE

There are many places you can find a Cherry Lime Rickey but only Vena's offers Lumber Jack Love. It's described as tasting like "a lemonade you are drinking in a pine forest," and "like gin, without the gin." Try it out and see what you think, if you dare:

- 1 ounce Dram Pine Syrup
- 1 ounce squeezed lemon juice
- 1/4 ounce Wilks & Wilson Sir Teddy's Tonic
- 5 drops Alpine Herb Bitters (SF Bitters Co)
- 5 drops Wormwood Bitters (Cocktail Kingdom)
- ice, seltzer

Mix it up in a 16-ounce mason jar.

For more recipes, or to share your own, please visit Seltzertopia.com.

AFTERWORD

I interviewed hundreds upon hundreds of people of all ages and from all walks of life for *Seltzertopia*. I am indebted to each and every one of them for helping me to understand the cultural landscape of seltzer.

Unfortunately, I could not include every single unique and fascinating way that seltzer had worked its way into their lives. To assure you that I was indeed listening, below is a less than comprehensive list of the runners-up, the interesting tidbits that failed to make it into this book.

Feel free to consider it the table of contents for my next book.

Or perhaps yours.

Drum roll please . . .

In no particular order:

- Lou Reed's song "Egg Cream"
- Allan Sherman's song "Seltzer Boy"
- How to remove a stain with seltzer
- How to clean aluminum siding with seltzer
- How to wash your hair, your car, your floor, your [fill-in-the-blank] with seltzer
- How to carbonate grapes, watermelon, Gummy bears, [fill-in-the-blank] like seltzer.
- The history of Seltzer as a surname
- The history and culture of seltzer consumption around the world
- The Marx Brothers, Soupy Sales, and other siphon-loving comedians
- Various Israeli kibbutzim that once offered seltzer at their public fountains
- Whether seltzer was used as a weapon in the Israeli War of Independence

- Seltzers and bartenders
- Joey Rao's seltzer conspiracy
- The entire industry of large-scale seltzer production for cans and bottles
- The untold history of African Americans taking ownership of New York City seltzer works
- Barbara Park's hilarious children's book *Junie B., First Grader: Boo . . . And I Mean It!*
- Jessica Edwards's documentary short *Seltzer Works*, on the Gomberg Seltzer Works
- Seltzer science projects
- Seltzer, the programming language
- Seth Front's Jewish Zodiac and Year of the Egg Cream
- Scarlett Johansson as spokeswoman for SodaStream
- Mayim Bialik as spokeswoman for SodaStream
- The controversy over SodaStream's West Bank production facility
- Add your own here: _____

  _____

- The other one you just remembered: _____

  _____

ACKNOWLEDGMENTS

Oh boy, do I have a lot of people to thank! A project that took as long as this—over a decade—required hundreds of interviews, scores of assistants pointing me in fruitful directions, dozens of translators, and an incalculable number of supportive and kind souls. Experiencing such generosity cannot help but leave one in deep appreciation of the kindness of strangers and the warmth of humanity (at least among those favorable to seltzer).

At the risk of writing something as long as this book, let me begin by sending out a spritz of the old siphon to Google: searching the web through Google got me started; Google Groups gave me instant access to a wide variety of communities of interest; Google Books let me take deep dives into obscure and remote haystacks to find those proverbial needles of seltzer; and Google's Ngram Viewer let me track seltzer popularity over time.

If Google, Evernote, many now-extinct generations of PDAs, smartphones, and Mac computers were my tools, let me next thank the safe and secluded place I found to write: the New York City subway system (where I am currently stuck on a Queens-bound F train, appreciating the delay). Without our daily writing sessions, which others called work commutes, this book could not exist.

For all the in-person and phone interviews that make up the core of this book, I want to send out a big seltzer spritz to:

- Thomasz Bednarz of the National Maritime Museum in Gdańsk (on marine archaeology)
- Nicholas J. P. Ryba and Charles Zuker (on the science of seltzer)
- Kelly B. Keller and Cathy Keller (on their beloved family relative, William B. Keller)
- Mel Shavelson (for living long enough to talk with me about Israeli seltzer bombs)
- Joan Howard Maurer (on her dad, the original Stooge)
- Richie Strell (on the love of siphon collecting)
- Rabbi Aaron B. Bisno (on Jews and seltzer)
- Mel Gordon (on Jews and comedy)
- Kelly and David Fox, and Daniel Humm (on egg creams)
- Lorri Trachtman (on working the soda fountain . . . and changing my diaper when I was a baby)
- Sam and Marion Edelmann, Paul Supowitz, and Andrea Brichacek (on the Pittsburgh Seltzer Works)
- Kathryn Renz, Ryan Pinnel, and Gustavo Leiva (on running a modern seltzer works)

- Amelia "Madame Bubbles" Nahman (on being Madame Bubbles!)
- Kenny and Alex Gomberg, Irv Resnick, and filmmaker Jessica Edwards (on Gomberg Seltzer Works and Brooklyn Seltzer Boys)

I want to give special thanks to both Eli Miller and Walter Backerman for letting me invade their workplaces as I rode along with them on deliveries, and to Randy Miller for letting me invade his memories.

This book found its structure following the adventures of John Seekings and Jim Rogal, and I will forever be indebted to them for all the time they spent with me and my endless queries.

I should add that I took some creative liberties turning many of these interviews into scenes; even though I often shared these segments with them in advance, I take full responsibility for any errors found within.

In addition, I would like to thank:

- Everyone who sent me material on Niederselters and/or helped me translate its history from the original German, including Dr. Norbert Zabel, mayor of Niederselters, his son Frank Zabel (who sent me the best package ever!), and the Goethe-Institut Washington.
- Andrew Kaplan, managing editor of *Beverage World*, and everyone else at the magazine who assisted me.
- Eddy Portnoy, for introducing me to the "bloody seltzer."
- Imre Kiss, for sending me the best seltzer exhibit catalog ever, in Hungarian!
- All the listeners to my podcast, readers of my blog, Twitter followers, and friends of the Seltzertopia Facebook page—your advice, encouragement, and interest have been invaluable throughout this project.
- Every organization who invited me to read excerpts from my book (and for serving egg creams afterwards).
- All the journalists and editors who interviewed me or gave me an opportunity to write about this project, none more so than Dan Friedman (of the *Forward*) and Julie Wiener (who also generously twice edited this book).
- Everyone who took the time to make an introduction, or send me a link, or mail me a book (and, in one instance, a case of seltzer—mango cilantro, booyah!).
- All my online fans who read versions of the manuscript and provided invaluable feedback.
- To all members of the private Facebook group Now Fizzing, the best place to find seltzer selfies, view fizzeos, and debate the value of a ghost over a Leroy.

I want to also thank the *Forward* for giving me my first opportunity to write about seltzer, and SodaStream for sending me the "review copy" that made it all possible.

The team at Behrman House has been remarkable, getting the book from day one and helping me take it places I had only dreamed of, specifically president David Behrman, partner Vicki Weber, editors Dena Neusner and Tova Ovits, designer Anne Redmond, and copyeditors Judy Sandman and Debra Corman.

My family was amazing, both my wife (who helped edit the book and put up with my endless excitement about the continuous stream of seltzer discoveries over the years) and both of my children, Akiva and Mira.

And lastly, a final carbonated thank you to Carolyn Starman Hessel, whose family kitchen had seltzer running on tap and whose email and early support made this project happen.

BIBLIOGRAPHY

Aiden, Erez, and Jean-Baptiste Michel. *Uncharted: Big Data as a Lens on Human Culture*. New York: Riverhead Books, 2013.

Anderson, Chris. *Makers: The New Industrial Revolution*. New York: Crown Business, 2012.

Andrae, Tom, Mel Gordon, Jerry Siegel, and Joe Shuster. *Siegel and Shuster's Funnyman: The First Jewish Superhero, from the Creators of Superman*. Port Townsend, WA: Feral House, 2010.

Balinska, Maria. *The Bagel: The Surprising History of a Modest Bread*. New Haven, CT: Yale University Press, 2008.

Carbonated Beverages in the United States: Historical Review. Greenwich, CT: American Can, 1972.

Chapelle, Frank. *Wellsprings: A Natural History of Bottled Spring Waters*. New Brunswick, NJ: Rutgers University Press, 2005.

"Early 19th Century Bottle of Mineral Water Found at Bottom of Sea." *The Telegraph*. Telegraph Media Group, July 2, 2014. Web. July 25, 2014. http:// www.telegraph.co.uk/news/worldnews/europe/poland/10941253/Early-19th-century-bottle-of-mineral-water-found-at-bottom-of-sea.html.

Fields, Armond, and L. Marc Fields. *From the Bowery to Broadway: Lew Fields and the Roots of American Popular Theater*. New York: Oxford University Press, 1993.

"For 112 Years, Pittsburgh Seltzer Works Has Been Tickling Tongues with Bubbles." *For 112 Years, Pittsburgh Seltzer Works Has Been Tickling Tongues with Bubbles*. Web. September 6, 2014. http://old.post-gazette.com/businessne ws/20010815seltzer0815bnp2.asp.

Funderburg, Anne Cooper. *Sundae Best: A History of Soda Fountains*. Bowling Green, OH: Bowling Green State University Popular Press, 2002.

Gies, Frances, and Joseph Gies. *Cathedral, Forge, and Waterwheel: Technology and Invention in the Middle Ages*. New York: HarperCollins, 1994.

"The History Blog." *The History Blog RSS*. Web. July 25, 2014. http://www. thehistoryblog.com/archives/31465.

Jenkins, Henry. *What Made Pistachio Nuts? Early Sound Comedy and the Vaudeville Aesthetic*. New York: Columbia University Press, 1992.

"JOHN MATTHEWS (1808–1870) | Green-Wood." *GreenWood*. Web. July 30, 2014. http://www.green-wood.com/2010/john-matthews/.

Johnson, Steven. *The Invention of Air: An Experiment, a Journey, a New Country and the Amazing Force of Scientific Discovery*. London: Penguin, 2009.

Kisseloff, Jeff. *You Must Remember This: An Oral History of Manhattan from the 1890s to World War II.* San Diego: Harcourt Brace Jovanovich, 1989.

"Narodowe Muzeum Morskie W Gdasku." *National Maritime Museum.* Web. July 25, 2014. http://www.en.nmm.pl/.

North, M. L., and John Bell. *Analysis of Saratoga Waters: Also of Sharon, Avon, Virginia and Other Mineral Waters of the United States: With Directions for Invalids.* New York: Saxton & Miles, 1846.

Page, Brett, and J. Berg Esenwein. *Writing for Vaudeville: With Nine Complete Examples of Various Vaudeville Forms by Richard Harding Davis, Aaron Hoffman, Edgar Allan Woolfe, Taylor Granville, Louis Weslyn, Arthur Denvir, and James Madison.* Springfield, MA: Home Correspondence School, 1915.

"Poland Spring® 100% Natural Spring Water." Poland Spring. Web. September 12, 2014. http://www.polandspring.com/#/assured/history_and_heritage.

Pollan, Michael. *The Omnivore's Dilemma: A Natural History of Four Meals.* New York: Penguin, 2006.

Priestley, Joseph. *Directions for Impregnating Water with Fixed Air, in Order to Communicate to It the . . . Spirit and Virtues of Pyrmont Water, Etc.* London, 1772. Print.

Priestley, Joseph. *The History and Present State of Electricity, with Original Experiments.* London: Printed for J. Dodsley, 1769.

Sagan, Carl, and Ann Druyan. *Comet.* New York: Random House, 1985.

"Small Batch Businesses." *Kottke.org.* Web. September 12, 2014. http://kottke. org/09/09/small-batch-businesses.

Soda Water, How to Make and Serve It with Profit: A Guide to the Successful Conducting of a Modern Soda Water Business. Chicago: Liquid Carbonic, 1905.

"Source of Trouble." *The Economist.* The Economist Newspaper, 28 Oct. 2006. Web. September 12, 2014. http://www.economist.com/ node/8091329?story_id=8091329.

"A Sparkling Local Tradition." *Pittsburgh Magazine.* Web. September 6, 2014. http://www.pittsburghmagazine.com/Pittsburgh-Magazine/ January-2010/A-Sparkling-Local-Tradition/.

Standage, Tom. *A History of the World in 6 Glasses.* New York: Walker, 2005.

Stec, Laura F., and Eugene C. Cordero. *Cool Cuisine: Taking the Bite out of Global Warming.* Layton, UT: Gibbs Smith, 2008.

"200-Year-Old Bottle of Seltzer Found in Shipwreck: DNews." *DNews.* Web. July 25, 2014. http://news.discovery.com/history/archaeology/200-year-old-bottle-of-mineral-water-found-in-shipwreck-140710.htm.

Zimmerman, Steve, and Ken Weiss. *Food in the Movies.* Jefferson, NC: McFarland, 2005.

NOTES

1. Although Carolyn Starman Hessel officially retired from the Jewish Book Council, she remained in 2017 as director of its Sami Rohr Prize for Jewish Literature.

2. Gary Rotstein, "Pittsburgh Seltzer Works Fizzes Away After 120 Years in Business," *Pittsburgh Post-Gazette*, June 2, 2009. See also Marilyn McDevitt Rubin, "Bottling Seltzer as a Sideline," *Pittsburgh Press*, October 3, 1982; Peter Mattiace, "Fizz, Fizz—Bubbles Are Bouncing for Bottler," *Free Lance-Star*, July 24, 1982; Michel Sauret, "Seltzer Works Has Bubbly New Owners," *Pittsburgh Post-Gazette*, September 4, 2009; Rick Sebak, "A Sparkling Local Tradition," *Pittsburgh Magazine*, December 18, 2009, http://www.pittsburghmagazine.com/ Pittsburgh-Magazine/January-2010/A-Sparkling-Local-Tradition.

3. Jayaram Chandrashekar et al., "The Taste of Carbonation," *Science* 16 (October 2009): 443–45.

4. Nell Greenfieldboyce, "Study: When Soda Fizzes, Your Tongue Tastes It," *All Things Considered*, NPR, October 15, 2009, http://www.npr.org/templates/ story/story.php?storyId=113831763.

5. Steve Levin, "For 112 Years, Pittsburgh Seltzer Works Has Been Tickling Tongues with Bubbles," *Pittsburgh Post-Gazette*, August 15, 2001.

6. Levin, "For 112 Years."

7. Sebak, "Sparkling Local Tradition."

8. Steven Johnson, *The Invention of Air: An Experiment, a Journey, a New Country and the Amazing Force of Scientific Discovery* (London: Penguin, 2009)

9. Johnson, *Invention of Air*, 48–51.

10. Johnson, *Invention of Air*, 50.

11. Johnson, *Invention of Air*, 48–51.

12. "Dr. Joseph Priestley," *National Bottlers' Gazette* 1, no. 2, 31.

13. "Dr. Joseph Priestley," 31.

14. Joseph Priestley, *Directions for Impregnating Water with Fixed Air; in order to communicate to it the peculiar Spirit and Virtues of Pyrmont Water, and other Mineral Waters of a similar Nature* (London: J. Johnson, 1772), 3.

15. *The Pharmaceutical Era*, February 1913, 65.

16. D. O. Haynes, *The Soda Fountain* 26 (1927): 33.

17. "John Matthews (1808–1870)," Green-Wood, accessed April 3, 2018, http:// www.green-wood.com/2010/john-matthews.

18. Anne Cooper Funderburg, *Sundae Best: A History of Soda Fountains* (Bowling Green, OH: Bowling Green State University Popular Press, 2002), 21–24.

19. William B. Keller, *National Bottlers' Gazette*, March 1882.

20. "The Proper Care of Horses," *National Bottlers' Gazette*, November 1882, 21.

21. Anonymous, *National Bottlers' Gazette*, 1882, 3.

22. *National Bottlers' Gazette*, September 1883, 22.

23. *National Bottlers' Gazette* 2, no. 1.

24. *National Bottlers' Gazette*, October and November 1885.

25. *National Bottlers' Gazette* 2, no. 1.

26. Wikipedia, s.v. "Woman's Christian Temperance Union, accessed April 3, 2018, http://en.wikipedia.org/wiki/Woman%27s_Christian_Temperance_Union.

27. "Teaching with Documents: The Volstead Act and Related Prohibition Documents," United States National Archives, accessed April 3, 2018, https://www.archives.gov/education/lessons/volstead-act.

28. *Carbonated Beverages in the United States: Historical Review* (Greenwich, CT: American Can, 1972), 13.

29. Frances Gies and Joseph Gies, *Cathedral, Forge, and Waterwheel: Technology and Invention in the Middle Ages* (New York: Harper Perennial, 1995), 112.

30. Richard Gazarik, "National Guard Summoned to Help," *TribLIVE*, April 27, 2012, http://triblive.com/x/pittsburghtrib/news/westmoreland/s_666651.html; Kathy Mellott, "Region, State Buried under Blowing Snow," *Tribune-Democrat*, February 10, 2010, http://www.tribune-democrat.com/local/x878600895/Region-state-buried-under-blowing-snow/print.

31. "SodaStream One2One Project," The Water Project, accessed April 3, 2018, https://thewaterproject.org/community/profile/sodastream.

32. Frank Chapelle, *Wellsprings: A Natural History of Bottled Spring Waters* (New Brunswick, NJ: Rutgers University Press, 2005), 209.

33. Chapelle, *Wellsprings*, 10.

34. Chapelle, *Wellsprings*, 12.

35. Tom Standage, *A History of the World in 6 Glasses* (New York: Walker, 2005), 23.

36. Standage, *History of the World*, 21.

37. Hippocrates, *On Airs, Waters, and Places*, Library of Alexandria, part 7.

38. Chapelle, *Wellsprings*, 112.

39. Matthew Day, "Early 19th Century Bottle of Mineral Water Found at Bottom of Sea," *Telegraph*, July 2, 2014, https://www.telegraph.co.uk/news/worldnews/europe/poland/10941253/Early-19th-century-bottle-of-mineral-water-found-at-bottom-of-sea.html; Rossella Lorenzi, "200-Year-Old Bottle of Seltzer Found in Shipwreck," Discovery, July 10, 2014, http://news.discovery.com/history/archaeology/200-year-old-bottle-of-mineral-water-found-in-shipwreck-140710.htm; "200-Year-Old Seltzer Water Bottle Found on Shipwreck," *The History Blog*, July 14, 2014, https://web.archive.org/web/20160918162432/http://www.thehistoryblog.com:80/archives/31465.

40. Mark Strauss, "Archaeologists Have Found an Unopened, 200-Year-Old Bottle of Seltzer," Gizmodo, July 23, 2014, http://io9.gizmodo.com/archaeologists-have-found-an-unopened-200-year-old-bot-1609630553.

41. "Unusual Discovery of Archaeologists," National Maritime Museum in Gdansk, June 27, 2014, http://www.en.nmm.pl/news/unusual-discovery-of-archaeologists.

42. This section is based in large part on the 1994 history of the town, *Geschichte von Niederselters*, written in German. It was sent to the author, signed by the town's mayor, Norbert Zabel. The author later had parts translated into English.

43. Milo Linus North, *The Invalid of Saratoga* (M. W. Dodd, 1840), 9.

44. North, *Invalid of Saratoga*, 10.

45. North, *Invalid of Saratoga*, 11.

46. North, *Invalid of Saratoga*, 63.

47. North, *Invalid of Saratoga*, 28.

48. Benjamin Colby, "A Guide to Health, Being an Exposition of the Principles of the Thomsonian System [. . .]" (Dr. Noble, 1844), viii.

49. Chapelle, *Wellsprings*, 47.

50. William Saunders, *A Treatise on the Chemical History and Medical Powers of Some of the Most Celebrated Mineral Waters* (W. Phillips, 1800), 226.

51. "Early Soda & Mineral Water Bottles," Soda & Beer Bottles of North America, accessed April 3, 2018, http://www.sodasandbeers.com/Articles/ArticleSoda0001/SABArticlesSoda0001_02.htm.

52. *Soda Water, How to Make and Serve It with Profit: A Guide to the Successful Conducting of a Modern Soda Water Business* (Chicago: Liquid Carbonic, 1905), 7.

53. *Soda Water*, 48–49.

54. The author interviewed Lorri Trachtman over a Chinese dinner in 2012.

55. The author interviewed David Fox in his office on February 24, 2011.

56. Anne Cooper Funderburg, *Sundae Best: A History of Soda Fountains* (Bowling Green, OH: Bowling Green State University Popular Press, 2002), 50.

57. Jeff Kisseloff, *You Must Remember This: An Oral History of Manhattan from the 1890s to World War II* (San Diego: Harcourt Brace Jovanovich, 1989), 57.

58. Kisseloff, *You Must Remember*, 65.

59. Kisseloff, *You Must Remember*, 80.

60. Brad Darrach, "*Playboy* Interviews Mel Brooks," *Playboy*, February 1975, 48.

61. The author interviewed Jeremiah Moss by email on August 26, 2011.

62. Alan M. Kraut, "The Butcher, the Baker, the Pushcart Peddler: Jewish Foodways and Entrepreneurial Opportunity in the East European Immigrant Community 1880–1940," *Journal of American Culture*, January 1983, https://doi.org/10.1111/j.1542-734X.1983.0604_71.x.

63. William B. Keller, "The Jew in the Bottling Business," *National Bottlers' Gazette*, July 5, 1903.

64. "Seltzer: A Renaissance in Fizz," *New York Times*, September 26, 1979, C1.

65. The author interviewed Mark Epstein by phone.

66. Chapelle, *Wellsprings*, 177–78.

67. Maine League of Historical Societies and Museums, *Maine: A Guide "Down East,"* ed. Doris A. Isaacson (Rockland, ME: Courier-Gazette, 1970), 398.

68. "Great Moments in Our History," Poland Spring, accessed April 3, 2018, https://www.polandspring.com/our-story.

69. Information provided by Beverage Marketing Corporation to author by email.

70. Michael Pollan, *The Omnivore's Dilemma: A Natural History of Four Meals* (New York: Penguin, 2006), 295.

71. Pollan, *Omnivore's Dilemma*.

72. Maria Balinska, *The Bagel: The Surprising History of a Modest Bread* (New Haven, CT: Yale University Press, 2008), 124–25.

73. Woodene Merriman, "For Him, a Shot of the Bubbly Means a Spritz of Seltzer," *Pittsburgh Post-Gazette*, July 29, 1981, 21.

74. "Perrier Brand Focus," Nestle, accessed April 5, 2018, https://www.nestle.com/investors/brand-focus/perrier-focus.

75. "Perrier Brand Focus."

76. "Perrier Brand Focus."

77. Chapelle, *Wellsprings*, 184.

78. "Seltzer: A Renaissance in Fizz."

79. Ted Okuda and Edward Watz, *The Columbia Comedy Shorts: Two-Reel Hollywood Film Comedies, 1933–1958* (Jefferson, NC: McFarland, 2013).

80. Steve Zimmerman and Ken Weiss, *Food in the Movies* (Jefferson, NC: McFarland, 2009), 129.

81. Zimmerman and Weiss, *Food in the Movies*, 130.

82. Zimmerman and Weiss, *Food in the Movies*, 130.

83. From an interview with Mel Gordon by the author, March 2011.

84. Tom Andrae and Mel Gordon, *Siegel and Shuster's Funnyman: The First Jewish Superhero, from the Creators of Superman* (Port Townsend, WA: Feral House, 2010), 4.

85. Andrae and Gordon, *Siegel and Shuster's Funnyman*, 10.

86. Henry Jenkins, *What Made Pistachio Nuts? Early Sound Comedy and the Vaudeville Aesthetic* (New York: Columbia University Press, 1992), 85.

87. Jenkins, *What Made Pistachio Nuts?*, 59.

88. Greg Goldin, "Randy Miller," *University Man*, Fall 1987, 64–66.

89. Goldin, "Randy Miller."

90. Samuel Greengard, "Alan and Randy Miller: No Soda Jerks," *Los Angeles Magazine*, January 1987.

91. Jessica Ellman, "The Whiz Kid of Fizz: Seltzer Seller Earns Top 10 Honor," *L.A. Times*, March 3, 1988.

92. Bob Weinstein, "The Fizz Biz," *Entrepreneur*.

93. Andrea Scott, "Seltzer Tickles Tastebuds," Boise, Idaho, March 27, 1986.

94. Lisa A. Lapin, "Flavored Seltzer: Old Recipe Adds Fizz to Beverage Sales," *Los Angeles Times*, October 20, 1986.

95. Lyrics to ONYS commercial used with permission.

96. Alphy Hoffman, "Hop On Over to Alphy's Soda Pop Club!," *Teen Beat*, 44.

97. "Fizz-biz Whiz Randy Miller Leaps into High-Rise Hype," *People Weekly*, March 2, 1987, 74.

98. William Franklin, "Taming the Fiz Biz," *Men's Fitness*.

99. *California Beverage Hotline*, September 21, 1986.

100. Weinstein, "Fizz Biz."

101. Barbara Lamprecht, "Walnut-Based Seltzer Maker Goes Big Time," *San Gabriel Valley Tribune*, October 14, 1986.

102. Brian H. Greene, "New York Seltzer Surviving Soda Wars," *Tribune/News*, February 19, 1989, E1.

103. Kathy Richer, "Future of Seltzer Drinks Sparkles," *Bell Gardens Review*, June 4, 1986.

104. Meg Grant, "Fizz Biz," *Seattle Times*, August 21, 1985, C1.

105. *California Beverage Hotline*, October 1986.

106. Judith Vandewater, "Busch Bellying Up to the Seltzer Bar," *St. Louis Post-Dispatch*, January 14, 1987, B1.

107. Todd S. Purdum, "Attorney General Abrams to Quit to Join a Law Firm in Manhattan," *New York Times*, September 9, 1993, A00001.

108. Lisa A. Lapin, "Small Southland Firms Start a Trend: Flavored Seltzer; Old Recipe Adds Fizz to Beverage Sales," *Los Angeles Times*, October 20, 1986.

109. "SELTZER: Flavorful Old Recipe Adds Fizz to Beverage Sales," *Los Angeles Times*, October 20, 1986, 5.

110. William Franklin, "Taming the Fiz Biz."

111. Alex Godfrey, "How to Train Your Dinosaur: Meet Jurassic World's Animal Wrangler," *Guardian*, October 28, 2015.

112. Chelsey Dulaney, "Buy into These Bubbles: Seltzer's Fizz Is Back," *Wall Street Journal*, June 16, 2015.

113. Millie Dent, "Tiny Bubbles, Big Business: How Seltzer Became the Hot New Drink," *Fiscal Times*, July 17, 2015.

114. Drew Harwell, "How Seltzer Water Became Cooler Than Coke," *Washington Post*, July 16, 2015.

115. Drew Harwell, "How Something as Tasteless as Seltzer Water Won America's heart," *Chicago Tribune*, July 17, 2015.

116. Charlotte Wilder, "The Cult of Polar Seltzer: Why One Brand of Carbonated Water Has New Englanders Obsessed," *Boston Globe*, November 8, 2015; Janelle Nanos, "A Sparkling New Era for Time-Tested Polar," *Boston Globe*, July 25, 2016; "Since 1882," Polar Seltzer, accessed April 3, 2018, http://polarseltzer.com/history-since-1882.

117. Polar Selzer, used with permission.
118. Emily Gowdey-Backus, "Latest Polar Flavor Puts Some Sparkle in Seltzer Sales," *Herald News*, March 31, 2016.
119. Alyse Whitney, "What's the Mystery Flavor Behind Polar's 'Unicorn Kisses' Seltzer?," *Bon Appétit*, November 6, 2017.
120. Nanos, "Sparkling New Era."
121. Steve Annear, "People Are Stocking Up on the New Polar Seltzer Flavors Like the Apocalypse Is Coming," *Boston Globe*, August 1, 2017.
122. Jamie Ducharme, "We Got Our Hands on Polar's Crazy New Flavors," *Boston Magazine*, July 25, 2017.
123. Elisabeth Sherman, "LaCroix Can Paintings Are the Ultimate Millennial Pop Art," *Food & Wine*, July 13, 2017.
124. Claudia McNeilly, "Why LaCroix and the World of Carbonated Water Will Not Go Out of Style Anytime Soon," *National Post*, July 6, 2017.
125. Caroline Goldstein, "LaCroix, Seltzer of Choice for Millennials, Is Now a Work of Pop Art," July 14, 2017, Artnet, https://news.artnet.com/art-world/lacroix-fnnch-pop-art-1023587.
126. Dent, "Tiny Bubbles, Big Business."
127. H. B. Duran, "LaCroix Sparkles with Millennials Thanks to Influencer Marketing," Influencer Orchestration Network, accessed April 5, 2018, http://www.ion.co/lacroix-sparkles-millennials-thanks-influencer-marketing.
128. Elisabeth Sherman, "Big Dipper's 'LaCroix Boi' Is a Sensual Ode to Seltzer," *Food & Wine*, June 1, 2017.
129. Daniel Reynolds, "'LaCroix Boi' Is the New Song of Gay Summer," *Advocate*, June 4, 2017, https://www.advocate.com/music/2017/6/04/lacroix-boi-new-song-gay-summer.
130. Big Dipper, "LaCroix Boi," used with permission.
131. Chris Crowley, "'LaCroix Boi' Is the New Sparkling-Water Ode Inspired by Midwestern Parents and Big Baby D.R.A.M.," *Grub Street*, June 5, 2017.
132. Jesus Garay, "How the Hell Did LaCroix Become So Popular?," Guff, accessed April 5, 2018, http://guff.com/how-the-hell-did-la-croix-become-so-popular/from-obscuriff.
133. "Original New York Seltzer Returns after 20-Year Hiatus," June 23, 2015, BevNET, http://www.bevnet.com/news/2015/original-new-york-seltzer-returns-after-20-year-hiatus.
134. Sarah Baird, "Vintage Soda Brand 'Original New York Seltzer' Is Making a Comeback," May 19, 2015, Yahoo Food, https://www.yahoo.com/style/vintage-soda-brand-original-new-york-seltzer-is-119365008687.html.
135. Baird, "Vintage Soda Brand."
136. Baird, "Vintage Soda Brand."
137. "SELTZER: Flavorful Old Recipe Adds Fizz to Beverage Sales."
138. Godfrey, "How to Train Your Dinosaur."
139. Brooklyn Farmacy, *The Soda Fountain*, used with permission.

CREDITS AND PERMISSIONS

The author gratefully acknowledges the following sources of photographs and graphic images:

Shutterstock/homunkang: cover bubbles; Anne Redmond: cover seltzerscape; Shutterstock/ Luis Fernandez: cover blue bottle; courtesy of Archives and Special Collections, Dickenson College, Carlisle, PA: 30; National Bottlers' Gazette: 35, 51, 59; Beverage World: 100 Year History, 1882-1982, and Future Probe, Beverage World, 1982: 41; The Complete Practical Bottler, by Charles Herman Sulz, 1888: 42, 50; courtesy of Richie Strell: cover green bottle, 43, 46, 217, 278; "John Matthews 1884 Siphon Filling Machine" from http://www.bottlebooks. com/siphons/mixing_it_up.htm: 68; courtesy of Seltzer Works Documentary/Film First Co: 72; courtesy of John Seekings: 91, 148, 261; courtesy of SodaStream: 128; courtesy of Dr. Norbert Zabel, Mayor of Niederselters: 141; courtesy of Frank Zabel: 141, 143; courtesy of Kelly Fox: 170, 171; Soda Water: How to Make and Serve It with Profit: A Guide to the Successful Conducting of A Modern Soda Water Business, Liquid Carbonic Co., 1905: 61; ©2018 C3 Entertainment, Inc. All Rights Reserved: 201; used with permission of Quartz (qz.com): 152, 197, 248; made with TheAtlas.com: 195, 196; Up From Seltzer image © 1981 by Peter Hochstein, Illustrations © 1981 by Sandy Hoffman, used by permission of Workman Publishing Co., Inc., New York. All rights reserved: 192; Wikimedia Commons/1881 Young Persons' Cyclopedia of Persons and Places: 136; Wikimedia Commons/ State Library and Archives of Florida: 158; Shutterstock/Elzbieta Sekowska: 185; Shutterstock/mandritoiu: 188; www.perrier.com: 194; Ngram Viewer graphs and data courtesy of Google Books Ngram Viewer, books.google.com/ngrams: 195; www.newyorkseltzer.com: 223; State Archives of Florida/Roy Erickson: 206; courtesy of Randy Miller: 225, 230, 242; used with permission of fnnch: 248; used with permission of Chelsea Steele: 250; used with permission of Big Dipper: 251; courtesy of Imre Kiss: 256. All other photographs are owned by Barry Joseph.

The author is grateful for the following text permissions:

Excerpt from "Water for Elephants" © 2011 Courtesy of Twentieth Century Fox. Written by Richard LaGravenese. All rights reserved.

Excerpt from For Two Cents Plain, by Harry Golden, used with permission of John Goldhurst.

Excerpt from interview with Mel Brooks: Archival Playboy Magazine material. Copyright © 1975 by Playboy. Used with permission. All rights reserved.

Excerpt from "The Mary Tyler Moore Show" (episode: "Chuckles Bites the Dust") ©1975 Courtesy of Twentieth Century Fox Television. Written by David Lloyd. All rights reserved.

Excerpt from Soda Water: A Cult Drink in Hungary, by Imre Kiss, 2008, used with permission of the Hungarian Seltzer Museum.

ONYS commercial lyrics used with permission.

Unicorn Kisses origin story used with permission of Polar Seltzer.

"LaCroix Boi" lyrics used with permission of Big Dipper.

Sam Edelmann's classic seltzer recipes used with permission of Sam Edelmann.

Brooklyn Farmacy Egg Cream used with permission of Brooklyn Farmacy.

Vena's Fizz House recipes used with permission of Johanna and Steve Corman.